Pro iOS and Android Apps for Business

with jQuery Mobile, Node.js, and MongoDB

Frank Zammetti

Apress·

Pro iOS and Android Apps for Business with jQuery Mobile, Node.js, and MongoDB

ISBN-13 (pbk): 978-1-4302-6070-7

ISBN-13 (electronic): 978-1-4302-6071-4

President and Publisher: Paul Manning
Lead Editor: Michelle Lowman
Development Editor: Douglas Pundick, Gary Schwartz
Technical Reviewers: Danny Swarzman and Andrew Zack
Editorial Board: Steve Anglin, Ewan Buckingham, Gary Cornell, Louise Corrigan, Morgan Ertel,
    Jonathan Gennick, Jonathan Hassell, Robert Hutchinson, Michelle Lowman, James Markham,
    Matthew Moodie, Jeff Olson, Jeffrey Pepper, Douglas Pundick, Ben Renow-Clarke, Dominic Shakeshaft,
    Gwenan Spearing, Matt Wade, Tom Welsh
Coordinating Editor: Kevin Shea
Copy Editor: Kim Wimpsett
Compositor: SPi Global
Indexer: SPi Global
Artist: SPi Global
Cover Designer: Anna Ishchenko

Distributed to the book trade worldwide by Springer Science+Business Media New York, 233 Spring Street, 6th Floor, New York, NY 10013. Phone 1-800-SPRINGER, fax (201) 348-4505, e-mail orders-ny@springer-sbm.com, or visit www.springeronline.com.

For information on translations, please e-mail rights@apress.com, or visit www.apress.com.

Apress and friends of ED books may be purchased in bulk for academic, corporate, or promotional use. eBook versions and licenses are also available for most titles. For more information, reference our Special Bulk Sales–eBook Licensing web page at www.apress.com/bulk-sales.

Any source code or other supplementary materials referenced by the author in this text is available to readers at www.apress.com. For detailed information about how to locate your book's source code, go to www.apress.com/source-code/.

Dedicated to Traci, Ashley, and Andrew—the only stars I ever need in my sky.

—Frank

Contents at a Glance

Contents

About the Author

Frank W. Zammetti is the author of seven other books under the Apress banner as well as a number of technical articles for a variety of publications.

Frank is a lead developer/architect for a major U.S. financial services company (but he wasn't responsible for the crash a few years back, we promise!). Frank has been a "professional" developer for more than 20 years, which simply means he's been getting paid to pretend he knows what he's doing for a *long* time.

Frank is a contributor to a number of open source projects, including a few he leads and even a few he founded.

Frank is an experienced mobile developer, having worked on a number of platforms over the years including PocketPC, webOS, iOS, and Android, in a variety of technologies.

When he isn't writing yet more technical books, Frank can be found forcing his wife and kids to watch old movies that he loved as a child and assuring them that "they're cool; you just don't get it!"

About the Technical Reviewers

Andrew Zack is the CEO of ZTMC, Inc. (ztmc.com), specializing in search engine optimization (SEO) and Internet marketing strategies. His project background includes almost 20 years of site development and project management experience and more than 15 years as an SEO and Internet marketing expert.

Mr. Zack has also been very active in the publishing industry, coauthoring *Flash 5 Studio* and serving as a technical reviewer on more than ten books and industry publications.

Having started working on the Internet close to its inception, Mr. Zack has continually focused on the cutting edge and beyond, including new platforms and technologies, in order to continually stay at the forefront of the industry.

He would like to thank his father, Edward, for his support on all of this work.

Danny Swarzman is a software engineer who has been developing software for Apple products since the Apple II. He has written many magazine articles about various computer systems, both for professional programmers and for beginners. He is an electronics hobbyist who has developed sketches and interfaces for Arduino. Throughout his career, he has created software to control conveyor systems, medical equipment, milling machines, and various custom devices. When not developing software, he enjoys the occasional game of go. His e-mail is danny@stowlake.com. His site is http://stowlake.com.

Acknowledgments

It's easy to think that a book written by a single author means that one person did all of the hard work, but that couldn't be further from the truth. In reality, a book of this size, in a sense, isn't actually written by just one person; you need a strong team to back you up every step of the way (just like Michael Weston on *Burn Notice*—hey, I do love yogurt after all, so that analogy holds, right?!).

Therefore, special thanks must go out to everyone at Apress who was involved in bringing this book to completion including Kevin Shea, Michelle Lowman, Douglas Pundick, Jill Balzano, Gary Schwartz, Kumar Dhaneesh, Kim Wimpsett, and Dominic Shakeshaft.

Thank you as well to my two technical reviewers, Andrew Zack and Danny Swarzman. With my previous books, I knew my technical reviewer going in; this time it was different, as I didn't personally know them, yet the experience was, from my side anyway, a good one. I appreciate their efforts helping to make this book as good as it could possibly be!

If by chance I left anyone out, please know that it was unintentional and you have my gratitude regardless!

Introduction

Anyone who says writing mobile applications is easy probably has never actually done it. Either that or they've been focused on a single platform only. If you're trying to hit multiple platforms, it's a challenge.

Fortunately, we have a ready-made solution at our disposal—web technologies. The combination of HTML, JavaScript, CSS, and HTTP represents a development platform that you can target, and the result is that your work will largely work across multiple platforms. If you already have skills in this area, having to learn a new technology, be it Objective-C, Java, or C/C++, not to mention the myriad of device APIs that are out there to support, isn't a particularly attractive concept.

When your boss says, "Hey, we need an app to run on iPhones and iPads," you can either try to pick up those new technologies (and probably on a tight deadline, as is typical in the business world) or apply the web development skills you already have to get the solution done in record time. That, concisely, is what this book will teach you to do.

The app you write in this way will work on all the Apple-branded devices, plus the vast majority of Android devices and even other platforms that don't quite have the market share of iOS and Android but that nonetheless represent users whom it's better not to ignore if you can help it.

Who This Book Is For

This book is designed for experienced web developers who now need to tackle developing mobile apps for iOS, Android, or both, and perhaps even other platforms such as webOS, Blackberry, and Symbian. This book is for you if you already know HTML5, JavaScript, and CSS reasonably well but you don't want to learn the "native" development model for all the various platforms out there. This book won't teach you the fundamentals of those web development technologies, but you don't necessarily have to be an expert in them either to find value here. You don't need any mobile development experience, though, and that's the key point: it's all about web development in this book. The fact you're creating a mobile app in the end is almost secondary.

How This Book Is Structured

I've split the book into three parts, each covering one broad aspect of writing a single application: My Mobile Organizer. This simple personal information management (PIM) app will demonstrate all of the core concepts you need to produce mobile business applications for iOS and Android.

Part 1 deals with building the client app, that is, the part of the overall solution that runs on the mobile device. In this part, you'll be exposed to jQuery Mobile, a nice front-end JavaScript library based on the ubiquitous jQuery library.

Part 2 covers the server side of the equation. Here, you'll use the popular Node.js framework, coupled with the NoSQL MongoDB product, to build a server that responds to REST requests from the client application and serves as your persistent data store.

Part 3 discusses PhoneGap and PhoneGap Build, the tools you'll use to take your HTML5-based client application and create from it a native application that you can run on iOS, Android, and even other mobile platforms. I'll also talk about getting your app published in the various stores where users expect to find their apps these days.

Downloading the Code

The code for the examples shown in this book is available on the Apress web site, www.apress.com. You can find a link on the book's information page on the Source Code/Downloads tab. This tab is located underneath the Related Titles section of the page. While you certainly could type in all the code, I make the rather sane assumption that you won't be doing that and that you have the code downloaded and available as you read through the book.

When you download the code, you'll find within the archive two directories: chapters and MyMobileOrganizer. The directory chapters contain code found in the various chapters. (Each chapter has a subdirectory there, although not all chapters have code.) The MyMobileOrganizer directory is where you'll find the app that is the subject of this book. Within that directory, you'll find four subdirectories. Naturally, the client subdirectory is where the client portion of the app is located, meaning the code you can load into a desktop browser to test the app or that can be built into a true mobile app and deployed to a device, which will be detailed in the chapters to come. The client_augmented subdirectory is a version of the client app enhanced with some advanced capabilities, as described in Chapter 10. As I'm sure you have guessed, the server subdirectory is where the server portion of My Mobile Organizer is stored. (To start the server, you have to execute only the run.bat file.) Finally, the test subdirectory has some command-line tools for testing the server independently of the client app.

Contacting the Author

If for any reason you'd like to get a hold of me, I'm a pretty easy guy to find online. You can always e-mail me: fzammetti@etherient.com. I'm also on "the Twitter," as I hear tell the cool kids call it, as @fzammetti, if you're into that sort of thing.

Part 1

The Client

It doesn't stop *being magic just because you know how it works.*

—Terry Pratchett

I am thankful the most important key in history was invented. It's not the key to your house, your car, your boat, your safety deposit box, your bike lock, or your private community. It's the key to order, sanity, and peace of mind. The key is Delete.

—Elayne Boosler

A good programmer is someone who always looks both ways before crossing a one-way street.

—Doug Linder

The only difference between death and taxes is that death doesn't get worse every time Congress meets.

—Will Rogers

When angry, count to four. When very angry, swear.

—Mark Twain

Designing My Mobile Organizer

Designing a mobile app is no easy task! The wide variety of devices in the world makes it difficult to target them all effectively. Because of this, one of the more popular paradigms for mobilizing an app is to use the same technologies you build websites with: HTML5, JavaScript, and CSS. Doing so is, for most companies and developers nowadays, a good reuse of existing knowledge and skills. However, even after making the seemingly simple decision to follow that path, there are still a bewildering number of technology choices to be made.

Do you write all the code of the app running on the mobile device, or do you use a library to save you time? There are pluses and minuses to both answers. On the server, what technology do you use? Do you go with Java, PHP, or maybe Ruby on Rails?

Moreover, once you make those decisions, how does the client application on the mobile device communicate with the server? Sure, you can simply say "HTTP" and you're probably correct, but there's almost certainly more to it than that, especially if you want a robust and extensible application because, as all professional developers know, applications aren't a steady-state thing. No, they change, grow, and evolve over time, and if they aren't designed to accommodate that change from the start, then they can become a real nightmare to maintain.

It didn't occur to me until I sat down to write this book, but I have in fact been doing mobile development, in one form or another, for more than ten years now. I got in early in the mobile trend. Yet, even with all that experience, I have to admit that all these decision points can be overwhelming still. It *should* be easy, and maybe it will be some day, but it is not this day, to quote Lord Aragorn.[1]

---

[1]This was a line from the speech given by Lord Aragorn, one of the central characters in *The Lord of the Rings* trilogy. This speech was in front of the black gate of Mordor before the start of the intended battle meant to draw away the forces and attention of Sauron to give Frodo and Sam time to reach Mount Doom and destroy the ring of power. Wow, *now* I see why I had no luck with the ladies in my younger years!

Until that day comes, there is an emerging option that's darned good right now. In this book, you'll learn that there is a popular "full stack" that many developers are using to write mobile business apps, in fact, not just business apps but really *any* type of mobile app—yes, even games in some cases. This stack is flexible, meaning you can swap out any part of it for another. That being said, this stack has become popular for good reason: the underlying pieces make up a powerful and coherent whole that allows you to build mobile apps quickly and effectively, something you know your boss is looking for! At the same time, it allows for that growth we all know will probably occur (well, certainly you *hope* it occurs anyway, as that's a sign of a successful app).

Before we get to discuss the stack and the parts that comprise it, we need to come up with an app that can serve as the vehicle to demonstrate its usage. The app has to be something that is simple enough, frankly, to be presentable in book form while not being overwhelming but still having enough "meat on its bones," so to speak, to be able to demonstrate the stack effectively. I considered many possible app concepts, but the one that jumped out at me is something we all need: the venerable personal information manager.

The Need for Organization

A personal information manager (PIM) is an application where you can store a variety of information and recall it quickly. All mobile devices worth their salt already have this sort of functionality built into them at a fundamental level. You have the option, though, of using any of the numerous third-party apps for this sort of functionality if you prefer. That's exactly what we're going to set out to build here.

A PIM, typically, contains four pieces of information: appointments, contacts, notes, and tasks. While you can probably come up with some other things, as I can, those four are generally the ones that come immediately to anyone's mind, and most other things can actually be fit into one of those four. Those will be the four things, *entities*, as I'll call them,that our app will deal with.

We'll model each of those entities as having a set of data that makes sense for each, but it will be a minimal set. If the intent were to sell this app to others, then the set of data would need to be more expansive or, more likely, extensible to the user in some way. However, as a learning experience, we don't want the app to get overly complex, so we'll keep the data set to a minimum.

Cross-Platform Considerations

As mentioned, one of the big considerations with writing a mobile app is that it should usually be cross-platform. You want this to be true for many reasons, but one that everyone can understand is money! The more users you can reach, the more income you can potentially generate. Even if you're developing a free app and money isn't a concern, you probably still want as many eyeballs as possible on your app, so, again, supporting as many platforms as possible is a good goal.

In terms of market share, Google's Android and Apple's iOS obviously lead the pack and account for the vast majority of modern mobile devices. Therefore, cross-platform, at a minimum, means supporting those two platforms.

However, there are others to be considered: Microsoft's Windows Phone and Blackberry's OS 10, for instance, as well as others that are generally much lower on the market share ladder. Even if you don't specifically target those platforms, I think you'd agree that it's not a bad idea to avoid doing anything that *precludes* you from supporting them at some point in the future. Better still, if you choose the right set of technologies, you can support them out of the gate without doing anything special, so while our direct goal will be support for Android and iOS, we'll also support other devices indirectly by choosing technologies, which we'll discuss shortly in the "Technology Decisions" section, that allow us to do that by design.

Using the Cloud

Another consideration is data storage. That is, where will the data from our PIM be persistently stored? Simply storing it on the device probably isn't the best idea for this sort of application because if the device is lost, stolen, or broken, then that might be a serious inconvenience for the user. Many people can't keep their lives organized at all without such devices and applications anymore.

There's a drive these days to use the cloud for storing data that you want to be "durable" and not be subject to destruction if something bad happens to the mobile device. In simplest terms, storing data in the cloud means storing your data on an Internet-connected server and making it available through some sort of interface that a client application can use.

The term *cloud* actually has a number of meanings and discrete forms besides simple data storage.

- *Software as a Service* (SaaS) means applications hosted on a server that you could access and use almost as if they were installed on your local device. SaaS also to some means web application programming interfaces (APIs) that you can access remotely. Some examples of SaaS include Salesforce (www.salesforce.com), a customer relationship management (CRM) service, and GoToMeeting (www.gotomeeting.com), an online virtual meeting service.

- *Infrastructure as a Service* (IaaS) means the hosting of real or virtualized systems. If you need a Linux machine, for example, you can have a virtual server built and hosted in the cloud with IaaS, removing the responsibility of building and maintaining the hardware yourself (whether that hardware is real or virtual doesn't really matter in this model; you don't care as the client of IaaS and in fact may not even know). The benefit of this is that most of the responsibility for maintaining servers, worrying about updates, ensuring proper virus protection is in place, and so on, are dealt with by the provider, allowing you to focus on what really matters most to you, namely, your business. Some examples of IaaS include Amazon EC2 (http://aws.amazon.com/ec2) and Google App Engine (http://developers.google.com/appengine).

- *Platform as a Service* (PaaS) is effectively an extension of IaaS where instead of just a virtualized server you get a virtualized "full stack" including things such as databases, web/app servers, and programming execution environments. Examples of PaaS include IBM's SmartCloud Application Services (www.ibm.com/cloud-computing/us/en/paas.html) and VCE's VBLOCK (www.vce.com/products/vblock/overview).

■ *Network as a Service* (NaaS) includes capabilities such as VPNs and "bandwidth on demand." Once again, this removes the need to administer the hardware and/or software for your networking capabilities yourself. Any VPN, such as GigaNews' VyprVPN (www.giganews.com/vyprvpn), is an example of NaaS.

■ *Storage as a Service* (also abbreviated SaaS) is similar to IaaS but deals specifically with data storage. Sites such as Dropbox, Google Drive, and Microsoft's SkyDrive are all examples of SaaS.

For the purposes of our little PIM application, we're going to use the SaaS model (where the first *S* is Software). We'll build a server-side component to the app that will present an API for our client application running on a mobile device to call on. This API will provide basic CRUD (create, read, update, and delete) operations for our four entity types of appointments, contacts, notes, and tasks. The data will be stored on the server in a database to ensure that if the mobile device needs to be reset, the data will persist.

What About Sunny Days?

Of course, we need to account for the possibility that our cloud-based API, and therefore our PIM data, won't be available at any given time. Perhaps the server is offline. Maybe we're hiking in the mountains and don't have a network connection (I'd question why someone in that situation needs to check when their next dentist appointment is, but who am I to judge?).

Therefore, we will need to do some caching of data on the client so that we can still, at a minimum, look at our existing data, even if we cannot create new items. As with the cross-platform issue, if we choose the correct technologies, we should be able to do this with a minimum of hassle and without writing code specific to each platform we want to support.

A PIM for All Seasons

With a general idea of what we're looking to build in mind, I present to you the admittedly not very creatively named My Mobile Organizer app!

This app will provide us with a user interface on any Android or iOS mobile device (as well as others) that communicates with a cloud-based API that we'll build for storing and manipulating our data. It will allow offline access to that data in a read-only fashion as well, and all of this will be done using technologies that allow us to have a single code base for all supported platforms.

Before we get to the technology decisions, let's look a little more closely at the four entity types My Mobile Organizer will help us organize, including mocking up what the screens for each will look like. We'll also talk about some overall navigation, a home screen for the app, and some other miscellaneous UI elements that we'll need to make a complete app.

Home Screen, Header, and Navigational Footer

When the app starts, we need a place for the user to land by default. Sure, we could try somehow to divine what entity they intend to deal with and show the appointment, contact, note, or task screen right away, but really, we don't know their intent going in. Therefore, we need a basic "home screen" instead. This doesn't need to be anything fancy and may be not much more than what you see in Figure 1-1.

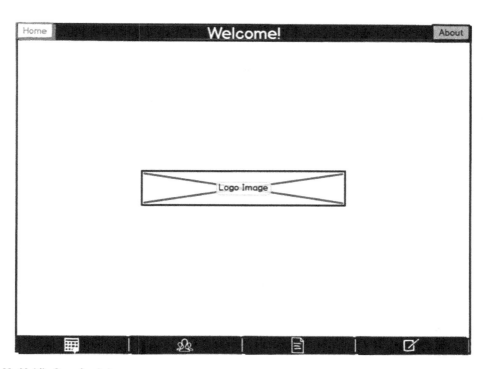

Figure 1-1. My Mobile Organizer's home screen

The basic layout is quite simple, beginning with two elements that will appear on all screens in the app: the header and the navigation bar (or *navbar* for short) at the bottom. The header at the top will always have a button on the left (disabled here of course because we're already there) that returns the user to the home screen and an About button on the right that will show the user a little "about this program" dialog. This button will change on other screens to a menu of functionality specific to the entity the user is dealing with, but on the home screen it's just the About button. In between them is greeting text because, after all, our app should be polite and friendly!

In the center of the screen is a little logo for the app. In keeping with the notion of "low-fidelity" mock-ups, I am using a simple placeholder.

More About Mocking Up Screens

Figure 1-1, as is the case with all of the screen mock-ups that appear in this chapter, was generated with Balsamiq Mockups, which you can find at www.balsamiq.com. The nice thing about this program is that, as you can see, it generates "sketches," not proper screens.

Any time you start to mock up a UI, you want to do "low-fidelity" versions first, often drawing them by hand or sometimes using bits of construction paper pinned to a board. This not only allows you to quickly make changes and iterate the design but also keeps the focus where it should be: on navigation, functionality, and overall layout. You don't worry about things such as colors and fonts (for the most part anyway) because those elements aren't important in the first phase of design and obviously won't be final in a low-fidelity mock-up. What's important is figuring out your overall navigation and basic screen layout, where functionality resides, and how the user accesses it. Especially when working with clients, it's easy for nondesigners (yes, which usually includes us developers) to get bogged down in details that shouldn't be the concern up front. Some people prefer doing basic HTML5 work to do such mock-ups, but even that level of "perfection" can distract from what's important because it becomes easy to focus on the color of things, the graphics used, and so on.

Balsamiq Mockups is ideally suited for this because it allows you to do these sorts of low-fidelity mock-ups without having to have any real artistic ability—something very much needed if, like me, you couldn't draw a straight line by hand to save your life! You get the benefit of the low-fidelity look while also having the benefit of being digital, so you get a more word processor type of capability while saving a few trees in the process. This neat little tool is available for multiple platforms too, so you shouldn't have an issue using it no matter what your preferred environment.

At the bottom is our omnipresent navbar. We'll use only icons rather than words (or icons and words together) to save some horizontal space. From left to right the icons are appointments, contacts, notes, and tasks—which, if I've done a reasonable job choosing icons, should be obvious!

About Dialog

When the user clicks the About button on the home screen, they should see some information about the app, as well as one small piece of functionality, for lack of a better place to put it. However, I didn't want displaying this information to require a transition to an entirely new screen. Instead, I wanted it to be shown on the home screen, overlaid on top of it to be more precise, as you see in Figure 1-2.

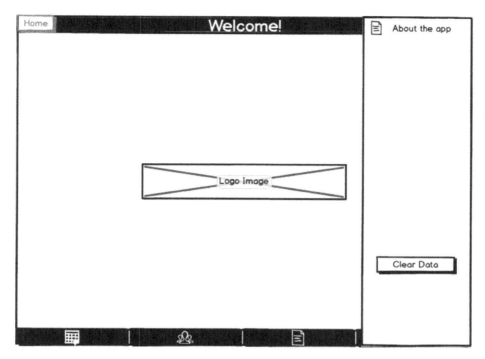

Figure 1-2. *The About overlay*

This overlay should slide in from the right and then slide away when the user taps anywhere outside of it. Note that I haven't detailed what information should be displayed, and this is by design. Remember, these are intended to be low-fidelity mock-ups, so getting into too much detail about specific content would be counter to that intention. Of course, it's a fine line determining what's too specific and what's not specific enough, and sometimes you might cross it, as you could argue I've done in a few of the mock-ups to come. The point is to put in as little detail as you think makes sense but that still gets the basic design across.

In addition to the "about" information, there will also be a single button that the user can use to clear all of their data. When tapped, the user should see an alert-type dialog, as shown in Figure 1-3.

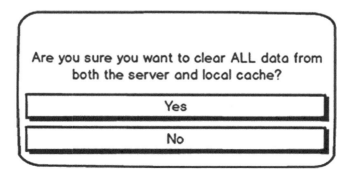

Figure 1-3. *Verification alert dialog for the Clear Data button*

Not only is this a good feature to provide to the user for security purposes, but it's also quite handy when developing such an application. During the time I was coding this app, I used this function a number of times to reset things to a "clean state" and make it easier to see whether things were working as expected.

Appointments

The first type of data entity that our little PIM application will manage is appointments. Clicking the leftmost button on the navbar, the one with the calendar icon, accesses this functionality.

Data Model

Before we get to the screen mock-ups, let's look at the data model, that is, what information about an appointment we'll store. Figure 1-4 diagrams an Appointment object.

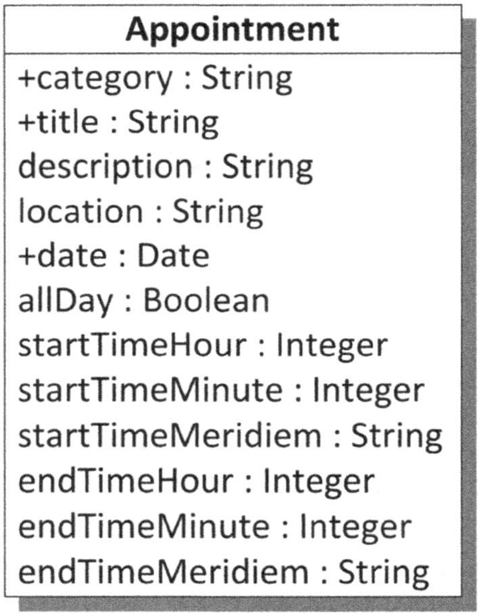

Appointment
+category : String
+title : String
description : String
location : String
+date : Date
allDay : Boolean
startTimeHour : Integer
startTimeMinute : Integer
startTimeMeridiem : String
endTimeHour : Integer
endTimeMinute : Integer
endTimeMeridiem : String

Figure 1-4. Appointment data model

category, a field that will be common to all the data models, lets the user determine whether this is a personal appointment or a business-related appointment. The title and description fields are arbitrary bits of text the user sets to identify their appointment. The location field stores where the appointment will occur, and the date field tells us when the appointment is. The allDay field is a Boolean flag that, when true, tells us the appointment lasts for the entire day. When false, the startTimeHour, startTimeMinute, startTimeMeridiem, endTimeHour, endTimeMinute, and endTimeMeridiem fields become relevant because they tell us when the appointment occurs on the specified date.

In this data model, and all the others to come, a plus sign in front of the field name denotes a required field. The client application will be responsible for enforcing these when an item is created.

> **Note**   Meridiem, in case you aren't aware (many people aren't, don't feel bad!), is the a.m./p.m. portion of a time.

I decided to break up the times like this more for learning reasons: it allowed me to demonstrate some features of jQuery Mobile, the UI library used to build My Mobile Organizer, which I might not have been able to otherwise. Whether it leads to the best user experience (UX) is debatable.

As you'll see in the chapters to come as we dissect the code, the data models described in this chapter represent a JavaScript Object Notation (JSON) structure that will be stored in a server-side database as well as a client-side data cache. In addition to the fields shown, all entities will therefore wind up having two "hidden" fields: _id and __v. The _id field is a system-generated ID unique to each object created, and __v is a version indicator that, while unused in this application, would allow us to identify whether a given object was created using a previous version of the database schema and possibly upgrade them if needed. This can be useful when you update the application later and need to change the data models underneath too. I haven't shown them in the data model diagrams, however, as they're a creation of the database we'll store the data in and so not part of our data model per se.

List View Mock-Up

With the data model described, we can now move on to screen mock-ups. Each entity type (appointment, contact, note, and task) will effectively have not one but *two* screens for working with it. The first is the list view, as shown in Figure 1-5, for appointments.

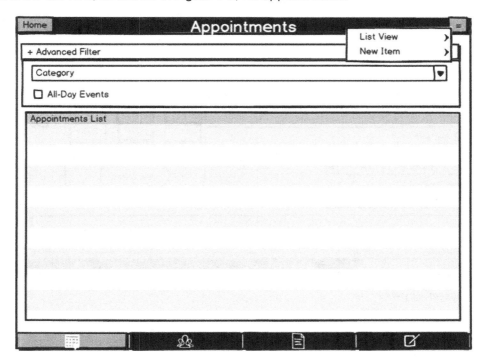

Figure 1-5. Appointment list view

At the top, we have an Advanced Filter section, which is in fact a collapsible section that starts out collapsed, but I've shown it expanded in the mock-up to provide a more complete picture of the screen. In the case of appointments, we can filter the list, which takes up the rest of the screen, by the category, as well as showing only all-day events.

Each of the entity screens has a menu in the upper-right corner, taking the place of the About button on the home screen. When the button is tapped, a menu expands that allows the user to flip back to the list view (which of course makes sense only when they're not on the list view) as well as an option to initiate creating a new appointment. On the mock-up, as with the Advanced Filter section, I've shown that menu as it would appear when the menu button is tapped, but the user would of course not see this until they actually do tap the button.

The list itself is just a simple list of appointment titles, sorted by date. The user can tap any list item to see further details, as well as update it.

Entry View Mock-Up

When the user taps an item in the list, they will be shown the entry view, as in Figure 1-6. This same screen serves double-duty: it allows the user to update an existing item as well as to create a new item.

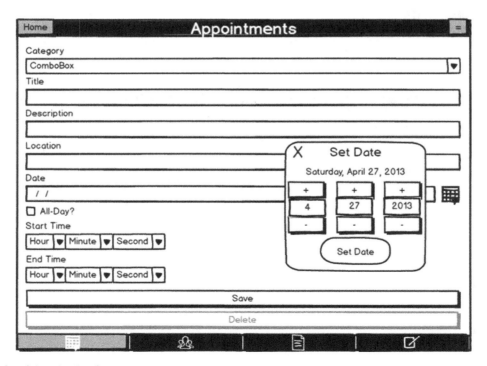

Figure 1-6. Appointment entry view

All the fields from the data model are represented here. Category is a combo box while Title, Description, and Location are simple text fields. The Date field is a text field as well; however, when it receives focus, it triggers a pop-up, which I've shown overlaid on the mock-up. This allows the user to set the date without actually having to type anything. The start time and end time fields are three combo boxes, one for each element of the time.

Finally, we have two buttons at the bottom, Save and Delete. The Delete button will be disabled, as shown in the mock-up, when creating an item but will be enabled if the user clicks an item from the list. When Save is tapped, one of the two dialogs in Figure 1-7 will be shown, depending on the outcome of the save.

Figure 1-7. *The possible outcomes of a save (or delete)*

When a delete of an existing item is done, one of these dialogs is shown as well, of course with the appropriate text in the case of success. In any case, the user is returned to the list view, with the list properly updated to reflect the outcome of the save (or delete).

Contacts

Now that you've seen the data model and screen mock-ups for appointments, the rest of the entities should be quick and easy to get through, as they're substantially the same, aside, of course, from the data fields involved. That is entirely by design: the app is designed such that there isn't much separate code for each entity type except in places where there truly *needs* to be. We'll get into how that's accomplished starting in the next chapter, but for now let's continue our journey through the entities and see what differences are present.

Data Model

The data model for contacts, as shown in Figure 1-8, is actually quite simple.

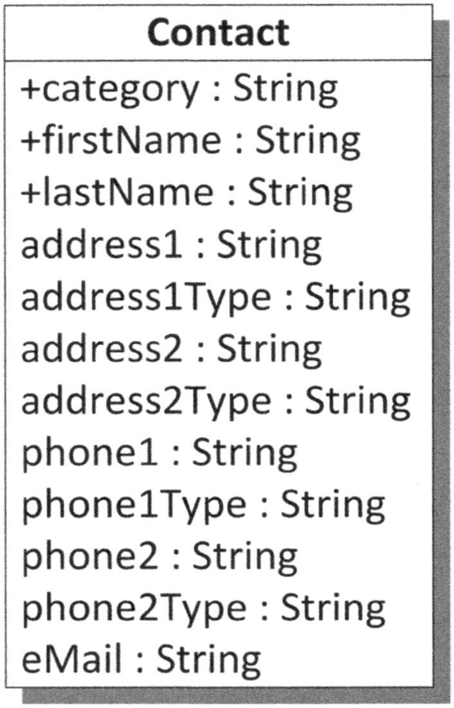

Figure 1-8. Contact data model

While there may be a fair number of fields, unlike appointments, we don't even have different data types this time around. Everything in a contact is a simple string. category, firstName, and lastName are all obvious I suspect. For every contact, we allow the user to save two addresses and two phone numbers. Further, they can determine whether each address is a home address, business address, or other address. Similarly, a phone number can be designated a home phone, business phone, cell phone, fax, or other. That's the purpose of the address1Type, address2Type, phone1Type, and phone2Type fields. The address1, address2, phone1, and phone2 fields are where the actual addresses and phone numbers are stored. Finally, we store an eMail address too as that's a common piece of information to want about a contact.

List View Mock-Up

The list view mock-up for contacts, shown in Figure 1-9, isn't much different from the one for appointments, but there *are* in fact a few minor differences.

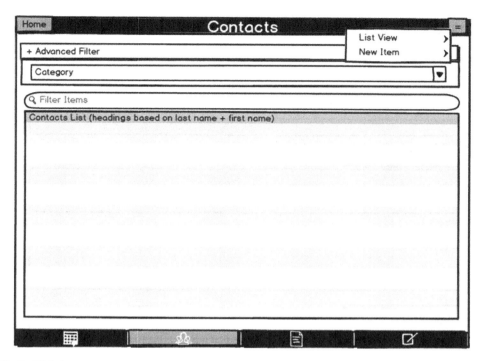

Figure 1-9. Contact list view

First, the Advanced Filter section has only a single filter field this time, Category. However, outside of that section is a Filter Items entry box. This is always present and allows the user to type into this field, and the list will be filtered such that only items matching what the user enters are shown. In addition, the list will have headings between items based on the last name and first name (combined as "last name, first name") and is alphabetized.

Entry View Mock-Up

When the user chooses to either create a new contact or edit an existing one, the entry view shown in Figure 1-10 is what they see.

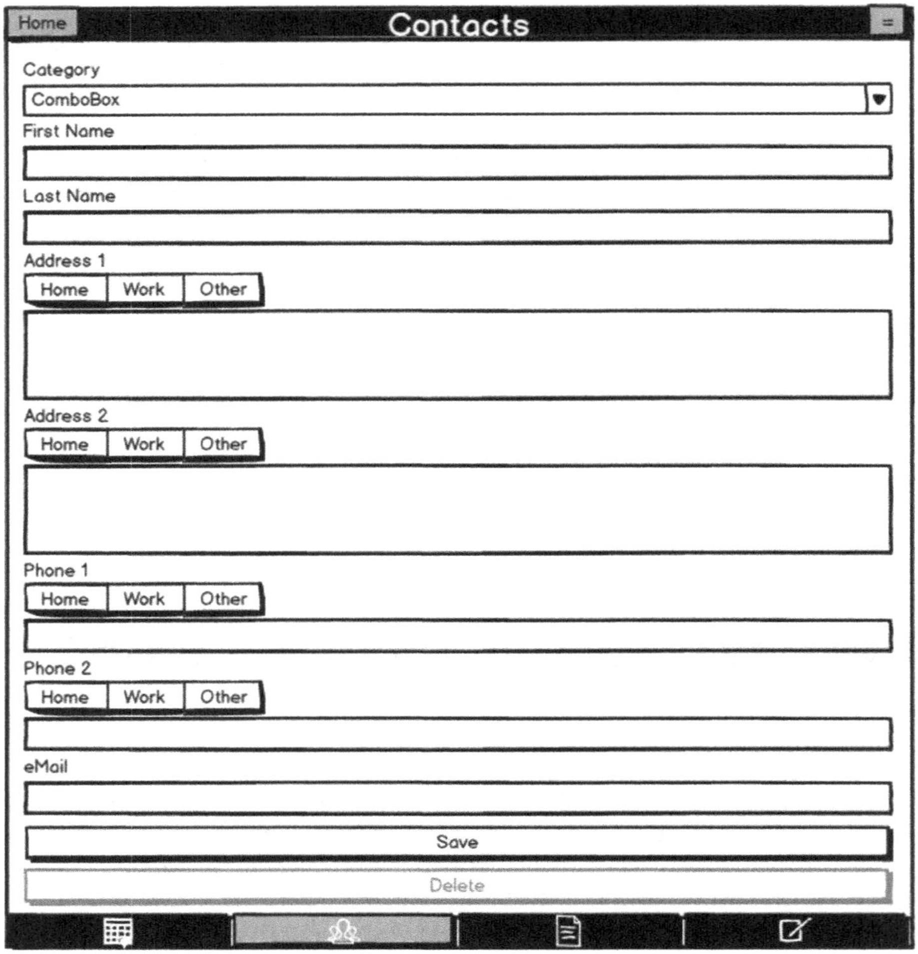

Figure 1-10. *Contact entry view*

For Address 1 and Address 2 we provide text areas to type in, larger than the single-line text fields used for First Name and Last Name. In addition, three buttons are above each section that function similarly to radio buttons in that only one can be selected at any given time. This is true for the two phone numbers as well.

The dialogs for saving and deleting are the same as for appointments but naturally have the appropriate text on them.

Notes

The notes entity is actually the simplest. After all, when you get right down to it, a note isn't much more than some text, right? Still, we'll look at everything for the sake of full disclosure if nothing else!

Data Model

The data model, shown in Figure 1-11, is rather sparse.

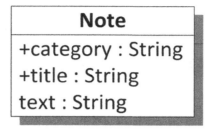

Figure 1-11. Note data model

As with all entities, we have a category field, along with a title and the actual text of the note. That's all there is to a note; it's very simple!

List View Mock-Up

The list view for notes is nearly identical to the one for contacts, except that what's shown is the title of the note. Figure 1-12 is the mock-up of this view.

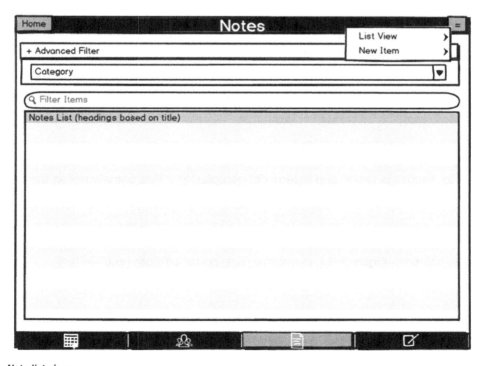

Figure 1-12. Note list view

We can again filter by category as well as type in the Filter Items box to find items with the text we type in the title.

Entry View Mock-Up

The entry view for notes couldn't be simpler, as you can see in Figure 1-13.

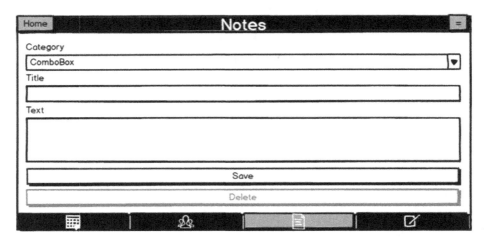

Figure 1-13. Note entry view

It's just the usual category combo box, followed by a text field for the title and a text area to type the text of the note. In addition, in all entry views where we have text areas, we want the text areas to expand vertically as the user adds text. That way, users can type as much as they like.

The Save and Delete buttons are once again present and work the same as for appointments and contacts, including the dialogs that can result from them.

Tasks

The final entity to discuss is tasks, and in terms of complexity, it falls somewhere in the middle of the previous three entities. It's not the simplest but probably not the most complex either.

Data Model

The data model, shown in Figure 1-14, is minimal, not too far off from notes in fact.

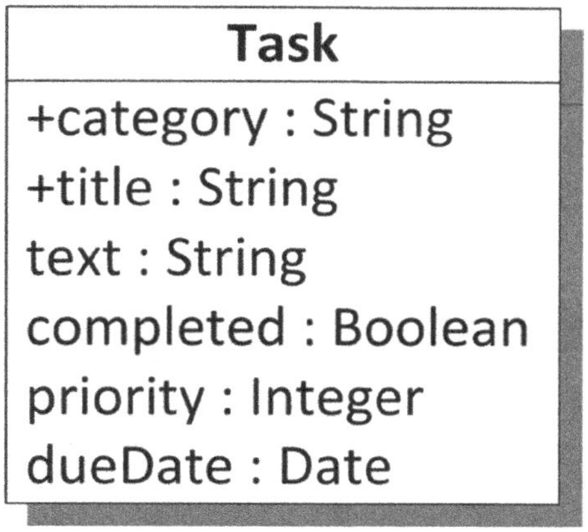

Task

+category : String
+title : String
text : String
completed : Boolean
priority : Integer
dueDate : Date

Figure 1-14. *Task data model*

The category, title, and text fields you're familiar with at this point. For a task, we also want a Boolean flag that tells us whether the task has been completed, and that's the purpose of the completed field. A task should also have a priority we can assign to it, and we'll arbitrarily have a five-level scale of priorities that the user can choose from. In fact, we won't even tell the user whether one is the highest priority or five is; that'll be up to them! Of course, a task needs a dueDate as well in most cases, so there's a field for that too.

List View Mock-Up

Figure 1-15 shows the list view for tasks, which should look quite familiar!

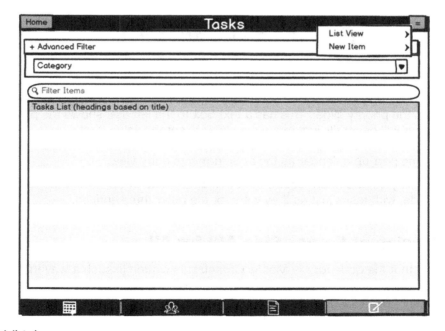

Figure 1-15. *Task list view*

Yes, this list view is identical to that for notes, including the filtering that is possible.

Entry View Mock-Up

The entry view for tasks, shown in Figure 1-16, is where we finally come to some more substantial differences and some new UI tricks too!

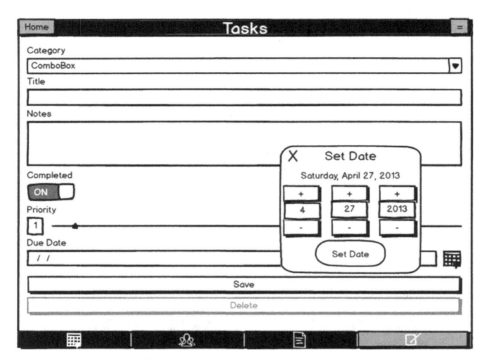

Figure 1-16. Task entry view

After the category, title, and notes, we have an on/off slider to indicate whether the task is completed. Next is the priority slider. This has a text box to the left that shows the priority as a number, but the user will generally just move the slider to set the value (that's up to them, though, because entering a number directly will update the slider as well). Finally, we have the Due Date field, which uses the same pop-up calendar as the appointments entry view.

At the risk of sounding like a broken record, the Save and Delete buttons, and the resultant dialogs, are along for the ride, with tasks just as they were for the other three entities.

... and a Consistent Server-Side API for All

I mentioned earlier that the code for My Mobile Organizer is written in such a way that all four types of entities are largely treated identically. As you'll see in the coming chapters, this reduces the amount of code needed and tends to simplify things a bit. It also allows the code to be written more generically, which is a plus because it means the app can be extended in the future easier (to add other entity types, for example) and also centralizes things such as error handling to avoid redundant, mostly identical code. There are of course places where writing generic code just isn't possible, but generic code was a guiding principle.

Nowhere is this more evident perhaps than in the server-side API that the client app uses. Simply put, we have four basic CRUD (create, read, update, and delete) operations available for every entity type. That is to say, there is *not* a separate API function for a contact versus a note, for example, to do an update; there's simply an update API call that knows how to handle a contact as well as a note. This is true for all entity types and all API functions.

The function to clear all data falls outside of this model, though, and that's where we see some nongeneric code. Even still, you'll see in later chapters that even it fits nicely within a common model, so even though it's something of a "special function," as compared to the basic CRUD operations, it's not *that* much different either.

How this is all accomplished is a deeper conversation that is presented in Part II of this book, starting with Chapter 5, but for now, you should be aware of this underlying design principle and expect to see it in the server-side API design when we get to that.

Offline Access and Synchronization

One other big consideration of any mobile application is what it does, or doesn't do, when no network connectivity is available. A few years ago, the idea of cloud-based data storage and APIs was ridiculous! The idea that you'd have an always-on Internet connection, especially from a mobile device, was borderline insane. Nowadays, though, it's the norm. Therefore, people expect their apps to continue to work, to at least some degree, even if they can't get on the Net.

My Mobile Organizer will be no different. However, it's not a simple concern because the concepts behind offline access and data synchronization can get hairy in a hurry!

For example, should we allow notes to be created when the user is offline? If so, what happens when connectivity is restored? How do we synchronize the added note with the database on the server? What if that database is also accessible from somewhere else, say a desktop web interface? How do we then synchronize if the user made a change to a contact on the offline mobile device while also making a change to the same contact from the web interface? How do we resolve such conflicts and ensure our data, both on the client and server, is always in a consistent state?

Caching and synchronization are expansive topics that can drive you crazy to get right and nearly always require a good amount of complex code to handle well. Fortunately, some much simpler approaches can largely alleviate the concerns and difficulty involved for you as a developer.

One of the easiest is simply to reduce the functionality of the app somewhat when offline. Some apps simply *can't* work offline under *any* circumstances because of their very nature, but others can, just with a reduction in their capabilities. We'll use that approach for My Mobile Organizer.

Put concisely, the app will go into a read-only mode when offline. The user can still view all their appointments, contacts, notes, and tasks, because we'll cache all that data on the device, but they will be unable to create, update, or delete any entities until connectivity has been restored. That's a fair compromise between an entirely useless app when offline and one that has a ton of complex and potentially brittle code to handle synchronization more robustly. It's not a perfect solution by any stretch, but if we make the simplifying assumption that the app will always have a single user accessing the server component from a single mobile device, then it works out reasonably well.

> **Tip**   One other approach that I considered that wouldn't be overly complex is the log approach: every update when offline is logged, meaning all the details of the change are stored locally on the device. Then, when connectivity is restored, the app runs through the log and executes the updates in the order they were originally done. The local copy of the data would already be up-to-date in this model, so only the server-side database would need to be updated. The downside to this is that it does nothing to deal with situation of multiple users or multiple devices; conflicting updates can still arise. Therefore, in order to ensure the complexity of this app didn't balloon too much and become unwieldy as a learning exercise (which, remember, is the point of why we're here!), I decided against that approach in lieu of the "reduced functionality" approach.

One other simplifying assumption we'll make is that if connectivity is available at app start-up, then it's available all the time for the current execution of the app, and likewise, if it's unavailable at start-up, then it's unavailable until the app is restarted and connectivity is checked again.

Technology Decisions

Now that you have a clear picture of *what* we're building and what it'll do, let's get into the questions of *how* to build it. This is the part where we get into those technology decisions I mentioned at the start of the chapter. Let's begin by discussing how we're going to build the client portion of the app.

Native or Mobile Web?

The first major decision point when thinking about creating a mobile app is whether to code it as a native app. In other words, do we write our app in Objective-C for iOS devices and then write it again in Java for Android and then in C# for Windows Mobile devices, and so on, for each platform we want to support, or do we instead use the power of web development to create a "mobile web" app?

It's more than just the programming languages used to consider: the underlying APIs you need to deal with will be different, as well as how you lay out and construct screens, and so on. Yes, if you're smart and architect your code reasonably well, then you'll find you can reuse some of the native code, if not directly, then close enough to lessen the burden of developing for multiple, disparate platforms. Even if you do a good job in this regard, though, you'll still be developing, and don't forget maintaining, multiple code bases going forward; there's just no way around it with true native development.

So, if it's such a hassle, why do people *ever* do native mobile development at all? Certainly, there are some good reasons, chief among them being performance and access to the full capabilities of the devices.

It's hard to argue that the performance of a native version of a given app will usually be superior to that of a mobile web solution. The question is whether that difference will be significant enough to offset the cost of doing that development. To be sure, some types of apps truly do require every ounce of performance and power a mobile device can muster. Games are a prime example. For those types of apps, native development *tends* to be better in terms of performance.

> **Note** In addition to mobile web solutions, there is also the notion of cross-platform "native" development. A number of fantastic cross-platform development tools can very nearly match the performance of native apps while abstracting away from you all those pesky native development issues. I actually wrote a book on one: the Corona SDK (the book is *Learn Corona SDK Game Development*, also published by Apress). While these tools don't provide "true" native development, the abstraction they provide allows a single code base to run at near-native performance on a number of platforms. It usually comes down to what type of app you're writing and what capabilities it truly needs in determining which approach is best, as well as what skill set you already have.

The other concern is that of full access to a device's capabilities. Mobile web development tends to have some limitations in this regard because those capabilities have to be presented in a JavaScript-exposed API that you have access to from your own code, and such APIs aren't always available in mobile web development environments. The situation there is most definitely improving with HTML5 and all it has to offer, but it alone isn't the answer just yet.

Oftentimes, though, the cost of native development, even using a good cross-browser tool, outweighs the performance benefits and device capability access that native development offers. It all comes down, of course, to the margins. How close is mobile web development in terms of performance? How much of the device's capabilities do we have access to from a mobile web app? If it's close enough and our app has some leeway in terms of what it needs, then mobile web development is the way to go.

Why is that? Well, first is reusing existing skills. Especially in the business world, developers, more often than not, are "web" developers. They already know HTML5, JavaScript, CSS, and related technologies. It's to everyone's benefit to use those existing skills. It saves time and money and usually leads to better solutions since there's a lot of experience getting things right to draw from. The knowledge gained over the years developing web applications can be transferred to mobile development, and the quality of the initial solutions will usually be better than they would be if you tried to do native development without the benefit of that experience.

Second, web technologies are by definition designed to be cross-platform. As long as you have a web browser on a given platform, you can target it. Even the best of the near-native cross-platform tools that are available can't usually target as many platforms as the mobile web approach can.

In addition, remember that most web technologies are open standards, not controlled by any one company. That's usually a better position to be in from a business perspective than going with a more proprietary solution.

Certainly, for an app like My Mobile Organizer, a mobile web approach makes a lot of sense, even if it wasn't just a learning exercise in a book! Here are some aspects to consider:

- It doesn't have intensive computational requirements.
- Its screens are, relatively speaking, not all that complex.

- While we of course want it to perform well, it isn't, by its nature, something that requires oodles of performance.

- It's the type of app that could be useful on any mobile device, so ideally we want to target every platform we possibly can.

Overall, it's not a terribly difficult decision to make in this case. Still, I wanted to walk you through some of the thought process and some of the other options because I'm not trying to convince you that a mobile web approach is The One True Approach To Mobile Development™. While a good answer in many cases, perhaps even in most cases, it's not always the best choice, and you should evaluate each project on its own to decide which way to go.

Choosing a Mobile Web Library

Now that we know we're building a mobile web app, the next question to ask is what technologies to use to build the client with. Of course, a mobile web app means we're using HTML5, CSS, and JavaScript. However, that's not all there is to it!

Do we do "naked" HTML5, CSS, and JavaScript? Meaning, do we write all of it by hand ourselves? While I'm an old-fashioned type of developer who likes to write as much of my own code as possible, I'm also a business developer in my day job, which means I can't be spending company money on things that don't truly *need* to be developed by hand.

Take, as a simple example, the navbar in our mock-ups. Writing that by hand wouldn't be the most complex undertaking by any stretch. However, there are aspects to it that could get tricky. For example, how do we maintain state when jumping between pages? How do we anchor it to the bottom of the page regardless of the size of our content? How do we style the buttons dynamically without needing a number of different images (that we'd have to develop ourselves too)? None of that is rocket science to be sure, but even if it takes just an hour or two to write ourselves, aren't there better ways to spend that time?

There's plenty of code we're going to have to write ourselves no matter what, so why not lessen the burden by smartly choosing some libraries to take care of at least some of the more mundane tasks? That's smart development if you ask me. After all, good developers code; great developers steal!

When you start to look at the mobile web libraries available, you'll come across a number of options. There's Sencha Touch (www.sencha.com), which is a very good library designed specifically for mobile web development. It allows us to develop screens using JavaScript and provides things such as widgets (grids, buttons, calendars, and so on) as well as a robust data-handling module, among lots of other things.

There's DHTMLX Touch (www.dhtmlx.com) that provides a full HTML5-based framework and widget set for developing mobile applications.

There are also some old favorites like Dojo (www.dojotoolkit.org) and Yahoo's YUI (www.yuilibrary.com) that, while not exclusively mobile-oriented, are capable of helping develop mobile web apps nonetheless.

However, one of the most popular general JavaScript libraries in existence (many polls indicate it is in fact *the* most popular) is jQuery (www.jquery.com). As a more general-purpose JavaScript library, however, jQuery isn't focused on mobile development. Although not an all-inclusive description, probably the main goal of jQuery is to make Document Object Model (DOM) manipulation easier, and it does this exceedingly well. It's extremely fast, lightweight, and, most importantly for the purposes of this discussion, extensible.

That extensibility comes into play with jQuery Mobile (`www.jquerymobile.com`), which is built on top of jQuery. This library is an HTML5-based system for developing mobile UIs. It contains widgets and helper functions for putting such apps together, among other things.

I don't want to get into too much detail about jQuery Mobile here as that's what Chapter 2 is focused on, but suffice it to say it is popular for a reason, as is jQuery underneath it. It's a fine choice for My Mobile Organizer, as you'll see in the coming chapters.

Server-Side Architecture

With the client-side decisions of mobile web app using jQuery Mobile decided, how do we build the server side? Clearly, there's a ton of choices there too.

Do you already know Java (`www.oracle.com`)? Then that might be a good choice. What about PHP (`http://us.php.net`)? Again, there's nothing wrong with PHP in my mind, even though some would argue that it isn't appropriate for "professional" development. I'm not here to pass judgment, though! If you know PHP already, then it's certainly worth considering. Are Microsoft technologies (`www.microsoft.com`) up your alley? If that's a skill set you already have, then they are not a bad choice. Ruby on Rails (`www.rubyonrails.org`) perhaps? Yes, it's worthy of consideration certainly, as are any of a dozen other possible technologies you might come across.

All of these also require potentially significant server infrastructures. Java requires an entire servlet container. PHP is an extension to an existing web server. Microsoft of course requires IIS, its proprietary web server, plus the appropriate extensions. Ruby on Rails is its own server product essentially. All of these also require administration expertise and are therefore somewhat complex to work with, depending on what you might already know.

At the end of the day, there's another option that's fast becoming very popular, and for good reason: node.js (`www.nodejs.org`). One of the key benefits to node.js is that the code you write on the server side is written in JavaScript, just as your client-side code is. Since one of the reasons I stated for going with a mobile web approach is reuse of skills, shouldn't that apply to the server side as well? I think so! The idea of the same language on both sides of the conversation, meaning client side and server side, and assuming performance isn't a problem, is attractive to many people.

The other big benefit of node.js is that it is designed for high performance and concurrency from the start. While neither of these concerns is particularly big for My Mobile Organizer frankly, there's no good reason to use technologies that hamstring us in either regard.

As with jQuery Mobile, we'll be getting intimate with node.js in Chapter 5, but just this little bit of introduction should give you a good foundation to go forward with before then.

What About the Database?

Of course, just deciding on node.js for the server side isn't quite the whole story. There's also data storage to consider. We need a database of some sort too, don't we?

Of course we do!

So then, which do we use? Oracle (`www.oracle.com`)? It's a great database supporting tons of massive, high-availability systems out there. Yet, it's expensive, so it's probably not the best choice for our relatively minor app. What about the popular MySQL (`www.mysql.com`)? It's very good, no question; I use it tons myself. To make a long story short, there are many choices to choose from in this area, too many to name.

Given that we've decided on node.js, are there any options that work well with it? Yes, all of the above in fact can be used with it. There's another choice, though, that is very popular and is part of the "NoSQL" movement: MongoDB.

The NoSQL movement is an approach to data storage that eschews the need for Structured Query Language (SQL) that all relational database management systems (RDBMSs) are based upon. It's fundamentally different in that you store "documents," as opposed to relational data in the form of tables and rows of data. It goes along fantastically well with JavaScript, and therefore node.js, because a "document" can be simply an object represented with JSON, which of course is native, even the lingua franca really, of JavaScript. MongoDB is one very popular implementation of this concept, and it integrates exceedingly well with node.js.

Chapter 6 is where we'll deep-dive into MongoDB so for now, suffice to say that its NoSQL approach, and the simple API made available to our node.js app for it, makes it easy to work with and provides a good data storage mechanism for our PIM app.

Client-Server Communications

The next piece of the puzzle is how our client app will talk to our server component. As My Mobile Organizer is really the combination of a mobile client web app and a server component, we know fundamentally we'll be dealing with HTTP to communicate between the two parts, but that's not the whole story.

If we were using a Java-based server, Direct Web Remoting (DWR; `www.directwebremoting.org`) is an option I'm particularly fond of. It provides a mechanism that makes remote server calls look like any other local JavaScript call.

Alas, we're not talking Java here, so that's out. Instead, we're almost certainly talking about Ajax, the well-known Asynchronous JavaScript and XML. This allows us to make "out-of-band" requests from a browser to a server without refreshing the entire page, as web browsers and web pages were originally designed to do. This is the most popular way, by far, for a modern web app to talk to a server. All modern browsers provide this simple mechanism.

However, in recent years, people have discovered that doing "naked" Ajax isn't the panacea they thought it was early on, and one of the big reasons is that there's no clearly defined API that Ajax demands. You can make an Ajax request to any arbitrary URL and send and receive any arbitrary data, and it's up to the client and server to agree on the communication protocol they'll use. What form does the data take? What kinds of commands can be used, and how do you specify a command?

Naturally, this isn't a particularly difficult thing to do, but having to define that contract means you have to maintain it going forward too, so things can break at the most inopportune time (usually when you're sipping a margarita on a beach on your vacation and a production app goes down!). Perhaps more importantly, putting another protocol on top of HTTP strikes many developers as superfluous. HTTP is itself a protocol, of course, so isn't it sufficient on its own?

To address these concerns, the notion of Representational State Transfer (REST) has emerged. REST really is not much more than a well-defined contract between clients and servers that they agree to follow in terms of what URLs, things you're already using everywhere on the Web anywhere, look like and represent. In that regard at least, it's no different from defining your own protocol. The difference, though, is that REST uses fundamental characteristics of HTTP to define that contract, so in a sense it's not really another protocol; it's merely defining HTTP requests consistently. In addition, REST is a well-defined standard now that has become popular fast because it's both simple to understand and easy to implement in code. A so-called RESTful API is quite easy to deal with in every way us developers would want, largely anyway.

Therefore, for My Mobile Organizer, REST is the way we'll go. Chapter 7 is, ostensibly, where we'll get into the details of REST; however, we'll necessarily have to touch on it in the chapters that precede it, so don't worry—it won't be long before we get into the details of REST!

Mobilizing the App

Simply deciding to write a mobile web app isn't the end of the story in terms of making our app truly mobile. While it's entirely true that you could host your app on a web server and people could just navigate to it any time they want with the web browser on their mobile device, that isn't what most people want. It's just not the most convenient way. Nowadays, people instead expect an app they can download from the app store of their choice and run on their device. They don't even want to know, and arguably *shouldn't* know, that what they're seeing and interacting with is a web app. Therefore, we'll need to figure out how to take our mobile app, which in essence is just a website designed for mobile devices and package it into a *proper* mobile app that runs just like a native app would.

There are actually fewer choices to accomplish this than most of the other technology choices we've talked about so far, and really one name floats to the top immediately when you go looking for such a solution: PhoneGap.

PhoneGap simply wraps your HTML5-based website in native code scaffolding and creates a properly packaged application that can be executed on a given mobile platform. It can create an iOS-based package, an Android package, a Windows Mobile package, and a number of others. These packages are installed and run just as with any other application is on a mobile device. What the app really is, though, is nothing but a full-screen web browser with your HTML5-based application inside of it! Pretty neat, isn't it?

PhoneGap also provides you with a set of APIs to access native capabilities of the device your app is running on that you wouldn't normally have access to from a plain old website. It does this in a cross-platform way so that you generally don't need to write any code specific to a single platform. If you write your code to target the PhoneGap API, it will, largely, work on any platform PhoneGap supports.

Part III of this book, starting with Chapter 9, is where PhoneGap will really come into play. Before then, we'll just be writing an HTML5-based application, on your desktop in fact, without concern for it being mobile until later.

Tip   That's actually one of the biggest benefits of the mobile web app model: you can, for the most part, do all your development on a desktop, with all the fancy development tools available there, and then later simply wrap up your work with PhoneGap to run on a real mobile device. Being able to use all the same tools you're used to using for web development and not, unless you want to, have to install any special tools, as you do for doing native development, is a big plus.

Finally, We Have It: The Full-Stack

Once we've made all these technology decisions, we find that what we've effectively done is rolled our own development platform! We now have a so-called full stack to develop with, that is, all the technologies, from client to server, needed to construct a modern mobile app based on open web technologies. Figure 1-17 visually represents the solid foundation this stack represents and that we'll build My Mobile Organizer on.

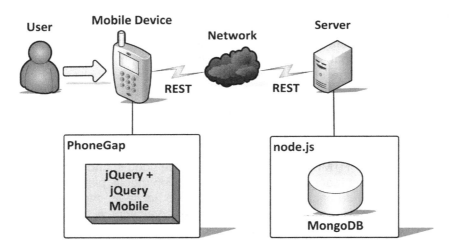

Figure 1-17. Our complete "full-stack" development platform

This stack, the combination of PhoneGap, jQuery, jQuery Mobile, node.js, REST, and MongoDB, is rapidly becoming a popular one because it is flexible, is easy to learn, performs well (if you do your job as a developer reasonably well at least), and is based on open, free technologies. It is therefore cost-effective and allows for cross-platform development without a "heavy lift," as the saying goes. The mobile web app approach using open standards such as HTML5, CSS, and JavaScript is powerful and well-known, allowing businesses and nonbusiness developers alike to leverage their existing skills to create great mobile apps effectively.

Summary

In this chapter, you looked at a number of technologies for building mobile apps using open technologies including jQuery, jQuery Mobile, node.js, and MongoDB. You got a brief introduction to each, and I discussed the reasons for choosing them over other options. You saw that PhoneGap allows you to take your existing web development skills and use them to build mobile apps quickly and easily. You got a quick introduction as well to the REST style of service APIs, and you saw how all of these disparate technologies together form a development stack that is quite popular because of its power, flexibility, and general ease of use.

My Mobile Organizer was designed at a high level as well in this chapter, and you got the chance to see some mock-ups describing its various screens. The notion of offline functionality and server synchronization was touched upon as well. You should at this point have a good feel for the application that this book presents as well as the technologies that are brought together to build it.

In the next chapter, you'll take a "deep-dive" into jQuery and jQuery Mobile to become familiar with what they has to offer, how they work, and how we'll use it to build My Mobile Organizer in the chapters that follow.

Chapter 2

Introducing jQuery and jQuery Mobile

In this book, we're building a handy little PIM in the form of a mobile web app. We know what the app is going to do and at least roughly what it will look like. We even have a good idea of what technologies we're going to use to do it. Now where do we begin?

To get started, you might take a number of approaches. Some people prefer to put together the server-side API first and then build the client application around it. Certainly, there's nothing wrong with that approach. For me, though, I prefer doing the client UI first. Since the server-side API will be tied intimately to the client and not to a general-purpose API that might be made available to the world at large, it makes a lot of sense to let the client dictate the server-side API.

More importantly, perhaps, is that UIs can be fun to make! So I ask you, why not have that fun up front?

In Chapter 1, we decided to use the very popular jQuery library and the related jQuery Mobile library to build our client UI. Before we start actually building that client app, however, let's look at jQuery and jQuery Mobile more generally so that you have a solid foundation from which to begin exploring the code of the app.

It's All About the DOM

Before we even get into those libraries, though, I need to make sure you have a more general foundation. In this book, I assume you are no stranger to HTML, CSS, and JavaScript. While you don't need to be an expert in any of these languages to get through this book, you do need to have some basic skill with these things. Most important of all, perhaps, is the concept that in fact underlies all of these things: the Document Object Model (DOM).

The DOM is (in this context anyway) the hierarchical structure of objects that results from a browser parsing an HTML document. For example, let's say you have the simple HTML document shown in Listing 2-1.

Listing 2-1. A Simple HTML Document

```
<html>
  <head>
    <title>Example</title>
    <style>
      .cssDiv2 {
        color : #ff0000;
      }
      </style>
  </head>
  <body>
    <div id="divGreeting">Hello!</div>
    <div class="cssDiv2">I am an HTML document</div>
  </body>
</html>
```

When you load this HTML document into a web browser, the DOM that is produced is what you see in Figure 2-1.

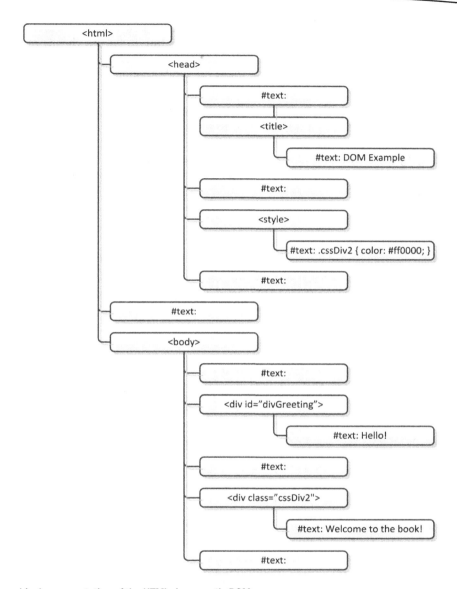

Figure 2-1. A graphical representation of the HTML document's DOM

Note If you download the source bundle, you'll find that the listing doesn't quite match this one. The difference is that the downloaded version will include some JavaScript and a button to perform the functions described next. However, the listing you see here is the essential document minus all of that stuff, and it is what the figure describes.

As you can see, the hierarchy starts with the `<html>` tag, which has children `<head>` and `<body>`. In turn, each of those has various children including the `<style>` tag under the `<head>` and two `<div>` tags under the `<body>`. Note that the closing tags for each of those tags aren't separate nodes in the tree. Also note that the boxes with `#text:` in them are whitespace in the document. Yes, those become part of the DOM as well.

Now, once the document is parsed and there is a corresponding DOM in the browser's memory, you can then go about manipulating the DOM, and that's really the underlying concept behind most modern web development. It's no longer just static HTML documents hyperlinked together; real apps require changing the DOM after the browser initially loads it. This is how you accomplish things such as animation, remote loading of data (AJAX), and numerous other capabilities that users expect from a modern web page or app.

> **Note**   Not to toot my own horn…ah, never mind, that's exactly what it is…if you're looking for a book or two on this kind of development beyond this one, you can check out mine, as most of them deal with rich Internet applications (RIAs), which is the label that describes this sort of web development. Check 'em out at www.apress.com/catalogsearch/result/?q=zammetti&submit=Go. *Practical JavaScript, DOM Scripting, and Ajax Projects* is perhaps the best choice.

JavaScript is the conduit into this dynamic changing of the DOM, and, as such, the DOM is exposed to JavaScript via various methods, objects, and properties. For example, let's say you want to change the text "Hello!" inside that first `<div>` element to "Go away, I'm tired!" Doing so is easy enough with this line of code:

```
document.getElementById("divGreeting").innerHTML = "Go away, I'm tired!"
```

The variable `document` is how the DOM is exposed to JavaScript. Through it, we can manipulate any element contained in the tree structure that is the DOM. The `innerHTML()` function allows us to set the content between the `<div>` and `</div>` tags.

Now what happens if we want to make the text in both of those `<div>` elements bold? It's easy enough to do that for `divGreeting`, since we have an ID for it. What about the second `<div>`, though? It has no ID, so we can't address it directly without doing some extra work. While there are a couple of ways you could do this, one straightforward approach is to iterate over the DOM nodes that are children of the `<body>` element and change their style like so:

```
var bodyNodes = document.body.childNodes;
for (var i = 0; i < bodyNodes.length; i++) {
  if (bodyNodes[i].tagName == "DIV") {
    bodyNodes[i].style.fontWeight = "bold";
  }
}
```

The `childNodes` attribute provides an array of all the elements that are direct children of a given element, `document.body` in this case. Once we have that, we iterate through the array and look for any elements that are `<div>` elements, and we set the `fontWeight` style attribute for each.

That' not so bad, but what about adding new elements to the DOM? We can do that as well, can't we? Most definitely, we can!

```
var e = document.createElement("div");
e.innerHTML = "I was inserted";
document.body.appendChild(e);
```

We can use the createElement() function of the document object to create any kind of element we want, given the tag type. We can then set the various attributes of the element as appropriate, and when it's all ready, we can then insert it into the DOM using the appendChild() function.

None of that is rocket science. However, the dirty little secret is that various browsers implement the DOM in subtly different ways, and sometimes (although this is less true now than it used to be) browsers even present a slightly different API with which to manipulate the DOM. While you can do an awful lot nowadays with direct DOM manipulation like this and have your app be cross-browser, when you do happen to run into differences, they can be extremely unpleasant to deal with.

Even if compatibility were truly 100 percent across all modern browsers, that's still a fair bit of code to have to write to do relatively simple things. Certainly, there must be a better way, right?

If you're guessing that jQuery is the answer, then get yourself to Las Vegas right now because you know how to make a good bet!

jQuery Saves Your Brain from the DOM

jQuery, created by John Resig in 2006 (or 2005, depending on how you define "created"), is, by most estimates, the most popular JavaScript library in existence today. Something like 50 percent of the top-rated sites on the Internet use jQuery, and for good reason: it makes working with the DOM far easier than it would be otherwise.

There's nothing fancy about getting started with jQuery: you simply download a .js file from the jQuery site at, not surprisingly, jQuery.com and include it in an HTML document like you do any other JavaScript source file. There's no installation, setup, or anything like that—just a single .js file and you're good to go! Not only will you find the jQuery JavaScript file on that site, but you will also find tons of documentation and examples, as you'd expect from any well-known and highly regarded library.

The core concept behind jQuery is that of *selectors*. The idea is that you "select" elements in the DOM to manipulate using common CSS selectors. For example, the <div> in the first listing named divGreeting can be accessed, thanks to it having an ID, with the selector #divGreeting. Where this comes into play is when you use the jQuery $() function, which is the gateway into jQuery land.

> **Note**   JavaScript has no problem with you defining a function simply named $ because that's a valid identifier. In addition to $(), you'll find that there is a function named jquery(). They are completely synonymous and interchangeable, but most developers use $() just because it's shorter.

With jQuery, instead of this…

```
document.getElementById("divGreeting")
```

you now would write the following:

```
$("#divGreeting")
```

Now, in and of itself, that's not too big a deal. Sure, less typing is good (and less error-prone), but conciseness isn't the be-all and end-all of programming. The real power of jQuery is what $() returns. It returns the $() function!

What happens is that the element (or elements) that your selector matches becomes the *context* of the $() function, at least temporarily. By returning a function, you get the ability to do something called *call chaining*, which means you can do something like this:

```
$("#divGreeting").html("Go away, I'm tired!")
```

That is, in fact, the jQuery equivalent of the following:

```
document.getElementById("divGreeting").innerHTML = "Go away, I'm tired!"
```

Even that may not seem like too big a change. It's still a single line of code. However, because of call chaining, you can also do this:

```
$("#divGreeting").html("Go away, I'm REALLY tired!").css("color", "#0000ff");
```

The css() function, along with the html() function, are functions that are members of $(). They're just functions defined within a function, in other words, and since functions are proper objects in JavaScript, they really should be referred to as *methods* at this point. And that's how I'll be referring to them from here on out.

> **Tip** You can use this style of programming in your own code too! If a function you write returns a reference to that function, then you'll have this same style of call chaining available to you. Whether this style of API is good or not is something you'll need to decide for yourself. Rest assured, there's plenty of debate about it on the Web (although with jQuery being as popular as it is, I think it's fair to say most people like it!).

Semantics aside, this approach means we can continue to call methods in a chain like this because each one returns $() again, which keeps the chain going. This is not only concise but also efficient: the selection of the DOM nodes is done only once at the start, not repeatedly, and it lets you avoid having to cache a reference yourself.

Speaking of that css() method, what's the equivalent of the earlier code that makes both <div> elements bold? It's simply this:

```
$("body div").css("fontWeight", "bold");
```

Here the CSS selector specifies all `<div>`elements that are children of the `<body>` element, and then it uses the `css()` method to set the `fontWeight` attribute. Yes, jQuery will happily deal with selectors that find one match or many all the same! It will also happily not blow up if there are no matches. If there were no `<div>` children of the `<body>` tag, this code would just silently do nothing and no error would be generated.

To complete the comparison, let's see how to insert a node using jQuery:

```
$("body").append("<div>I was inserted</div>");
```

Now this is pretty simple and obvious! However, it's also a little bit of a cheat: the earlier code used DOM manipulation methods directly, creating an intermediary element in the process. Here we just pass a snippet of HTML and let jQuery do all of that work behind the scenes. However, it's possible to do the same thing without jQuery as well just by inserting the HTML using an element's `innerHTML` property. However, some cross-browser issues can arise with doing it that way … issues that jQuery hides from us! That's another big advantage of using jQuery.

You get top-notch performance, concise code, and no cross-browser concerns using jQuery, and that's why it has quickly become as popular as it has.

Now these were just a few simple examples that only scratch the surface of what jQuery has to offer. There are a ton of methods and properties of `$()` that provide all sorts of other functionality, aside from these basics (although these basics are without question the bread-and-butter of jQuery usage). Now let's look at some other capabilities that jQuery provides.

Note   This is in no way, shape, or form an exhaustive look at jQuery—and it's not meant to be. As we explore the code of My Mobile Organizer beginning in the next chapter, you'll see a bit more, but even still, this book isn't focused on jQuery specifically, so we're not covering it in exhaustive detail. If you really want to get into all that jQuery can do, `http://jquery.com` is the URL to hit up. In addition, Apress has a number of excellent books on jQuery including *Beginning jQuery and Pro jQuery 2.0* (both by Adam Freeman) and *Pro jQuery Mobile* (by Brad Broulik), just to name one directly relevant to this topic in this book.

Effects Aren't Just for Movies

The term *effects* has a wide range of meanings depending on the context. However, within the context of jQuery, an effect is an animation of some sort. That's great, but what's an animation? you ask. Simply put, an *animation* is the changing of one of more of the properties of an object over time. It's not necessarily something moving on the screen, as the more typical meaning of *animate* would imply. You can animate the color of a bit of text, for instance, by changing it from red to green over, say, one second.

In fact, Listing 2-2 shows the code to do just that.

Listing 2-2. My First jQuery Animation Example

```
<html>
  <head>
    <title>Example</title>
    <style>
      #divGreeting {
        color : #ff0000;
        color : #ff0000;
        position : absolute;
        left : 50px;
        top : 50px;
      }
    </style>
    <script src="jq/jquery-1.9.1.js"></script>
    <script src="jq/plugins/jquery.animate-colors.js"></script>
    <script>
      function testme() {
        $("#divGreeting").animate({ color : "#00ff00" }, 1000);
      }
    </script>
  </head>
  <body>
    <div id="divGreeting">Hello!</div>
    <input type="button" onClick="testme();">
  </body>
</html>
```

The `animate()` method is your one-stop shop for all sorts of animations. With it, you can animate virtually any CSS attribute you want. All you do is pass to it, as the first argument, an object that contains properties that define the target values for whatever attributes you want to animate. That's the only thing required, but you can also pass the duration that the animation should take as the second argument, one second in this case (1000 milliseconds = 1 second). jQuery takes care of the mechanics of the animation for you.

While you can animate most attributes, there are some exceptions. As it happens, `color` is one such exception! To be able to animate color, you need to include the `jQuery.Color()` plug-in. *Plug-ins* are one of the things that helps make jQuery so powerful and useful. They allow you to extend jQuery to add features and help speed the development process by helping you avoid "reinventing the wheel." All it takes to use a plug-in generally is to include its JavaScript file, and you can explore the hundreds of plug-ins available by visiting `http://plugins.jquery.com`. That's the purpose of the `jquery.animate-colors.js` import here. Once it's included, we can animate the `color` attribute the same as any other attribute.

You can also pass a third argument to `animate()` to specify an easing function. An *easing function* defines how the animation proceeds over its lifetime. For example, the default easing, swing, causes the animation to not transition directly from source color to target color, but instead it "swings" between them with an intermediate color in the middle. Another easing function, linear, is available, which makes the animation more direct. Other easing functions are available via plug-in.

A fourth optional argument is available as well, which is in the form of a function reference. When present, this function will be called when the animation completes. This allows you to do timed chains of animation with precise timing. For example, let's say we want to move the text in divGreeting in the previous example to left position 250, but we want to do that only after the color change has completed. To do that, we can change the animate() call to the following:

```
$("#divGreeting").animate({ color : "#00ff00" }, 1000,
  function() {
    $(this).animate({ left : "250px" }, 1000);
  }
);
```

Now, after the animation of color finishes, the left CSS attribute will be animated to do the movement. Also note the use of the handy $(this) selector. This works because the context of the function is set to be the element itself, so the keyword this points to it, and $() understands that when you pass this to it. This becomes useful if you have a long chain of animations nested many levels deep. (Though nesting like that is not necessarily the best approach, extracting those nested functions so that they're stand-alone functions instead is usually preferable. It's not at all uncommon to see code written this way either.

While the animate() method is the primary entry into jQuery animations, a number of common premade animations are also available via a number of methods. For example, the show() and hide() methods can be used to quickly show or hide all matched elements. Although, by default, these methods perform their function almost instantaneously, they are still technically animations (and you can change the time they take just like any other animation). The slideDown() and slideUp() methods perform a show and hide function as well correspondingly, but they do so with an animated "wipe" effect. The fadeIn() and fadeOut() methods similarly do a show and hide, but this time by animating the opacity of an object so that it fades out or in to view.

While being an exceedingly simple API, jQuery provides a tremendous amount of power to do all sorts of animations with just a single line of code. Just don't get carried away! After all, we got rid of the <blink> tag for a good reason; we shouldn't be in a rush to reimplement it with JavaScript.

Stuff Happens: Events

jQuery also has support for various events that can occur over the lifetime of a web page. Perhaps the most important is the ready event. This event is triggered when the DOM is fully created but potentially (likely even) before all assets, such as images, have been loaded and displayed. This differs from the basic load event, which is triggered only after everything has been fully loaded and rendered. In most cases, you can and probably even want to manipulate the DOM before everything is fully loaded for performance reasons. jQuery makes this easy.

```
$(document).ready(function() {
  // Do something
});
```

This effectively attaches an event listener, that is, a function to execute when a given event occurs, for the ready event, to the document object. You can then perform whatever functions are necessary, perhaps deactivating some form fields based on user privileges as an example.

If the load event is what you're interested in, though, you can use the load() method in the same way. Similarly, there is an unload() method that can fire some code when the document is unloaded, like occurs when the user navigates away from the page.

Various methods for dealing with both keyboard and mouse events are present, and you can attach them to any element you want, at least, any that supports the underlying events naturally. For example, to attach an event handler to a button, rather than specifying the event handler inline as was done in the previous example, you can do what you see in Listing 2-3.

Listing 2-3. Attaching an Event Handler the Nonintrusive Way

```
<html>
  <head>
    <title>Example</title>
    <script src="jq/jquery-1.9.1.js"></script>
    <script>
      $(document).ready(function() {
        $("#button1").on("click", function() {
          alert("You clicked me!");
        });
      });
    </script>
  </head>
  <body>
    <input type="button" id="button1">
  </body>
</html>
```

The on() method allows you to attach arbitrarily named events to any matching elements. You can also use the click() method directly, rather than naming the method with the first argument, as shown in Listing 2-3. These two approaches are equivalent, and this is true of all the similar methods that jQuery makes available, such as mouseover(), mousedown(), mouseup(), keyup(), keydown(), dblclick(), change(), scroll(), resize(), and so on.

> **Tip**   jQuery also provides the off() method to remove previously attached event handlers (attached with the on() method).

With just these few simple methods, jQuery lets you work with events in a nonintrusive manner, meaning that you don't need to sprinkle event handlers on elements throughout your page. This allows for graceful degradation. This means you design your page to work properly without JavaScript but then add enhanced capabilities when JavaScript is available. By attaching all event handlers with jQuery in this way, then this will obviously occur only when JavaScript is available. Nevertheless, as long as you designed the page to work without it, even if in a reduced functionality manner, you don't need to do anything more to reach the widest possible audience and provide the best possible experience for all.

Working with Forms

Beyond effects and events, which are such a common need, jQuery has some handy methods specifically designed for working with forms. Look at Listing 2-4 to get a feel for some of these methods.

Listing 2-4. Some jQuery Form Goodness

```html
<html>
  <head>
    <title>Example</title>
    <script src="jq/jquery-1.9.1.js"></script>
    <script>
      function testme() {
        var t = $("#myForm").find("input[name='text1']").val();
        alert(t);
        alert($("#myForm").serialize());
        alert($("#myForm").serializeArray());
      }
    </script>
  </head>
  <body>
    <form id="myForm">
      Text1: <input type="text" name="text1">
      <br><br>
      Text2: <input type="text" name="text2">
      <br><br>
      <input type="button" onClick="testme();">
    </form>
  </body>
</html>
```

First, although it's not specific to forms, the `find()` method allows you to find all descendants of a given element (or set of elements) that matches a selection criteria. Here we're asking for the input element with a name of `text1` that is a child of the form with the ID `myForm`.

Now, though that's useful on its own, it's a bit pedantic with respect to the most common need these days regarding forms: submitting them to a server. Imagine having to write code to get each form field individually and then construct a properly formatted string (perhaps JSON, maybe XM—whatever) from it to submit to the server. That's a lot of work! For that common use case, jQuery provides the `serialize()` and `serializeArray()` methods.

The `serialize()` method returns a string representation of the form in a URL-encoded format. So, for example, if I enter Frank in `text1`, enter Zammetti in `text2`, and click the button, the output of the `serialize()` method would be `text1=Frank&text2=Zammetti`.

Sometimes, you may want to get all of the values of the form as an object with which you can work in JavaScript. The `serializeArray()` method can be used for that. For the same form and values, it generates an object with the following form in JSON:

```
[
  { name : "text1", value : "Frank" },
  { name : "text2", value : "Zammetti" }
]
```

You can then do whatever you need to with that object—iterate over its members, for example, and perhaps construct an XML document to submit to the server, whatever your needs are.

Working with CSS

Aside from animation, jQuery provides a number of methods to make working with CSS a lot nicer. The `addClass()` and `removeClass()` methods allow you to add one or more classes to an element. For example, to add a CSS class named `highlighted` to an element with ID `message`, you might do the following:

```
$("#message").addClass("highlighted");
```

Conversely, to remove that class, you might do this:

```
$("#message").removeClass("highlighted");
```

To discover that an element has a given class applied, you can use `hasClass()`, like so:

```
$("message").hasClass("highlighted");
```

This will return `true` if the message has the highlighted class applied, or `false` if not. All of those methods allow you to specify multiple classes, so you could see whether the message is both highlighted and large, assuming that the CSS class `large` exists, by calling this:

```
$("message").hasClass("highlighted large");
```

Various methods are available for obtaining sizing information about elements. The `innerWidth()` and `innerHeight()` methods return the current computed width and height, respectively, or the element(s) selected. Similarly, `outerWidth()` and `outerHeight()` give you the width and height of the element including box model attributes (`padding`, `border`, and, optionally, `margin`). The `width()` and `height()` methods also give you the computed width and height, but they also allow you set those values simply by supplying an argument when you call them.

Miscellaneous Niceties

Finally, jQuery provides a number of what I term "miscellaneous" functions, that is, things that generically make working with JavaScript and the DOM easier. Some of these methods are as follows:

- `extend()`, which merges the contents of two or more objects to create a single object with all the properties from all the specified objects.

- `inArray()`, which searches an array for a given value and returns the index of the first match, if any.

- `isArray()`, `isFunction()`, and `isNumeric()`, which tell you whether a given object is an array, a function, or a numeric value, respectively.

- `merge()`, which returns an array resulting from merging two other arrays.

- `parseJSON()`, which takes in a string of properly formed JSON and returns an object based on it.

- `trim()`, which trims whitespace from both ends of a string .

- `type()`, which tells you the internal JavaScript class of a given object. For example, `alert($.type(new Array()));` displays "array."

- `unique()`, which sorts an array of DOM elements and removes duplicates in the process.

As stated earlier, this chapter is not meant to be an exhaustive look at jQuery by any stretch of the imagination. There are plenty of other great books in the Apress stable if you want a deep-dive. jQuery has plenty more to offer, and you'll see some of it in action in the code for My Mobile Organizer starting with the next chapter, including Ajax functionality, which I purposely haven't mentioned here. I hope, though, that this brief introduction has provided the foundation you'll need to understand the code to come and to give you a high-level view of the jQuery library.

jQuery Isn't UI *per se*—jQuery Mobile Is!

For all the awesomeness jQuery brings to the table, the one thing you'll notice that I never mentioned was user interface widgets. Many apps today, perhaps even most, use some sort of library that provides widgets— buttons, grids, sliders, and so forth—and they don't use plain old HTML. You tend not to see plain old forms that much anymore, and instead you see forms built up from specialized components that provide all sorts of extended functionality. Perhaps it's a pop-up calendar instead of a plain old text box or a text area with rich edit capabilities rather than just a plain text area.

jQuery doesn't provide any of this. Although it makes working with forms easier, they're still plain old HTML forms in the end. While you can use jQuery to enhance a form's capabilities and appearance, you take on the responsibility. The implementation details are entirely up to you.

What you need is a proper GUI toolkit. Thanks to the extensibility of jQuery, there's an extension available that provides exactly that: jQuery Mobile. (I'll refer to it as JQM from here on out.) Not only does it provide such a toolkit, but it does so with a focus squarely on mobile development. Its design is geared toward this and all the unique challenges that entails.

Unobtrusiveness and Progressive Enhancement Is Where It's At

One of the best aspects of JQM is that you actually have to write very little code to do most things with it. Considering it is, ostensibly, a JavaScript library, that's surprising! You can accomplish most basic tasks without writing any code because JQM takes an unobtrusive approach to JavaScript and a progressive enhancement approach generally.

In a nutshell, this means you build a page using plain old HTML, and JQM then "enhances" that page using JavaScript, assuming it's available, to transform that HTML-based page into a much richer version.

This approach also means you really are focused on separating the display from other concerns. You focus on building the overall layout and not so much on individual elements on the page and what they do. Those concerns are effectively added after the fact as the page is progressively enhanced.

When an HTML document that imports JQM (and jQuery, by extension) loads into a browser, JQM parses the DOM after the browser has built it and automatically converts some elements into richer versions. For example, a `<button>` tag on a page is transformed into a more aesthetically pleasing version of a button that is better suited to a small mobile display, like a smartphone, by stretching across the screen and thereby making it easier for the user to tap it. A number of elements are transformed automatically in this way without you ever having to lift a finger!

Data-* Attributes

Of course, a good library provides many options to you as a developer, and JQM is no exception. While it may be great that a `<button>` tab is automatically converted to a better version designed for mobile, you will likely want more control over what JQM actually does with the button. This sort of configuration is very much possible by using `data-*` attributes on elements. This is a key concept to working with JQM.

> **Note**   The HTML5 specification states that you can add arbitrary attributes to any tag as long as you name it beginning with `data-`. This will allow your HTML document to be considered valid HTML even though a `data-*` attribute isn't a known valid attribute for a given tag, something that will normally cause an HTML document to fail validation. Although browsers will ignore unknown attributes, the document cannot be said to be "valid" with them present. The `data-*` attributes get around that issue entirely, allowing you to add information to tags at will and still have a valid document. This is just the sort of flexibility that JQM needs, so by extension, JQM requires an HTML5-compliant browser to work.

Let's look at an example in Listing 2-5.

Listing 2-5. A Simple JQM Example

```
<!DOCTYPE html>
<html>
  <head>
    <link rel="stylesheet" href="jq/jquery.mobile-1.3.1.css">
    <script type="text/javascript" src="jq/jquery-1.9.1.js"></script>
    <script type="text/javascript" src="jq/jquery.mobile-1.3.1.js"></script>
  </head>
  <body>
    <button onClick="alert('clicked');">Click Me</button>
  </body>
</html>
```

If you removed the CSS and two JS imports in the head of the document, you would see a plain old HTML button, as shown in Figure 2-2.

Figure 2-2. A plain old HTML button

Well, it'll look *something* like that at least. It depends on your browser and operating system, of course, but you get the idea. Now with those imports in place, the button looks like Figure 2-3 instead.

Figure 2-3. The JQM-ified version of the button

As you can see, that's somewhat different! The width of the button, by default, will stretch across the entire browser window. On a desktop, that's likely to be too big, although it's still perfectly usable. On a smaller smartphone screen, however, it's likely to be exactly what you want.

Now say you want to put a small icon on the button, a star perhaps. That's where the data-* attributes come into play. To add a star icon, modify the button tag to this:

```
<button data-icon="star" onClick="alert('clicked');">Click Me</button>
```

With that attribute in place, the button now looks like Figure 2-4.

Figure 2-4. This button is such a star!

By adding various data-* attributes to elements, you control what JQM does with them. Each type of widget supports numerous such attributes, which let you manipulate many facets of the widgets that JQM produces. We'll see many of them as we progress through the remainder of this chapter, and of course we'll meet them in the code of My Mobile Organizer.

Before we get to that, though, let's talk about what a "page" means to JQM.

The Page Paradigm

A page has a subtly different meaning in JQM. Perhaps it's more precise to say it has a more *evolved* meaning. With JQM, a page is still an HTML document and is still a unit of a user interface, which may be one of many such units that the user navigates between. However, now a page has a more rigid form. A JQM *page* consists of three components: a header on top, content in the middle, and a footer at the bottom.

While it's true that these elements are optional, in practice you'll rarely see a page that doesn't contain all three. Furthermore, it will be downright rare to see a page without a content section.

In terms of markup, a basic page template looks like Listing 2-6.

Listing 2-6. A Basic JQM Page Template

```
<!DOCTYPE html>

<html>

  <head>

    <meta name="viewport" content="width=device-width,initial-scale=1">

    <link rel="stylesheet" href="jq/jquery.mobile-1.3.1.css">

    <script type="text/javascript" src="jq/jquery-1.9.1.js"></script>
    <script type="text/javascript" src="jq/jquery.mobile-1.3.1.js"></script>

  </head>
  <body>

    <div data-role="header" data-position="fixed">
      Header
    </div>

    <div data-role="content">
      Content
    </div>

    <div data-role="footer" data-position="fixed">
      Footer
    </div>

  </body>

</html>
```

This results in Figure 2-5, which I admit isn't much to look at!

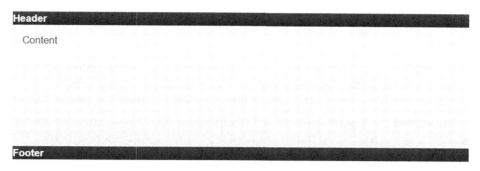

Figure 2-5. Yes, I know, it's not going to win any awards!

The nice thing about this is that if the content area happened to be vertically larger than the area you see here, it would scroll, while the header and footer would remain in place. If you think about any mobile app you've ever seen, you'll recognize that's exactly how you want it to work in most cases because the header normally contains app navigation controls and the footer normally stores menus and function buttons and such.

Looking back at the markup, you'll notice the use of a couple of data-* attributes. The data-role is an important one as it tells JQM what purpose a given <div> serves in the page, be it a header, footer, or content area. The data-position attribute, when set to fixed, is what causes the header and footer to remain fixed in place and not scroll out of view if (and when) the user scrolls the content area.

You'll also notice the <meta> tag that defines a viewport. This is important, especially on a mobile device, because it ensures that the width of the viewport; that is, the area your app fits within needs to be equal to the size of the devices' screen, and it does not start out zoomed in or out, as might otherwise happen by default. This ensures that your UI fills the entire screen, assuming the browser is full-screen, and is displayed without zooming, as any native app would be.

A JQM-based app can be a single-page app, in which case you'll have just one HTML file, like the template shown in Listing 2-6, that contains all of the functionality of your app, or it can be multipage. JQM includes a robust navigation system to deal with multipage apps, including Ajax-based loading (and/or preloading) of pages. I'm going to skip going into detail about that here as it will be dealt with when we look at My Mobile Organizer's code, as it is such a multipage application.

Whether you write a single-page or multipage app is entirely up to you and your goals. In fact, as I wrote My Mobile Organizer, I initially had it built as a multipage app; then, at some point, I decided a single-page design was better. Nonethgeless, I ultimately went back to a multipage design for reasons I'll get into in the next two chapters. The fact that you can change your mind so easily is a testament to the flexibility of JQM.

Theme Support

JQM provides a rich theming framework out of the box, and it provides the ability for you to add your own themes built using the ThemeRoller tool (http://jquerymobile.com/themeroller).

A *theme* is a set of visual cues that a page, and any widgets on it, will use. A theme includes some global items such as font family, drop shadow settings, and corner radiuses for elements, such as buttons, that have rounded edges. In addition, each theme can have a number of color "swatches," where a swatch is a set of colors for various elements (such as header and footer bars, buttons, and list items).

A theme is simply a CSS file and associated image files, which you import onto your page. The ThemeRoller tool will provide you with a ZIP file that includes all of these resources. If you choose not to roll your own theme, though, that's fine, as JQM ships with a default theme.

To switch color swatches for a given element, you include the data-theme attribute and specify a letter. Each swatch is given a letter so that there are 26 possible swatches in a theme. The default theme contains five swatches. Swatch A is a black-based, swatch B is blue-based, swatch C is light gray-based, swatch D is dark gray-based, and swatch E is yellow-based. By default, if no swatch is specified, then swatch A is used.

You'll see the usage of different swatches in My Mobile Organizer, but you really need to play with the app to get the full effect. Since there's no color on the printed page here, I encourage you to do that at some point.

A Rich Set of Widgets

JQM ships with a number of different widget types for you to use. You've already seen buttons, but there's much more where they came from!

Form Elements

Forms for user data entry are the bread-and-butter of most web-based applications. A JQM-based application is no exception, and, as such, JQM provides a number of form widgets, as shown in Figure 2-6.

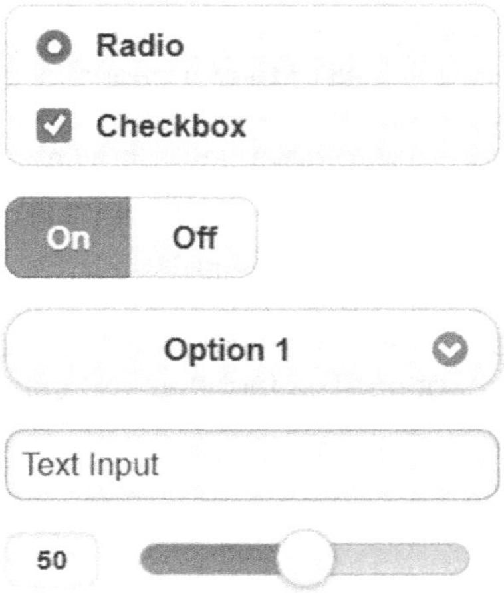

Figure 2-6. The few…the proud…the form widgets

Although I refer to them as form widgets, it's probably in fact more accurate to call them "data entry widgets," because they don't necessarily need to be part of a form. However, that being said, it really is most common to see them in a form, and forms are a well-known construct besides, so I feel the term fits just fine.

Radios and check boxes are well-known form elements, of course, and JQM just fancies them up a bit. The On/Off widget you see here is similar, functionally, to a set of radio buttons. However, its visual presentation is one that is common in the world of mobile development. The standard <select> element is, again, just a fancy version of the plain HTML version.

The text input box is also like its standard counterpart, and yes there's a text area analog as well. JQM can provide a small icon on the right to clear the field, however, which is a nice addition. The text area widget can also be set to expand as the user enters content. Again, JQM enhances what you'd have with plain old HTML.

The slider widget, however, is something that's not represented in standard HTML forms. It's quite a common widget nowadays for entering values across a continuum of possible values, so JQM provides it for you.

Collapsible Sections

Aside from the page layout structure, JQM also allows you to include collapsible sections. For instance, you may want to present data about an individual but group that data so that it isn't just one big list of attributes to scroll through. A collapsible set allows the user to expand one section while collapsing all others to focus on one particular set of data. Figure 2-7 shows what that may look like.

Figure 2-7. *A collapsible set*

An individual section can be made collapsible as well, as shown in Figure 2-7. You'll see this in practice in My Mobile Organizer. It is used to hide the advanced filter abilities until the user is interested in seeing them.

Some Other Goodies to Look Forward To

What's presented in this chapter is just a quick glimpse of the widgets and capabilities that JQM offers. As we explore My Mobile Organizer together, you'll get some hands-on exposure to a number of other elements.

For example, lists of data are a big part of many applications, be they mobile or other application types. As such, JQM provides a listview widget that offers a lot of flexibility in how it presents its data, as well as how the user can interact with it, as you can see demonstrated in Figure 2-8.

Figure 2-8. A listview widget

Things like the count bubbles are possible, as well as hiding or showing the arrows to indicate that the user can click an item to interact with it. The items themselves can show arbitrary amounts and types of data, so you can show multiple lines of text if you want, or even images, arranged as you like.

Dialogs are something else that you'll get a look at as you explore My Mobile Organizer. Dialogs are, in a sense, "subpages" that pop up over the main UI for the user to interact with. *Panels* are similar to dialogs—they can slide over the main content temporarily. Both of these elements build upon the basic page model that JQM uses, so you get a consistent construction in terms of the code as well as what it winds up looking like on the screen. Figure 2-9 shows a simple example of a dialog.

Figure 2-9. A dialog widget

A panel can actually overlay the main content, as shown in Figure 2-10, or it can push the content aside to make room for itself. This is an example of the type of flexibility JQM provides for all of its widgets. I could easily fill hundreds of pages showing all of the variations possible just by manipulating some data-* attributes!

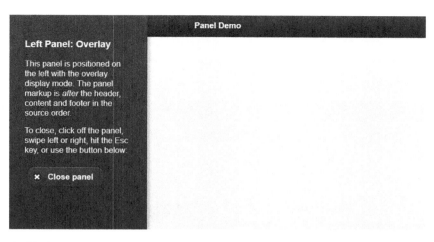

Figure 2-10. A panel widget

Finally, the navbar widget, as shown in Figure 2-11, is very important, as you'll see in My Mobile Organizer. This widget gives you a standard way for the user to move around your application, and it is tailor-made for My Mobile Organizer.

Figure 2-11. A navbar widget

> **Note**   In addition to what you've seen here, JQM, by virtue of the `data-*` attributes, provides a number of variations on these widget themes. You'll be seeing some of them in My Mobile Organizer, but you probably will want to spend some time with the JQM documentation, where lots of examples are presented for all of the different variations that are possible for each widget type.

Summary

In this chapter, you received a brief introduction to the two libraries that My Mobile Organizer is based on: jQuery and its close relative jQuery Mobile. You got to see some simple examples of using them, and you got a feel for what they have to offer, including simplified DOM manipulation, effects, event handling, and UI building.

In the next chapter, we'll begin to look at the actual code of My Mobile Organizer, starting with the user interface of the client application. That is, after all, why we're here!

Writing the Application with jQuery Mobile, Part I

Here we are, Chapter 3, and guess what? The preliminaries are out of the way, the setup is done, and now it's time to jump into some real code!

There are a myriad of ways you can approach writing an application, be it mobile or otherwise, and likely each of them is valid in some way. The approach I typically take is to create the user interface first, minus functionality. I do this because I'm a bit more of a visual person when it comes to fleshing out an application. That is, I prefer to see what the user will see first, ensure that it all "flows" when I pretend to use it, and then I "back fill" the implementation details. You may prefer to create the server-side API first, and there's a lot to be said for that approach too. The same is true, as I said, for any number of other approaches.

Of course, when you write the book, you get to choose the approach. As such, we're going to kick off our review of the code of My Mobile Organizer by looking at just the HTML and CSS files that make it up. In the next chapter, we'll look at the JavaScript that makes it, well, do stuff! Then, of course, in the chapters that follow, we'll get into the server-side code. For now, however, we'll start with the first file that will be loaded into the browser to launch the client.

First Steps

At this point, it isn't essential for you to have played with My Mobile Organizer. However, I recognize that you may want to do so before starting to explore the code.

If you simply want to see the screens without all the actual functionality, you can load index.html in your browser off your local file system. To start, you'll get a message about no network connectivity, but you should be able to click around and do most of the things you'd expect to able to do, except for saving and deleting. However, if you want to see the whole thing in action, you'll need to jump ahead to Chapters 5 and 6 and install Node.js and MongoDB (and Mongoose so that Node.js can work with MongoDB) as described there. Those chapters discuss the server-side part of My Mobile

Organizer. You don't need to read them at this point, just the sections in them about installing Node.js, MongoDB, and Mongoose.

My suggestion, though, would be to hold off on that for now and just play with the screens a bit by loading `index.html` in the browser of your choice. (You don't have to be on a mobile device; it should work either way.) This should suffice for this chapter and the next.

index.html

As with many websites, the first file that gets loaded into the browser when the client application is launched is `index.html`. Perhaps the most interesting thing about it is that it is, in a sense, unremarkable—it's just plain old HTML!

> **Note**   As for all of the code explored in this and the chapters to come, I'll break each file down into easily digestible chunks where each chunk encapsulates some logical unit of code. In the process, I've removed all comments, but rest assured, they are there in the actual code. In a few instances, I have also compressed the code to save some space on the printed page. I'll note those instances as we encounter them.

```
<!DOCTYPE html>

<html>
  <head>

    <meta name="viewport" content="width=device-width,initial-scale=1">
```

As described in Chapter 2, the `meta` viewport tag sets up the scaling of the screen so that the UI fills the entire screen. The `<!DOCTYPE html>` tag is required to tell the browser that the page makes use of HTML5 constructs, such as custom attributes. Without it, the app wouldn't render properly (the browser would probably "cover for us," as browsers do in some cases, but we certainly don't want to count on that!).

```
<link rel="stylesheet" href="jq/jquery.mobile-1.3.1.min.css">
<link rel="stylesheet" href="jq/plugins/jqm-datebox.min.css">
<link rel="stylesheet" href="styles.css">
```

A few CSS files are required for this app to look right. Of course, JQM has one, and it contains all of the styles necessary for all of the UI components that the framework provides. In addition, we'll be using a single plug-in, which we'll discuss later in this chapter. It has its own stylesheet that we need to import, though, and that's the important piece of information here. The `styles.css` file contains all of the style specifications specific to My Mobile Organizer. So, unlike the other two that are supplied by others, `styles.css` was put together by me.

> **Note**   We'll be looking at the contents of the `styles.css` file as we progress through the code. I'll show you the style declarations it contains in the appropriate context, not all together as a separate file as with the five HTML files. I think it'll make more sense that way.

```
<script type="text/javascript" src="jq/jquery-1.9.1.min.js"></script>
<script type="text/javascript" src="main.js"></script>
<script type="text/javascript" src="jq/jquery.mobile-1.3.1.min.js"></script>
<script type="text/javascript"
  src="jq/plugins/jqm-datebox.core.min.js"></script>
<script type="text/javascript"
  src="jq/plugins/jqm-datebox.mode.datebox.min.js"></script>
```

After all the style imports, we then need to import all the JavaScript files needed to make the app work. This begins with importing jQuery itself. After that, `main.js` is imported. This, like `styles.css`, is the JavaScript code that I wrote that implements the client-side functionality of My Mobile Organizer. Next up is the JQM file. Note that the order here is important: because there are a few default values that I want to provide for JQM to use and since those defaults are set in `main.js`, the file must be imported before JQM is imported. JQM will see those defaults and use them as appropriate when it loads. Finally, two JavaScript files for the DateBox plug-in need to be imported.

We won't be looking at the code behind this plug-in, be they the CSS or JS files. The general intention is that you use plug-ins without knowing how they implement their functionality, so that's the way they are treated here: as "black boxes" that perform a function for it; how they do it isn't terribly important to us.

> **Tip**   As a side exercise, you might want to look at the code behind this plug-in anyway. You're likely to pick up some neat tricks by doing so!

```
</head>
<body>
```

The `<head>` of the document is closed, of course, so we have a well-formed HTML document. The `<body>` is opened, where the real action is!

```
<div data-role="page" id="homePage">
```

The first bit of "action" is to create a page for the home screen, which you'll recall being described in Chapter 1. Thanks to JQM, all it takes, of course, is to add the `data-role="page"` attribute to a `<div>`, and we magically have a page!

Now, of course, what's on the page is where the interesting bits are located, so let's jump right into that.

About Panel

The About panel that you see when you click the About button in the upper-right corner of the home page is built using the following simple bit of markup:

```
<div data-role="panel" data-position="right" data-display="overlay"
  id="aboutPanel">
  <h2>My Mobile Organizer</h2>
  <h3>Frank W. Zammetti</h3>
  <div class="cssHomeAboutSection">As presented in the Apress book</div>
  <a href="http://www.apress.com">Practical iOS Apps For Business</a>
  <div class="cssHomeAboutSection">Navbar icons courtesy of</div>
  <a href="http://www.glyphish.com">Glyphish</a>
  <div class="cssHomeAboutSection">Thanks to Jonathan Sage for</div>
  <a href="http://dev.jtsage.com/jQM-DateBox">jQM DateBox</a>
  <br><br>
  <button data-icon="alert" data-theme="e"
    onClick="$.mobile.changePage('#confirmClear');">Clear Data</button>
</div>
```

The first thing to note is that this is a child of the homePage <div>. This is important because it ensures that it will appear properly, transposed on top of the home page, when it is shown.

This about information is shown using a *panel*, which is a generic widget that JQM provides that can be used to show information in roughly a windowed way. In other words, the content of a panel will usually appear superimposed over the main content of a page. Alternatively, as is also possible with a panel, it can temporarily push the main content out of the way to show itself.

In any case, to turn a <div> into a JQM panel, we need to add the data-role="panel" attribute to it. In addition, you'll generally want to specify where a panel will be shown, in this case, from the right side of the screen, using the data-position attribute. The other possible value for this attribute is, naturally enough, left.

Related to data-position is data-position-fixed. When set to true, the panel will persist in its location even when the page is scrolled. However, the JQM docs caution you to refrain from using this on Android devices because there's a hefty performance penalty and potential display issues, so it isn't used here (and it wouldn't matter if it were since the home page doesn't scroll in any case).

The data-animate attribute is also available. This defaults to true, but when set to false, it causes the panel to appear and disappear without animation. If you are very performance-conscious, you may want to forgo the animations . . . but I like to see things happen, so I've left this attribute off as well.

Two other related attributes are data-dismissible and data-swipe-close. By default, clicking anywhere outside of the panel causes it to close, but if you set data-dismissible to false, then this won't be possible. Optionally, you can allow it to be closed with a swipe rather than a click by setting data-swipe-close to true (which is its default).

> **Note** For full options of the Panel widget, see the jQuery Mobile documentation at
> http://api.jquerymobile.com/panel.

Remember that I said that a panel could be configured to push the main content of the page out of the way to make room for itself? Well, you specify that you want that to occur by setting the data-display attribute to push. The default value, reveal, makes the panel overlay the main content instead.

As with every JQM widget, the data-theme attribute allows you to select the color swatch from the current theme that you want to use. In this case, as with most of these options, the default is used.

There is just some straight HTML inside the panel—there's nothing special about it. The styles, specified by virtue of the class attributes, are quite straightforward, just some settings for colors, padding, font sizes, and that sort of stuff, as you can see here:

```
.cssHomeAboutSection {
  padding-top : 20px;
}
```

As I said, it's plain old, almost *boring* HTML, that is, until you hit that <button> tag. This button will be enhanced and, in a sense, "transformed" into a JQM widget version of a button, as all <button> tags are by default. This button uses the "e" color swatch from the theme, which, although you can't see it on the printed page, is a yellow coloring and has a warning sign icon (a triangle with an exclamation point in it) by virtue of the data-icon="alert" attribute.

Figure 3-1 shows the About panel, as it has morphed from the wireframe in Chapter 1 to become a real screen.

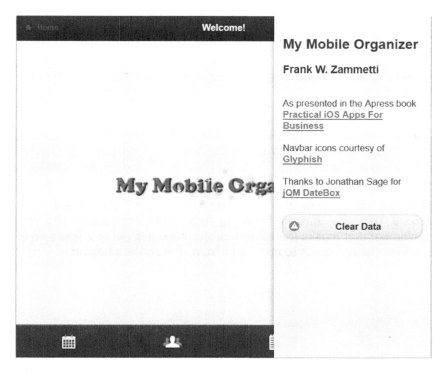

Figure 3-1. The About panel

> **Tip** If you ever want a specific page element that JQM enhances by default to not be enhanced, add
> `data-role="none"` to it. You can also stop all elements within a given container, a `<div>` say, from being
> enhanced by adding `data-enhance="false"` to the container.

The `onClick` event handler on the button is responsible for clearing the data, indirectly at least, as
you'll see when we look at the JavaScript in the next chapter. The important thing here is that the
`$.mobile.changePage()` JQM method is used. As you'll recall, `$()` is the main entry point into jQuery.
JQM enhances this by adding the `mobile` namespace to it to house all of the JQM-specific methods,
including `changePage()`. You pass the ID of a page you want to show to this (or a reference to the
page object itself if you already have it), and JQM handles navigating to that page for you. In this
case, we're actually going to be showing a pop-up dialog to let the user confirm whether they want
to clear the data. That dialog is defined as part of `index.html` as well, as you'll see shortly.

I'm jumping ahead a bit here, though! Before we get to that, we need to look at the rest of the home
page content, beginning with the page header that you can see behind the About panel in Figure 3-1.

Page Header

The page header, which you'll see on all of the pages of the app, is quite simple.

```
<div data-role="header" data-position="fixed">
  <div class="ui-loader-background"></div>
  <button class="cssHomeButton" data-icon="home"
    disabled="disabled">Home</button>
  <h1>Welcome!</h1>
  <a href="#aboutPanel" class="cssFunctionButton" data-icon="bars"
    data-theme="b">About</a>
</div>
```

The `data-role="header"` attribute is all JQM needs to turn this `<div>` into a proper page header.
The `data-position="fixed"` attribute ensures that the header will remain at the top of the page even
when scrolling of the main content occurs. While that isn't a problem on the home page, it is on
other pages, as you'll see shortly.

Within the header, in fact within the main content and footer as well, you'll see a `<div>` with the class
`ui-loader-background`. This `<div>` has the following style information applied to it whose purpose is
to ensure that the element that masks the screen covers the entire screen, floats on top of everything
else on the page, and is colored so as to appear to "dim" the content behind it:

```
.ui-loader-background {
  width : 100%;
  height : 100%;
  left : 0px;
  top : 0px;
  margin : 0px;
  background : rgba(0, 0, 0, 0.3);
```

```
  display : none;
  position : fixed;
  z-index : 100;
}
.ui-loading .ui-loader-background {
  display : block;
}
```

This is needed to make the "please wait" spinner work whenever we call the server. Without this, the spinner would appear, but the header, the main content, and the footer wouldn't be dimmed and, more importantly, disabled from user input. This would allow the user to navigate while a request was in flight to the server, something that could cause problems under some conditions, so it is better to avoid the possibility entirely. This action of dimming the screen and making its content unavailable to user input is sometimes called *scrimming*.

> **Note** If this were an app I intended to sell in an app store, I likely would not have done it this way. Instead, I would have written the code "defensively," so as to allow navigation while requests were in flight to and from the server. This would make the UI more responsive. However, writing that sort of code can get tricky in a hurry, and, as a learning example in a book, it's not all that important to deal with. The "cheap" solution of scrimming will do the trick just fine.

After the scrim `<div>` is another button for returning to the home page. Of course, the user is already on the home page in this case, so the `disabled` attribute is used to…wait for it…*disable* the button! The `data-icon="home"` attribute is used here to put a little house on the button, the typical graphical representation for a home page. Note that this value, as well as most of the values that you have seen throughout the app, are built into JQM and are always available to you as one of a set of basic icons. When we look at the footer, at the `main.css` file more precisely, you'll see how you can also use custom icons if you want.

The `cssHomeButton` and `cssFunctionButton` classes are responsible for adding some padding around the button so that it doesn't bump up to the left edge of the screen. Here are those declarations:

```
.cssHomeButton {
  margin-left : 10px!important;
}

.cssFunctionButton {
  margin-right : 10px!important;
}
```

After that button is a plain old `<h1>` element with some friendly greeting text for the user. Following that is an anchor tag. Huh? Wait a minute, if you look at Figure 3-2, there's a button after the greeting text on the right, not an anchor! What gives?

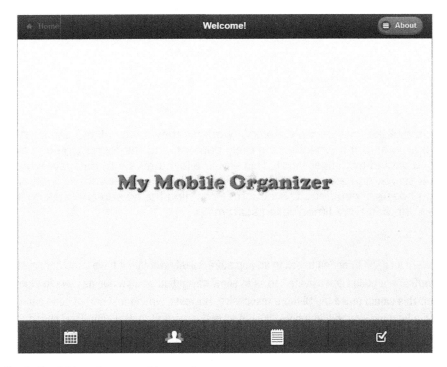

Figure 3-2. A button to the right . . . for some odd reason!

The answer is that JQM can transform `<a>` tags into buttons as well as it can transform `<button>` tags! All of the same attributes that you can use on buttons can be used here as well, including some others that aren't used here, including the following:

- `data-corners`: When `true` (the default), the button has rounded corners. When `false`, they will be square.

- `data-iconpos`: Allows you to specify whether you want the icon, if any, on the `left` (the default), `right`, `top`, or `bottom` of the button.

- `data-mini`: When `true`, the button graphics create a somewhat smaller version of a button—a bit more compact if you will. When `false` (the default), the regular version of a button is created, as shown in Figure 3-2.

- `data-shadow`: When `true` (the default), a drop shadow is applied to the button.

For this button, `data-icon="bars"` provides an icon that is typically used to represent a menu, and `data-theme="b"` uses a dark blue color swatch from the theme.

The last important thing to know about this button is that there is no `onClick` event handler. So, how does something ever happen when the link is clicked? As with any link, we use the `href` attribute for this, but the value here is interesting: it's the ID of an element on the page. This will, effectively, cause JQM to do a `$.mobile.changePage()` call behind the scenes when that button is clicked. Look back at the markup for the About panel earlier, and notice its ID. Yep, it's `aboutPanel`! So, by using the selector `#aboutPanel`, we're telling JQM to navigate to the "page" that just so happens to be in the form of a panel, and that's all we need to do to get that panel to show up! There's no JavaScript and no real manual effort on our part as a developer, just some declarative HTML5-compliant markup.

That's the beauty of JQM!

Page Content

The main page content section is quite sparse, as you can see:

```
<div data-role="content">
  <div class="ui-loader-background"></div>
  <img src="img/title.png" class="cssHomeTitleHeader">
</div>
```

The data-role="content" attribute turns this <div> into the main content of the page as per JQM, and of course we have the scrim <div> as previously discussed. Aside from that, it's just one simple image, our title graphic, with a style applied that is responsible for centering it on the page, with the style declaration being simply this:

```
.cssHomeTitleHeader {
  position : absolute;
  top : 0;
  bottom : 0;
  left : 0;
  right : 0;
  margin : auto;
}
```

Page Footer

The page footer is probably the most complex portion of this page, and really, it's not such a big deal either!

```
<div data-role="footer" data-position="fixed">
  <div class="ui-loader-background"></div>
  <div data-role="navbar" class="cssNavBar">
    <ul>
      <li><a href="appointmentPage.html" class="cssNavAppointmentPage"
        data-icon="custom" data-prefetch="true"
        data-iconpos="notext"></a></li>
      <li><a href="contactPage.html" class="cssNavContactPage"
        data-icon="custom" data-prefetch="true"
        data-iconpos="notext"></a></li>
      <li><a href="notePage.html" class="cssNavNotePage"
        data-icon="custom" data-prefetch="true"
        data-iconpos="notext"></a></li>
```

```
            <li><a href="taskPage.html" class="cssNavTaskPage"
              data-icon="custom" data-prefetch="true"
              data-iconpos="notext"></a></li>
        </ul>
      </div>
  </div>

</div>
```

Like the header, we apply the data-position="fixed" attribute to anchor the footer to the bottom regardless of whether the main content scrolls. (Again, this is not really an issue on the home page, but on other pages it is, and I prefer consistency, so I put it here regardless.) Then a scrim <div> is set up, the same as in the header and main page content.

After that comes the meat, the reason the footer is needed: a navbar. A *navbar* is a simple widget that, more times than not, sits at the bottom of a page and allows the user to flip between different pages. It's constructed by letting JQM enhance a plain old unordered list. Each list item is a navigation point for the user. In this app, that means it's a link to one of the four pages corresponding to our entity categories: appointments, contacts, notes, and tasks (in that order). Each of these categories is enclosed in an anchor tag with an href that points to another HTML file, one for each entity type. The navbar widget itself has little in the way of configuration options. In fact, it has just one, data-iconpos, which tells the widget where you want the icons on the buttons—to the left of the text, to the right of the text, on top of the text, or on the bottom of each button. If you want no icon at all, set a value of none for this attribute. Likewise, you can set a value of notext, as is done in our navbar, to indicate that you want an icon-only button.

The navbar also has the following cssNavBar style applied:

```
.cssNavBar .ui-btn .ui-icon {
  width : 32px!important;
  height : 40px!important;
  margin-left : -15px!important;
  box-shadow : none!important;
  -moz-box-shadow : none!important;
  -webkit-box-shadow : none!important;
}
```

The purpose of this styling is to ensure that the icons that wind up centered on the buttons are of a consistent size. Without this, the buttons shift around in unpleasing ways and generally make the navbar look lousy.

Two other things are of particular interest with regard to the navbar. First, data-icon="custom" allows for a custom icon on the buttons of the navbar. The actual icon used is part of the style class applied to each button.

```
.cssNavAppointmentPage .ui-icon {
  background : url(img/icoAppointment.png) 100% -20% no-repeat;
}
.cssNavContactPage .ui-icon {
  background : url(img/icoContact.png) 100% -20% no-repeat;
}
```

```
.cssNavNotePage .ui-icon {
  background : url(img/icoNote.png) 100% -20% no-repeat;
}
.cssNavTaskPage .ui-icon {
  background : url(img/icoTask.png) 100% -20% no-repeat;
}
```

The other big news is the `data-prefetch` attribute. When this is set to `true`, the page that the link references will be loaded via Ajax in the background immediately after `index.html` is completely parsed and the page is built. Assuming that happens quickly, it means there should be no real delay from the user's perspective when they click one of the navbar buttons; that is, the page the user selects will have already been loaded (and enhanced by JQM as appropriate). This is something you should more or less always do since it ensures a well-performing application. If you have a reason not to preload pages like this, then of course you just need to drop the attribute (or set it to `false` explicitly) to ensure that no preloading occurs.

Info Dialog

With the main content of the page out of the way, we need to examine two other elements that are defined in the file, outside of the home page. The first is a dialog.

```
<div data-role="dialog" id="infoDialog" data-close-btn="none">
  <div data-role="header">
    <h1 id="infoDialogHeader"></h1>
  </div>
  <div data-role="content" id="infoDialogContent"></div>
  <div data-role="footer" class="cssInfoDialogButtons">
    <a href="javascript:void(0);" data-rel="back" data-role="button">Ok</a>
  </div>
</div>
```

This dialog is used throughout the app, anywhere an informational-type message needs to be shown to the user. A dialog is defined simply by attaching the `data-role="dialog"` to a `<div>` and letting JQM enhance it for us as usual. Any page can be presented as a modal dialog like this, and the content of the dialog is, in fact, a page. This means it can have a header, footer, and main content, just like any page can. In this case, we have all three of those, but you'll notice that the header and main content is empty. That's by design. Later, when this dialog is shown, you'll see that those `<div>` elements are populated with the message to be shown to the user.

The `data-close-btn="none"` attribute on the dialog, when set to `none` as it is here, means that there won't be a close button in one of the top corners of the dialog. This ensures that the Ok button in the footer that you see is the only way the user can navigate away from the dialog. I prefer this treatment as it's a little simpler: the user doesn't have to choose whether to tap Ok or the close button, which could be confusing for some (and having *just* a close button doesn't seem right to me either as it doesn't directly acknowledge the message, which is really the intent behind a modal dialog in the first place).

That button has the `cssInfoDialogs` style applied, which ensures that the button is centered on the footer and is defined thusly:

```
.cssInfoDialogButtons {
  margin : 0 auto;
  text-align : center;
}
```

Now you'll notice that the `href` of the anchor tag that becomes the Ok button is just a void JavaScript function call. This has the effect of ensuring that the browser in which the app is viewed doesn't try to do what it normally does with an anchor: navigate somewhere. The `data-rel="back"` attribute is what's ultimately responsible for that. In this case, it tells JQM that we want to navigate back to whatever page launched the dialog. Remember, this dialog can be used from numerous places in the app, from a number of different pages; so hard-coding something here wouldn't work. We need it to be generic like this.

In addition to the `data-close-btn` attribute, you can also choose to show the dialog with square corners instead of the default round ones by setting the `data-corners="false"` attribute. As with most widgets, you can set the color swatch to use for a dialog, this time by selecting a suitable value for the `data-overlay-theme` attribute (a–e in most themes).

Confirm Clear All Data Dialog

Finally, another dialog is in the `index.html` file, the one we saw launched from the About panel for clearing data.

```
<div data-role="dialog" id="confirmClear">
  <div data-role="content">
    <p>Are you sure you want to clear ALL data from both the server and local cache?</p>
    <a href="#" id="confirmClearYes" data-role="button" data-theme="b"
      data-rel="back">Yes</a>
    <a href="#" data-role="button" data-theme="c" data-rel="back">No</a>
  </div>
</div>
```

It's no different from the info dialog really, except that this time we have only main content, and it is defined here in the markup, not inserted later as with the info dialog. You'll also notice that the `href` attributes of both `<a>` tags are set to a hash mark, which serves the same basic purpose as the void JavaScript call in the info dialog. Effectively, both of these buttons will dismiss the dialog and nothing more. If you're paying attention, you'll be scratching your head a bit asking yourself: "OK, self, how exactly does the data get cleared then?" Rest assured that the answer is coming in the next chapter when we examine the JavaScript for the app found in `main.js`. For now, though, we have a couple more pages to look at as well as the stylesheet that I've been saying will be "coming later," so let's keep movin' right along, shall we?

Appointment Page

We have four pages now to examine—one for each of our entity categories. You'll find that each of them has a very similar structure, and that's very much by design. The first one we'll be looking at is the appointment page, which you can see for yourself in its list view mode in Figure 3-3. Nope, no more wireframes for us now; we're on to the real thing!

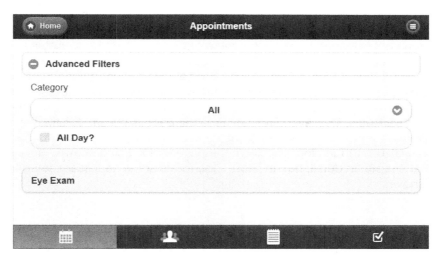

Figure 3-3. *The appointment page in list mode*

The `appointmentPage.html` file is what we're dealing with here, as it contains everything related to the appointment page—the list view and entry view alike. It also happens to be the biggest and most complex, relatively speaking, of the four entity pages, so we're jumping right into the deep end!

The first thing you'll notice as you look at the file is that it isn't a complete HTML document. It can be, and JQM will handle it just fine, but it doesn't *need* to be since its content will be inserted into the DOM of the document created from opening `index.html`. Recall that, in the navbar, these four pages are loaded via AJAX. This of course means that the `index.html` document isn't overwritten. Therefore, we're really just dealing with HTML "snippets" in these four files, and they all start in a similar fashion, as follows:

```
<div data-role="page" id="appointmentPage" data-dom-cache="true">

  <script>
    $(document).delegate("#appointmentPage", "pageshow", function(inEvent) {
      pageShowHandler("appointment");
    });
  </script>
```

We're still creating a JQM page, of course, so it all begins with a `<div>` with a `data-role="page"` attribute on it. The `data-dom-cache="true"` attribute is important for performance reasons: it ensures that the DOM created from parsing this document (well, a snippet really, as I said!) is kept in memory and not reloaded every time the user navigates away and back to it.

Tip   Instead of specifying this on every page you create, you can instead tell JQM to cache all pages via the JavaScript snippet `$.mobile.page.prototype.options.domCache=true;`. This is one of a number of options available to us that we can set in this way, but we'll look at those a bit more in the next chapter.

The other important bit is the script section you see. The purpose of this is to set up an event handler that will fire any time this page is shown. Since this handler could properly be set up only when this document is loaded because the page's `<div>` wouldn't be available until then, it makes sense to do it as a `<script>` block like this since it will be executed when this file is parsed. The `delegate()` method that JQuery offers allows us to set up an event handler on the matched element(s) based on a set of root elements. The root element in this case is `document`, and the handler is to be attached to the page's `<div>`. We also need to tell it what event we want to handle, and in this case, it's `pageshow`. That even fires any time the page is shown. Finally, we pass a function to it to execute for this event, an anonymous inline function in this case. All this function does is to call the `pageShowHandler()` function, passing it the page that is being shown. We'll look at this function in the next chapter in detail, but, in short, it performs some necessary setup tasks for the new page being shown.

Menu

The next bit of markup you encounter as you walk through this file is responsible for setting up the menu in the upper-right corner, which you can see in Figure 3-4.

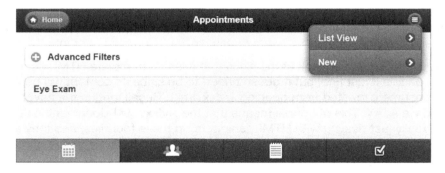

Figure 3-4. *The menu (the same on all four entity pages)*

```
<div data-role="popup" id="appointmentMenu">
  <ul data-role="listview" data-inset="true" class="cssFunctionsMenu"
    data-theme="b">
    <li><a href="javascript:showListView('appointment');">List View</a></li>
    <li id="appointmentNewLink">
      <a href="javascript:newItem('appointment');">New</a>
    </li>
  </ul>
</div>
```

As you can see, there's not much to it. It's just a `<div>` with a `data-role="popup"` attribute. A popup widget, which this creates, is similar conceptually to a dialog except that a pop-up is typical "attached" to some triggering element. It's used to create menus, context menus, and that sort of thing. The content of a pop-up is entirely up to you. However, in this case, it's an unordered list transformed into a `listview` widget by virtue of the `data-role="listview"` attribute. We'll get to that in a minute, though. For now, let's stick with the pop-up discussion. A pop-up has a number of interesting attributes, some of which will look familiar to you at this point, including the following:

- `corners`: When `true` (the default), the corners of the pop-up are rounded (`false` makes them square).

- `dismissible`: When `true` (the default), the pop-up can be closed by clicking outside of it or hitting Esc on a keyboard (`false` disallows this).

- `overlayTheme`: This allows you to choose the color swatch from the theme applied to the pop-up.

- `positionTo`: When set to `origin` (the default), the pop-up appears relative to the coordinates passed to its `open()` method. (When done automatically, as is the case here, it means effectively relative to the element to which it is attached.) You can also set this to `window` to center it in the window, or you can set this to a jQuery selector value to center it on the specified element.

- `shadow`: When `true` (the default), the pop-up is given a drop shadow.

- `transition`: You can use this to determine what transition animation to use to show and hide the pop-up. By default, `none` is used, but you can use any valid jQuery animation, such as `pop` or `fade`.

Two menu items are present here, one for switching to the list view and one for creating a new appointment. Each of them fires a JavaScript function that is present in `main.js`, which we'll look at in the next chapter. For now, it's enough to know that those functions switch the view as appropriate and do some needed setup tasks. Of course, if you click the List View option while already on the list view, nothing happens.

Speaking of list view, let's talk a little bit about the listview widget that is created by JQM enhancing the `<ul>` element here. This widget is one of the more robust and flexible that JQM has to offer, and you'll see it in a number of places throughout My Mobile Organizer. Here it takes on a simple form with just two static elements. A listview can be constructed dynamically too, of course, and this is the case for the list of appointments (as well as contacts, tasks, and notes) in the list view of each entity.

> **Note** Don't confuse the `listview` with the list view of each entity. The former is a JQM widget, while the latter is a type of view of a given entity, be it appointments, contacts, notes, or tasks. It's easy to tell them apart: if it's `listview` with no space, it's the widget. If it's list view, with a space, then it's the view of the entity.

Usually, items in a listview are clickable; hence, they are usually anchor tags for each `<li>` in the unordered list. The `data-inset="true"` attribute on the listview gives the items an inset view; that is, they are indented. In addition, this enhances the effect of the rounding of the pop-up. Ultimately, this is purely aesthetic—I just happen to like the way the menu looks better with this attribute applied.

One last item to mention: the `cssFunctionsMenu` style class is used to ensure that the pop-up has a consistent width. That style class is defined like this:

```
.cssFunctionsMenu {
  min-width : 200px;
}
```

Without this, it would shrink or expand to size itself according to the width of the items in the list. While that might be a good thing in some situations, I prefer the consistent look.

Page Header

As described earlier, a JQM page will, more times than not, consist of a header, main content, and footer—and the appointment page is no exception. Here's the header markup:

```
<div data-role="header" data-position="fixed">
  <div class="ui-loader-background"></div>
  <a href="index.html" class="cssHomeButton" data-icon="home"
    data-theme="b">Home</a>
  <h1>Appointments</h1>
  <a href="#appointmentMenu" class="cssFunctionButton" data-icon="bars"
    data-iconpos="notext" data-rel="popup" data-theme="b"></a>
</div>
```

If you recall the header markup from the home page, you'll realize that it's not very much different. In fact, aside from the text in the middle being obviously different, it's all about the Home and menu button.

First, the Home button isn't a `<button>` at all, as it was on the home page. Instead, it's a link here. The reason for this is that it needs to be enabled here, and a link doesn't have an explicit `disabled` attribute as a `<button>` does. Sure, you can simulate it with some styling and perhaps some JavaScript, but why bother? Just make it a `<button>` on the home page, and disable it the HTML way. Then make it a link here, and let it be active.

The menu button is a little different too since it's actually the About button on the home page. Still, they are very similar. Here we want to launch the pop-up we looked at earlier, and that's done by just using ID selector `#appointmentMenu` as the `href` of the link. JQM will take care of making that work for us when the button is clicked, although we also have to add the `data-rel="popup"` attribute to let JQM know that we want to launch a pop-up. Also, unlike the About button, there isn't any text on the menu button, just the three-bar menu icon. It's the `data-iconpos="notext"` that gets rid of the text for us, and it's the `data-icon="bars"` that puts the icon in its place.

Page Content

The page content is where the real action is, and it begins simply enough.

```
<div data-role="content">

  <div class="ui-loader-background"></div>
```

Yep, we've seen that before—nothing too exciting. We denote this as being the page content with `data-role="content"`, and we need a `<div>` for the scrim as previously discussed, but after that is where it gets interesting.

List View

The page content on all four entity pages is further broken down into two sections: a list view and an entry view. The list view for appointments is simply a `<div>`, and inside that `<div>` is the content that you saw in Figure 3-3. Here's the markup for it:

```
<div id="appointmentList">

<div data-role="collapsible">
  <h3>Advanced Filters</h3>
  <form name="appointmentFilterForm" id="appointmentFilterForm">
    <label for="appointmentFilterCategory" class="select">Category</label>
    <select name="filterCategory" id="appointmentFilterCategory"
      onChange="populateList('appointment', 'category', this.value);">
      <option value="all">All</option>
      <option value="personal">Personal</option>
      <option value="work">Work</option>
    </select>
    <label for="appointmentFilterAllDay">All Day?</label>
    <input type="checkbox" name="filterAllDay"
      id="appointmentFilterAllDay"
      onChange="populateList('appointment', 'allDay', this.value);" />
  </form>
</div>
```

The first `<div>`, with the ID appointmentList, contains all the content you see in Figure 3-3. The entry view will be in another `<div>`, as you'll see shortly. It's important to know that this `<div>` and the entry view `<div>` have a specific format for their IDs, and this is further true of all the entity pages to come. Simply stated, they take the form xxxList and xxxEntry, where xxx is the entity type, appointment in this case.

This will become important in the next chapter when we look at the JavaScript for the client app because it allows the code to be generic.

> **Tip**   *<SpoilerAlert>*We can have methods that accept an entity type as an argument, and we can then construct the IDs of the various page elements with which we need to work dynamically while the overall code is otherwise the same in all cases.*</SpoilerAlert>*

Inside that first `<div>`, we find a child `<div>` with a `data-role="collapsible"`. JQM will enhance this `<div>` to become a collapsible section. The user can tap it to expand and collapse it, and this is perfect for our advanced filters, which the user might typically not need to use.

The advanced filters are constructed by creating a plain old HTML form. We have a <select> element that allows the user to filter by category, whether they want to see personal appointments, business appointments, or all appointments. Then we have a check box so that they can choose to see only all-day events. Each of these form elements has an onChange event handler attached that calls the populateList() function. Again, we'll explore that function in detail as part of the next chapter, but you can see what I was talking about earlier: the first argument is the entity type, which implies that this function is generic. Indeed, it will be used by all of the advanced filter form fields on all entity pages in the same way with just some different arguments.

> **Note**   Not to get too ahead of ourselves here, but in addition to the entity type, we need to pass to populateList() the name of the attribute of the entity by which we're filtering and what matching value we want to see items for in the list. Again, though, the next chapter is where we get into that. For now, it's all markup, all the time!

JQM will of course enhance all of these form fields automatically for us and create more visually appealing versions that are also more suited to mobile user interaction, that is, easier to use on a touchscreen by being bigger.

The final bit of markup in the list view is a simple one.

```
<ul data-role="listview" data-inset="true" id="appointmentListUL"></ul>
```

```
</div>
```

This is another listview widget, similar to how the menu was built. However, you'll notice that there's no data within it this time—no <ul>s and <li>s embedded within it. That's because this listview will be populated with rows for appointments later, by JavaScript code, so the markup really is just providing us with a target in the DOM in which to put those rows.

Entry View

The entry view for appointments, shown when you either select the New menu item or tap an item in the list, is what you see in Figure 3-5.

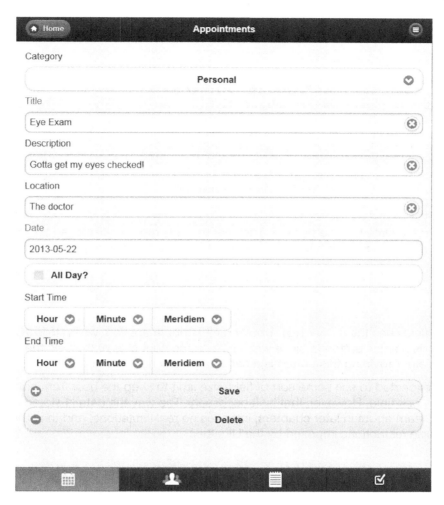

Figure 3-5. The appointment page in entry mode

The code behind this view begins with this snippet of markup:

```
<div id="appointmentEntry" style="display:none;">

  <form name="appointmentEntryForm" id="appointmentEntryForm">
```

The way the app flips between list view and entry view is simply to change the display style attribute of the appointmentList and appointmentEntry <div>s, and appointmentEntry starts out set to none since we always start in list view. Inside this <div>, we're again constructing a plain old HTML form that JQM will then enhance for us.

```
<label for="appointmentCategory" class="select">Category</label>
<select name="category" id="appointmentCategory">
  <option value="personal">Personal</option>
  <option value="work">Work</option>
</select>
```

The first element in the form allows the user to select the category of the appointment, be is personal or work-related.

Next we have a series of text input fields.

```
<label for="appointmentTitle" class="cssRequired">Title</label>
<input type="text" name="title" id="appointmentTitle"
  data-clear-btn="true">
<label for="appointmentDescription">Description</label>
<input type="text" name="description" id="appointmentDescription"
  data-clear-btn="true">
<label for="appointmentLocation">Location</label>
<input type="text" name="location" id="appointmentLocation"
  data-clear-btn="true">
```

The Title field and the Date field come next. They are the only required fields, so they have the cssRequired style attached to them to make them red. Thus, that style definition is simply this:

```
.cssRequired {
  color : #ff0000;
}
```

Each of the text fields has the data-clear-btn="true" attribute applied, which tells JQM that we want to provide a small button (a circle with an *X*) on the right side of the field that clears the contents of the field. Providing this button is a handy convenience for the user.

You might have expected to see some sort of field-size limit to keep the user from entering too much data in any one field. However, that isn't necessary. The way the data is stored on the server, something you'll learn about in later chapters, imposes no real limitations, and thus there doesn't need to be any size restrictions imposed by the UI either.

> **Note** The <label> tags are semantically tied to each of the input fields. This isn't required by JQM, but it's a good habit to get into nonetheless, as it makes your HTML document more meaningful when parsed by browsers that can, in some cases, do extra things because of that meaning (perhaps reading the labels aloud for the vision-impaired, as an example).

The Date field is next, and it has something new for you to see!

```
<label for="appointmentDate" class="cssRequired">Date</label>
<input name="date" id="appointmentDate" type="text" data-role="datebox"
  data-options='{"mode":"datebox","enablePopup":true,"useFocus":true,"useButton":false,"useNewStyle":true}'>
<label for="appointmentAllDay">All Day?</label>
```

For entering dates, I decided to use the DateBox widget provided by JTSage (http://dev.jtsage.com/jQM-DateBox). This JQM plug-in provides a nice pop-up type of date entry mechanism, as shown in Figure 3-6.

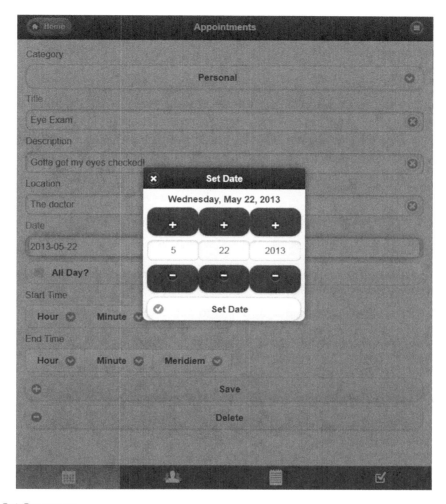

Figure 3-6. The DateBox pop-up

This not only is easier for the user to work with on a touchscreen, but it also imposes rules automatically that keep invalid dates from being entered (as opposed to a plain old text field, for example, where formatting and such would need to be taken into account). Not only do you wind up getting a consistently formatted date, but you also get only valid dates; that is, you can't select June 31st.

This widget provides quite a few options, all of which are made available to us by virtue of the data-options attribute. The value of this attribute is a JavaScript object (in JSON form). The first, and probably most important option, is mode. This widget can present itself in a wide range of modes, or display formats including the DateBox as shown in Figure 3-6, a typical calendar, a flipbox (picture wheels that you can "spin" instead of the +/- buttons of the DateBox), and a slidebox (where years, months, and days are in rows, and you can slide the rows to find what you want). There are also others for entering just times and durations, for example. It's an extremely flexible widget in this regard.

In addition, the enablePopup option allows you to control whether you want the widget to open in a pop-up, as in My Mobile Organizer, or whether you want it to be inline with your content and thus always present on the screen.

> **Tip** As I said, it's a very flexible widget for sure; it's one I like quite a lot. However, as a plug-in for JQM, it is, in a sense, tangential to the goal of this book. As such, I haven't gone into depth regarding all of the options available. The URL given earlier will provide all of that, though, and if you're thinking of using this widget, something I recommend, then that's the place to go to learn about what else it can do. In short, it can do a lot!

Following the Date field is a check box.

```
<input type="checkbox" name="allDay" id="appointmentAllDay" />
```

Obviously, this field allows the user to indicate that this appointment is an all-day event, rather than one that occurs between specific times.

Speaking of which, the following markup shows how to define the fields used to enter the time:

```
<fieldset data-role="controlgroup" data-type="horizontal">
  <legend>Start Time</legend>
  <select name="startTimeHour">
    <option>Hour</option>
    <option value="01">01</option><option value="02">02</option>
    ...and so on up to 12...
  </select>
  <select name="startTimeMinute">
    <option>Minute</option>
    <option value="00">00</option><option value="01">01</option>
    ...and so on up to 59...
  </select>
  <select name="startTimeMeridiem">
    <option>Meridiem</option>
    <option value="am">AM</option>
    <option value="pm">PM</option>
  </select>
</fieldset>
```

When indicating a start time for an appointment, the user must select an hour, minute, and meridiem value (a.m. or p.m., as they're more commonly known). Each of these elements is a plain old <select> element, however, and all three of them are melded together by wrapping them in a <fieldset> tag that is given the data-role="controlgroup" attribute. JQM will enhance the contents of this tag and create controlgroup widgets, which essentially look like one data entry control.

The `data-type="horizontal"` attribute tells JQM to lay the contents of the fieldset out across the screen. The default value is actually `vertical` to combine them all going downward instead. Some other options of the resultant JQM `fieldset` widget include the following:

- `data-mini`: When set to `true`, this results in a slightly more vertically compact version of the resultant combined control (defaults to `false`).

- `data-shadow`: When `true`, a drop shadow is drawn around the widget (defaults to false).

- `data-corners`: When `true` (the default), the resultant control has rounded corners.

Note that in order to save some space on the page here, I have removed most of the `<option>` elements in all three `<select>` elements.

The markup for the end time field follows the markup for the start time as you read through `appointmentPage.html`, and it is different from the start time only in the label text and element name attribute values. Therefore, I've saved a bit *more* space and not printed it here.

The final bit of markup in the entry form consists of the two buttons: Save and Delete.

```
<button type="button" data-theme="e" data-icon="plus"
  onClick="doSave('appointment');"
  id="appointmentSaveButton">Save</button>
<button type="button" data-theme="e" data-icon="minus"
  onClick="doDelete('appointment');"
  id="appointmentDeleteButton" disabled>Delete</button>
```

The Delete button is enabled only when the user selects an item from the list, as it wouldn't make sense to enable it when creating a new item. These buttons, when tapped, call the not very creatively named doSave() and doDelete() functions. Like the updateList() function, those functions are generic; that is, we pass to them the entity type we're saving or deleting and that's it. These functions know how to get the appropriate data from the correct form and work with it as needed, as you'll see in the next chapter.

Page Footer

The page footer is the last part of the `appointmentPage.html` file, and it's not much very much different from what you saw in `index.html`.

```
<div data-role="footer" data-position="fixed">
  <div class="ui-loader-background"></div>
  <div data-role="navbar" class="cssNavBar">
    <ul>
      <li><a href="javascript:void(0);"
        class="cssNavAppointmentPage ui-btn-active ui-state-persist"
        data-icon="custom"> </a></li>
      <li><a href="contactPage.html" class="cssNavContactPage"
        data-icon="custom"> </a></li>
      <li><a href="notePage.html" class="cssNavNotePage"
        data-icon="custom"> </a></li>
```

```
        <li><a href="taskPage.html" class="cssNavTaskPage"
          data-icon="custom"> </a></li>
    </ul>
  </div>
</div>

</div>
```

In fact, the only real difference is that the button for the appointment page has two new styles applied: ui-btn-active and ui-state-persist. These two styles combined result in the button having the "pressed" appearance to indicate this is the current page. In addition, the href of the <a> element for it is a void function call, so tapping it won't do anything. We're already on the appointment page, so that just makes sense!

Contact Page

Next up, we come to the contact page—the second button from the left on the navbar. The contactPage.html file is where this page is housed. Its list view looks not unlike the appointments view, although there are in fact some important differences, as you can see in Figure 3-7. It has a collapsible section for the advanced filters, although this time there is only a single filter for the category. The list is below that, and you'll notice here some interesting additions, namely, the text entry field that says, "Filter items" in it and the fact that there are headers for each letter of the alphabet to break up the list. There's only a single name in this screenshot, but trust me, if the rest of the crew of the Enterprise were listed, you'd have headers like S with "Scott, Montgomery" underneath it, C with "Checkhov, Pavel" underneath it, and so on.

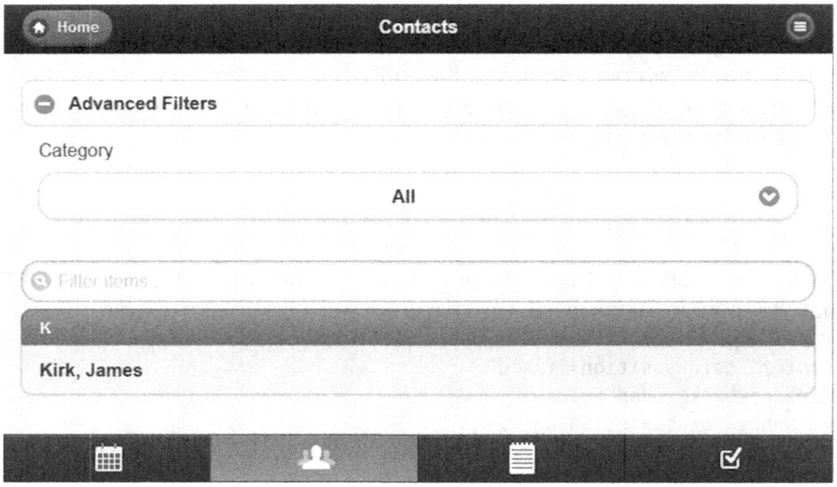

Figure 3-7. The contact page in list mode

> **Note**   As a total geek aside (and if you don't like *Star Trek*, feel perfectly free to skip this), you'll note that I didn't mention Spock. That's because there's some controversy surrounding everyone's favorite Vulcan: is Spock his first name or his last name? In the original series, in one episode he says that his first name is unpronounceable by humans, implying that Spock is indeed his last name. However, in a deleted scene from the 2009 *Star Trek* movie, we learn that Spock is actually his first name. Is the movie considered canon, as the original series certainly is? If so, which is right? I choose to take the coward's way out and simply not use Spock in this example!

In terms of the code, the contact page starts just as the appointment page did with regard to the `pageshow` event handler being attached. In addition, the menu section is identical. The only difference is the values passed to the methods: `contact` rather than `appointment`. The page header is also virtually unchanged, save for the text being different, of course. So, let's not spend any time rehashing that stuff and move on to the page content straightaway.

Page Content

The page content also starts like the appointment page: with a `<div>` for the page itself and a `<div>` for the scrim for when a call to the server is made.

List View

The list view section comes next and, as mentioned previously, is the same as the appointment page (are you seeing a pattern here?), except that it has only the `<select>` element for category.

The first real difference we encounter comes immediately after the Advanced Filters section.

```
<div> </div>
```

Although a trivial snippet of HTML, it serves an important purpose: it results in there being a space between the Advanced Filters section and the text entry field below it, which just plain doesn't look good.

As with the appointment page, after that is a listview widget constructed from a simple unordered list element:

```
<div>
  <ul data-role="listview" data-filter="true" data-inset="true"
    data-autodividers="true" id="contactListUL"></ul>
</div>

</div>
```

Two new attributes make an appearance here, though. First is the `data-filter="true"` attribute. This is what's responsible for creating the "Filter items" text entry field. The beauty of this is that JQM takes care of all of the details for us, not just in creating that field but also in implementing its functionality! As you enter text in the field, the list is filtered to show only items that contain the text you enter. You don't need to write any code. Just throw that attribute on the listview widget, and you're good to go!

The same is true of the data-autodividers="true" attribute, which is responsible for putting those headers in the list. JQM will use the value displayed in the list in creating these headers, and again it takes no more on your part than dropping that attribute onto the <ul> that is transformed into a listview widget!

Entry View

The entry view for contacts is next, as shown in Figure 3-8. Most of it will look rather familiar, but there is one new widget to explore.

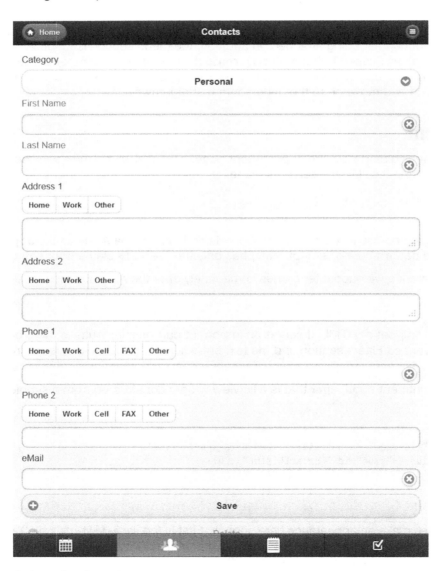

Figure 3-8. The contact page in entry mode

Before we get to it, though, we have some markup that should look familiar to you.

```
<div id="contactEntry" style="display:none;">

<form name="contactEntryForm" id="contactEntryForm">

  <label for="contactCategory" class="select">Category</label>
  <select name="category" id="contactCategory">
    <option value="personal">Personal</option>
    <option value="work">Work</option>
  </select>
```

Yep, the same category `<select>` element that was present for appointments is also present for contacts . . . and if you're guessing that it is present for notes and tasks too, you're right!

Following that, we have two `textinput` widgets, one for first name and one for last name.

```
<label for="contactFirstName" class="cssRequired">First Name</label>
<input type="text" name="firstName" id="contactFirstName"
  data-clear-btn="true">
<label for="contactLastName" class="cssRequired">Last Name</label>
<input type="text" name="lastName" id="contactLastName"
  data-clear-btn="true">
```

As you can see, there's nothing new or special about them. The same is not entirely true for the two address elements, though.

```
<fieldset data-role="controlgroup" data-type="horizontal"
  data-mini="true">
  <legend>Address 1</legend>
  <input type="radio" name="address1Type" id="contactAddress1TypeHome"
    value="home" />
  <label for="contactAddress1TypeHome">Home</label>
  <input type="radio" name="address1Type" id="contactAddress1TypeWork"
    value="work" />
  <label for="contactAddress1TypeWork">Work</label>
  <input type="radio" name="address1Type" id="contactAddress1TypeOther"
    value="other" />
  <label for="contactAddress1TypeOther">Other</label>
</fieldset>
<textarea cols="40" rows="4" name="address1"></textarea>
```

Sure, you've seen a `controlgroup` widget before—it was used for the start and end times for the appointment entry view. However, here we're using it to combine a series of radio buttons. Combining the radio buttons in this fashion effectively creates one unique widget, one that allows the user to select from one of a number of mutually exclusive options, whether an address is a work, home, or other address in this case. An important thing to recognize here is that each of the radio buttons must have a unique ID. Otherwise, you'll find that the control doesn't work as expected. Of course, as with radio buttons on a plain HTML form, the name attributes must all match.

After the `controlgroup` widget is a `<textarea>` element, and this, like an `<input>` element of type text, is enhanced to become a `textinput` widget. However, this type can expand as the user types text into it.

> **Tip**   The clear button is not available for `<textarea>` elements; that's somewhat unfortunate, but so be it.

There are two chunks of HTML for entering two addresses, but being that the second block looks just like the first one that we just examined, save for different IDs, let's move on to the chunk for entering the first phone number.

```
<fieldset data-role="controlgroup" data-type="horizontal"
  data-mini="true">
  <legend>Phone 1</legend>
  <input type="radio" name="phone1Type" id="contactPhone1TypeHome"
    value="home" />
  <label for="contactPhone1TypeHome">Home</label>
  <input type="radio" name="phone1Type" id="contactPhone1TypeWork"
    value="work" />
  <label for="contactPhone1TypeWork">Work</label>
  <input type="radio" name="phone1Type" id="contactPhone1TypeCell"
    value="cell" />
  <label for="contactPhone1TypeCell">Cell</label>
  <input type="radio" name="phone1Type" id="contactPhone1TypeFAX"
    value="fax" />
  <label for="contactPhone1TypeFAX">FAX</label>
  <input type="radio" name="phone1Type" id="contactPhone1TypeOther"
    value="other" />
  <label for="contactPhone1TypeOther">Other</label>
</fieldset>
<input type="text" name="phone1" data-clear-btn="true">
```

As you can see, it really doesn't look much different from the block for address. The radio buttons are different, that is, in terms of their label values; aside from that, the code is virtually identical.

As with addresses and the first phone number block, the second phone number block is basically the same markup, so there's no real need to examine it again. Instead, we have just the eMail field left:

```
<label for="contactEMail">eMail</label>
<input type="text" name="eMail" id="contactEMail" data-clear-btn="true">
```

Just a boring old `textinput` widget. . . or at least it will be once JQM enhances the `<input>` element.

Finally, in this entry view are the two buttons; once again, they are virtually identical to the appointment page, differing only by the values passed to the `doSave()` and `doDelete()` methods.

Page Footer

To close out the contact page, you have the page footer. Again, we'll be able to save some time because it's no different from the one for the appointment page, save for the fact that the contacts button has the styles applied to it to make it appear selected, as well as having the void JavaScript function call as its `href` value.

Note Page

After the contact page is the note page, as seen in `notePage.html`, the third button from the left on the `navbar`. This page is, by quite a bit, the simplest of all the pages. Figure 3-9 shows the list view for this page.

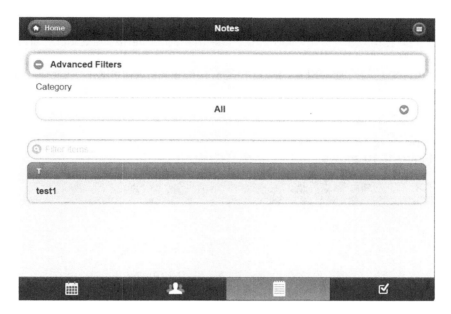

Figure 3-9. The note page in list mode

The note page is identical to the contact page in terms of the list view, including the advanced filter for category and the "Filter items" textinput widget below that. Also, as with contacts, the list has divider headings to break up the list alphabetically.

Once more when it comes to the code, we find that `notes.html` starts just like `appointments.html` and `contacts.html` before it in terms of the initial `<script>` block, menu, and header. So, let's save a few trees and move on, shall we?

Page Content

Another day, another `<div data-role="content">` page element and another `<div class="ui-loader-background"></div>` scrim element! That's how the page content begins, the same as with the previous two pages.

List View

As you've come to expect, the list view for notes begins with `<div id="noteList">`, and that is followed by a `collapsible` widget. The markup for this widget matches that of contacts with just the names of elements changed (to protect the innocent, I suppose?).

Also as with contacts, a `<div> </div>` follows that for proper spacing. After that is the listview widget definition.

```
<div>
  <ul data-role="listview" data-filter="true" data-inset="true"
    data-autodividers="true" id="noteListUL"></ul>
</div>
```

Once again, `data-filter="true"` is applied to provide the "Filter items" text input, and `data-autodividers="true"` creates the alphabetical headings in the list. The `data-inset="true"` part gives the list items a 3D "pushed-in" sort of look, purely an aesthetic choice on my part.

Entry View

The entry view for notes is, as you'd expect for an entity with just two attributes (title and text), quite simple, as Figure 3-10 shows.

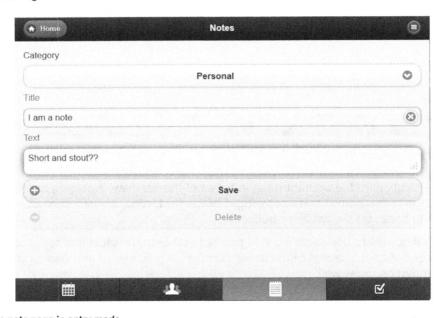

Figure 3-10. The note page in entry mode

The form that contains those two elements, as well as the buttons, is shown in its entirety here:

```
<div id="noteEntry" style="display:none;">

  <form name="noteEntryForm" id="noteEntryForm">

    <label for="noteCategory" class="select">Category</label>
    <select name="category" id="noteCategory">
      <option value="personal">Personal</option>
      <option value="work">Work</option>
    </select>
```

```
<label for="noteTitle" class="cssRequired">Title</label>
<input type="text" name="title" id="noteTitle" data-clear-btn="true">
<label for="noteText" class="cssRequired">Text</label>
<textarea name="text" id="noteText"></textarea>

<button type="button" data-theme="e" data-icon="plus"
  onClick="doSave('note');" id="noteSaveButton">Save</button>
<button type="button" data-theme="e" data-icon="minus"
  onClick="doDelete('note');"
  id="noteDeleteButton" disabled>Delete</button>

</form>

  </div>
</div>
```

There shouldn't be any surprises here, as each of these elements has been seen before on the previous two pages. Once again, a `<textarea>` is used so that the text of the note can be as large as the user wants it to be, and the field will expand to accommodate their input.

Page Footer

All that's left after the entry form on the note page is the page footer with the navbar widget. Once again, we find that . . . surprise! It's just like the one for contacts! Naturally, the notes button is the one highlighted as current and unclickable this time, but otherwise it's the same.

Rest assured, the task page has a few surprises, and guess what? That's our next stop!

Task Page

The final page of the My Mobile Organizer client app is for viewing, modifying, and creating tasks. Figure 3-11 shows what this page looks like. The file taskPage.html is the one to look at.

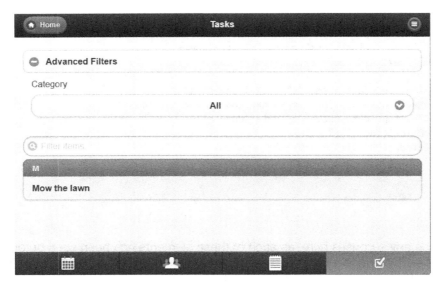

Figure 3-11. The tasks page in list mode

Not to sound like a broken record, but I will nonetheless. The list view for tasks is truly identical to that of notes! A single advanced filter is available for category, and the "Filter items" `textinput` widget is back, followed by a listview with alphabetical dividers.

Down at the code level, this page starts just as all others with the `pageshow` event handler being attached. In addition, the menu section is, once more, identical to the others, as is also true of the page header.

Yes, I said there was some new stuff to see here, but we haven't hit it quite yet.

Page Content

In fact, it's not even in the page content! Once more, we have a `<div>` for the page content and a `<div>` for the activity scrim.

List View

The advanced filters and the listview widget are just as identical; only the field names and IDs and text labels have changed.

With that being said, since you've effectively seen the markup by virtue of having viewed it on previous pages, let's march on.

> **Note**   Although I've said a number of times that various bits of code are identical to bits you've previously looked at, I want to encourage you to look at this code as you read through this chapter nonetheless. I assume you've downloaded the code package at this point, so you can open the appropriate file and walk through it. Yes, you'll see that indeed a lot of it is very similar—even boilerplate—but it's important that you see it for yourself if for no other reason than to become accustomed to what the code looks like before JQM enhances it.

Entry View

That's enough foreshadowing; let's get to some new stuff! The entry view for tasks, as shown in Figure 3-12, has two new widgets to check out: `slider` and `range`.

Figure 3-12. The task page in list mode

We have to create a form first, inside a `<div>` for the entry view.

```
<div id="taskEntry" style="display:none;">

  <form name="taskEntryForm" id="taskEntryForm">
```

Also, we have some other fields to deal with initially, namely, category, title, and notes. The category is, as usual, built with a `<select>`. Title uses a `textinput` widget created when JQM enhances an `<input>` of type `text`. The notes field is a `<textarea>`, also transformed into a `textinput` widget when the page is parsed.

```
<label for="taskCategory" class="select">Category</label>
<select name="category" id="taskCategory">
  <option value="personal">Personal</option>
  <option value="work">Work</option>
</select>
<label for="taskTitle" class="cssRequired">Title</label>
<input type="text" name="title" id="taskTitle" data-clear-btn="true">
<label for="taskNotes">Notes</label>
<textarea name="notes" id="taskNotes"></textarea>
```

The completed element on the form is a binary value, yes or no, to indicate whether the task has been completed. A common way for such a value to be entered in a mobile UI is by using a sliding on/off type of button. JQM provides the `slider` widget for this, and it creates this from a `<select>` with `data-role="slider"` attached to it.

```
<label for="taskCompleted">Completed</label>
<select name="completed" id="taskCompleted" data-role="slider">
  <option value="no">No</option>
  <option value="yes">Yes</option>
</select>
```

Aside from that single attribute, we have to create only two `<option>` elements, the values of which can be anything we like (also true of the text displayed for each option). Thus, while you can have a Yes/No slider as we do here, you can also do a Male/Female slider or Living/Deceased slider, if that's the type of app you're building.

The priority field allows us to set the priority of this task by choosing a value from 1 to 5. Interestingly, this app imposes no meaning on those values. If you decide that tasks with a priority of 1 are more important than those with a priority of 5, that's fine. In fact, you might decide priority 3 is the most important! It doesn't matter; all that matters is that a value from 1 to 5 is chosen.

```
<label for="taskPriority">Priority</label>
<input type="range" name="priority" id="taskPriority"
  value="1" min="1" max="5" step="1" data-highlight="true" />
```

An `<input>` element of type range is a new type of control offered by HTML5. A browser that supports this input type will produce some sort of slider, although it really could produce any sort of input widget it chooses that makes sense (it might be a spinner, that is, a text box with an up and down arrow next to it, for instance, or a more traditional slider, as mobile Safari and Chrome do on iOS and Android, respectively). JQM will enhance this to produce a slider independent of browser support! You can set the initial value via the value attribute, and you can set the minimum (min) and maximum (max) values. The data-highlight="true" attribute results in the line of the slider, the track if you will, to be filled in from the left edge up to the drag handle based on what value is currently set.

Note   Interestingly, this input type isn't supported by Firefox, which is something I learned while writing this chapter! However, this won't stop My Mobile Organizer from working in Firefox because JQM will be producing the widget you see on the screen rather than in the browser. Thus, the fact that Firefox doesn't natively support it doesn't matter. For reference, it appears that Firefox is, at the time of this writing at least, the only browser that doesn't support it.

After the priority slider is the Due Date field, which uses the DateBox widget plug-in, as shown on the appointment page.

```
<label for="taskDueDate">Due Date</label>
<input name="dueDate" id="taskDueDate" type="text" data-role="datebox"
   data-options='{"mode":"datebox","enablePopup":true,"useFocus":true,"useButton":false,
"useNewStyle":true}'>
```

Finally, the Save and Delete buttons close out this form in the same fashion as all three of the previous pages.

Page Footer

Now, finally, we come to the end of the last page to explore. It ends, of course, with the navbar, exactly as we've seen three times previously. Consequently, you can consider this early dismissal from school! You have now essentially explored all of the markup that makes up the client application of My Mobile Organizer, even if we seemingly skipped over a lot of it on the grounds that it wasn't anything new. A lot of it was repetitive to be sure, but that's actually by design; the four entity pages are all quite similar, all looking and functioning in much the same way, so it only makes sense that the markup on all of them would look quite similar. You'll find that this paradigm continues into the JavaScript that you'll see in the next chapter, and even in the server-side code in later chapters.

Tip   As a fun exercise, you might want to try combining all four of the pages into one, just to make it even more repetitive! You can create a single page that contains all the fields in list and entry views, and then when a navbar button is tapped, you just hide or show the appropriate fields. That would, in fact, improve the performance of the app a bit by reducing the DOM size and removing some Ajax loads at initial launch.

Summary

In this chapter, we covered a lot of ground indeed! We tore through all the markup that makes up the client portion of My Mobile Organizer, encapsulated within five HTML files. In the process, you saw how JQM is used to enhance plain old HTML to create a mobile UI. You also saw things such as the navbar, dialog, panel, textbox, and datebox widgets in use—some of them via plug-in. Furthermore, you saw how navigation is handled and how the preloading of pages can provide for an application that performs well. Finally, you saw how to create data entry forms and data lists and how to flip between them using a menu. We also touched upon a number of options available to you through JQM, even those that weren't used directly in the app.

In the next chapter, we'll look at the other half of the client equation, namely, the JavaScript that makes the client app work for us.

Chapter 4

Writing the Application with jQuery Mobile, Part II

It used to be that "just a little HTML would do ya," as the saying goes (well, if there **was** such a saying - which there should be!). So-called brochureware sites were all the rage, especially for companies taking their first tentative steps onto the fledgling Internet market. Nowadays, though, it's not nearly enough! The Internet-using public, including you and me of course, demand more. They demand interaction. They demand movement. Most of all, they demand that a website, and certainly a web *app*, do more than just sit there and burn itself into the screen-reddened eyeballs of the user viewing them.

For the most part, providing this interactivity demands JavaScript (putting aside things like CSS3 animations, plug-ins, HTML5 media tags, and such). Most definitely in the case of My Mobile Organizer, we're talking about JavaScript.

In the previous chapter, you saw a number of calls to JavaScript functions that I promised we'd "get to shortly." Well, shortly has arrived! In this chapter, we will explore that code, as housed in the `main.js` file. There is, in actuality, surprisingly little code to see when you consider the functionality of the app.

So, without further ado, let's get to it!

Some Global Variables to Kick Things Off

The `main.js` file begins with a few global variable declarations. In general, global variables should be considered a Very Bad Thing™. However, given the generally small size of this app and the truly global nature of the data these variables convey, I felt breaking this rule did not merit a capital crimes trial!

```
var ajaxURLPrefix = null;
```

The first variable declared (and defined, if you want to get all computer science-y) is `ajaxURLPrefix`. This is used as the base of the URL accessed when making any of the Ajax calls to the server to create, read, update, or delete a given entity. When you run the application on a desktop, as you might do when developing it (as I did, in fact), then the value of this variable would be something like `http://127.0.0.1:80`, assuming you have a web server running on the machine, of course. When it's run on a real mobile device, though, that URL would have to be something different—something that points to a real server, perhaps `http://www.etherient.com:80`, for example. Actually, it can be just some remote machine—it doesn't have to be a proper server; that's the real point here.

> **Tip**   It could conceivably be a server running on the device itself, in which case that same typical local machine address might work fine. In addition, `localhost` can be used in place of `127.0.0.1` on most machines, barring any unusual configuration.If you're thinking that you could do development on the go with your mobile device, you're completely right; that's why I mention this!

The value of this variable is actually determined dynamically in some JavaScript code that executes when the app starts, which is something we'll see in the upcoming section "Start Here: The mobileinit Event Handler." The value it is set to here doesn't really matter. (It's just a habit of minealways to define the value of variables initially, even if just to `null` as is done here.)

The next variable declared is `updateID`.

```
var updateID = null;
```

This variable is used by the code to determine when an item, be it an appointment, contact, note, or task, is being added or updated. If the value is `null`, then it's an add; otherwise, it's an update, and the value is the ID of the entity being updated.

```
var networkAvailable = true;
```

The `networkAvailable` variable is a simple flag that tells the code whether network connectivity is currently available. More precisely, it tells the code whether connectivity was available *when the app was last started*. If connectivity isn't available at app start-up, then it is assumed not to be available for the remainder of that execution. That isn't the user-friendliest approach, but it is fairly fail-safe and simple to implement.

> **Note**   At this point, the keen reader will realize that there is a problem: if connectivity is available at start-up but becomes unavailable later, the app will fail at some point when the server is accessed. I invite you to take on that issue as a challenge and correct it.However, be warned: the subject of handling changing connectivity more robustly can get complex very fast, especially when you add the notion of how to do data synchronization in light of that changing connectivity.Keep in mind too that there's no one true, correct answer to how to do this—there are many approaches.If you're interested in exploring it further, I suggest an article by Christopher Coenraets as a starting point: `http://coenraets.org/blog/2012/05/simple-offline-data-synchronization-for-mobile-web-and-phonegap-applications`. Note that it gets into some of what is discussed in later chapters about PhoneGap, so you may want to hold off reading it until later, just to have some extra context when you do.

Finally, the `pageVisited` structure is defined.

```
var pageVisited = {
  appointment : false,
  contact : false,
  note : false,
  task : false
};
```

This structure is used whenever the user flips to a new entity page. If the page hasn't been visited before, say when the user accesses the notes page, the flag will be `false`. The code will see that, set it to `true`, and populate the list of notes. This needs to happenonly the first time the page is visited since only adds, updates, and deletes can occur after that, and the code will handle those elsewhere.

Start Here: The mobileinit Event Handler

The first real executable code you find as you explore `main.js` is a bit of a misnomer. What it really does is set up an event handler for an event that won't occur until a later point (relative to the point where `main.js` is loaded and parsed by the browser).

```
$(document).on("mobileinit", function() {
```

JQM triggers the special `mobileinit` event on the document object very early on (the JQM documentation says "immediately," in fact), and it is where you must perform any setting of JQM defaults. JQM will do its page enhancements once the DOM is constructed, but `mobileinit` will fire even before that. In fact, if you look back at `index.html`, you'll notice that `main.js` is loaded before JQM's JavaScript file. This is necessary because if it weren't done in this order, then you'd find that JQM does the page enhancements before you have a chance to set its defaults, and you would lose that degree of control over what JQM does. It's always important to pay attention to the order that JavaScript files are loaded and to remember that each is evaluated before the next one is loaded because this can have major impact on what the code in the various files do and even on whether things will work as expected. That's a general rule, of course, when dealing with JavaScript in a browser in any situation, but it's even more important if you need to set these JQM defaults because if you get the order wrong, it simply won't work, and you'll be left scratching your head wondering why.

When the `mobileinit` event fires, the following code executes:

```
$.mobile.defaultPageTransition   = "none";
$.mobile.defaultDialogTransition  = "none";
$.mobile.phonegapNavigationEnabled = true;
$.mobile.loader.prototype.options.text = "...Please Wait...";
$.mobile.loader.prototype.options.textVisible = true;
```

Here we set the defaults that we want JQM to use. First, for the sake of performance, we'll turn off both transition animations between pages and animations of dialog open and close events.

> **Tip**   Feel free to change these defaults to any of the animations JQM and jQuery support to see what they look like and how they affect performance. You will find that they work greaton some devices, while on others, not so much. For the sake of good performance across all devices, turning them off is a good bet, if a less aesthetically pleasing one.

Next, the `phonegapNavigationEnabled` flag is set to `true`. This won't have any impact except when the app is wrapped with PhoneGap for deployment on a mobile device, as you'll see in Chapters 9 and 10. The purpose of this is to make JQM use PhoneGap's navigation helper when it is available. This is done to address some page refresh issues that you might otherwise see when running a PhoneGap-based app on Android with regard to navigating between pages. In short, it does no harm where it's not needed and it helps where it is, so why not?

The last two defaults deal with the spinning icon and message seen when the server is called. The text is set to something I prefer, and the `textVisible` flag being set to `true` tells JQM to show that text, which by default it wouldn't do.

The final `mobileinit` code that needs to execute has to do with determining the value of that `ajaxURLPrefix` global variable we saw earlier.

```
if (document.location.protocol.toLowerCase().indexOf("file") != -1) {
  ajaxURLPrefix = "http://127.0.0.1:80";
} else {
  ajaxURLPrefix = "http://www.etherient.com:80";
}
```

The logic is quite simple: any time we load the app off the local file system, the code assumesthe server is running on the same machine, as is typical during development. Any other time, a hard-coded server URL is used. Obviously, you'd need to change these URLs as appropriate for your environment.

> **Caution**   By default, browsers have restrictive policies with regard to Ajax calls made from JavaScript loaded off the local file system. Unfortunately, these rules vary by browser and even by versions of eachbrowser. At the time I wrote this, I found that Chrome 27, Opera 12, and Safari 5, at least on Windows, would allow this without any problem. For Firefox 21, you need to set the `security.fileuri.strict_origin_policy` option under `about:config` to `false` to allow it. I was unable to determine the mechanism that would allow IE 10 to make these calls. (I'm sure it's in the security policy settings, but I tried for a good hour without luck. Hit me up on Twitter if you find the answer—I'd love to hear it!)

No Wait, Start Here: The ready Event Handler

A little more initialization-type code needs to execute when the app starts. This time, though, we need to ensure that it executes when the DOM is fully built, even after JQM has enhanced it. The perfect event to hook into for that purpose is the document's well-known `ready` event.

```
$(document).on("ready", function() {
```

Once the document is ready, we can first check to see whether network connectivity is available.

```
if (navigator && navigator.connection &&
  navigator.connection.type == Connection.NONE
) {
  showConnectivityMsg();
} else {
  downloadServerData();
}
```

The `navigator.connection` object is one that PhoneGap makes available to determine the status of network connectivity as well as the type of connectivity. If this object is available and if the type of connection is `Connection.NONE` (a constant that PhoneGap also provides), then network connectivity isn't available, and, as a result, `showConnectivityMsg()` is called. This will be the next function we explore (not counting the anonymous functions that are the `mobileinit` and document `ready` event handlers). However, if `navigator.connection` is not available or if indeed `navigator` isn't available (which can be the case in some desktop browsers), and then it is assumed that network connectivity is available. That's a safe assumption in the sense that the only other *valid* way this app can run is on a desktop and then only for development. In that case, PhoneGap wouldn't be involved and so `navigator.connection` wouldn't be available. On a desktop, though, it's safe to assume that connectivity is available most of the time. Besides, even if it's not, it's likely that a developer will encounter the issues that would result, and they can handle it (right?).

> **Tip**   It might be an interesting exercise to run this app from a web server rather than as a PhoneGap-wrapped native app, in which case you'd need to make some modifications to this logic. Other than that, I suspect that there's nothing that would make the app not function in this mode, although it's not designed for it as such.

The final bit of setup-type code that needs to occur at this point relates to the Clear Data button on the About panel: there needs to be an event handler attached to its click event.

```
$("#confirmClearYes").on("click", function() {
  clearData();
});
```

Yep, that's it! However, you can now understand why this has to execute only in response to the document's ready event: if we tried to do this sooner, it's quite possible that the DOM node involved isn't available, and, at best, we'd wind up with no event handler attached (or, at worst, a page load error).

By the way, it would have been just as valid to write that code like this:

```
$("#confirmClearYes").on("click", clearData);
```

In general, I suggest that's the way you *should* write it. Removing this level of indirection would result in better performance (although the difference would be miniscule in a case like this that depends on user intervention). That being said, if there was more work to do before the call to clearData(), then the way it's written in the app would be the way to go. I just wanted to demonstrate both for you so that you know the alternatives.

When Networks Fail: Showing a Message When No Connectivity Is Available

When connectivity isn't found to be available in the document ready event handler, the showConnectivityMsg() function is called. It has a simple purpose in life: to ensure that the networkAvailable flag gets set tofalse and that the user knows what's up.

```
function showConnectivityMsg() {

  networkAvailable = false;
  $("#infoDialogHeader").html("No Network Connectivity");
  $("#infoDialogContent").html(
    "Network connectivity is currently unavailable. The ability to " +
    "create new items, update items and delete items has been " +
    "disabled. You can still browse locally-cached data. Restart " +
    "the app when connectivity has been restored."
  );
  $.mobile.changePage($("#infoDialog"), { role : "dialog" });

}
```

If you remember from our exploration of index.html, there was a dialog marked up that contained some placeholder elements. At that point, I told you that this info dialog is used in a number of places to show informational pop-up dialogs to the user. Well, this is the first use of that!

To make it work, the code needs to set some header text and some main content text on the dialog. The <h1> element with ID infoDialogHeader and the <div> element with ID infoDialogContent are the elements that we need to populate. Once we use jQuery to get a reference to them, the html() method that the jQuery object provides is used to set the content of those elements. Once that's done, showing the dialog is a simple matter of calling $.mobile.changePage()and passing to it a reference to the <div> with ID infoDialog. We also need to tell JQM that this dialog page, which you'll recall is what a dialog is built from, is to be used as a pop-up dialog. That's what the second argument, an object with a single role attribute set to a value of dialog, does. JQM takes care of dimming the main page and showing the dialog over it, which is just as we want.

Poor Man's Synchronization: Downloading Data from the Server

As you saw in the document ready event handler, when network connectivity is available, the first task to be performed is to call downloadServerData(). This function represents a simplistic client-server synchronization model. Put simply, the server's copy of the data is assumed canonical, and the client downloads it in its entirety when it starts. This is just about the least efficient way to do client-server data synchronization, but it has the benefit of being very simple to implement, and it also ensures perfect synchronization (assuming that the client can't make any changes locally, which aren't always immediately reflected in the server's copy of the data).

This function begins simply enough.

```
function downloadServerData() {

  $.mobile.loading("show");

  var fetching = {
    loaded_appointment : false, loaded_contact : false,
    loaded_note : false, loaded_task : false,
    data_appointment : null, data_contact : null,
    data_note : null, data_task : null
  };
```

The call $.mobile.loading("show") is used to scrim the screen and show the spinning activity indicator icon, along with the "please wait" text defined earlier as the default text for this. The fetching structure is definednext, and it is used to keep track of what has and hasn't been loaded. The loaded_* members are Boolean flags that record whether a given entity type has been loaded, and the data_* members are the actual data retrieved from the server.

Spoiler alert: the code will be making four simultaneous Ajax requests to the server to get the data—one request per entity type. Ajax requires that we have a callback function to execute when the response comes back from the server. To keep the code as concise as possible, I decided to write a single callback function rather than one for each entity type. That function is defined and assigned to the completeLoad variable.

```
var completeLoad = function(inType, inResponse) {

  fetching["loaded_" + inType] = true;
  fetching["data_" + inType] = inResponse;
```

As you'll see shortly, the Ajax calls perform some indirection by each having their own callback function, which then calls the `completeLoad()` function. Regardless, this function is where the action is. It is passed the entity type that was retrieved and the response from the server, of course. With that information, the appropriate flag in the `fetching` structure is set to `true` and the response is recorded. That flag is important because of the next statement:

```
if (fetching.loaded_appointment && fetching.loaded_contact &&
  fetching.loaded_note && fetching.loaded_task) {
```

This function will ultimately be called four times, each time flipping the appropriate flag in the `fetching` structure and recording the response. Once all four flags are `true`, then the rest of the function will execute, beginning with the next statement:

```
if (fetching.data_appointment && fetching.data_contact &&
  fetching.data_note && fetching.data_task
) {
```

At first glance, you might think this is redundant and that it does the same thingas the previous `if` statement, but that isn't the case. If a network error occurs while fetching any of the entities, the `fetching.loaded_*` flag for that entity will get set to `true`, but the `fetching.data_*` member will be `null`. If this happens for any of the entities, then essentially this callback function will throw away all of the data. Again, it's a simplistic synchronization scheme, but in order for it to be consistent, we need to ensure we get *all* of the data back, or instead we act as if we got *none* of it back. That's what this `if` statement essentiallydoes.

Now if we *did* get all the data back, then it's time to make use of that data.

```
window.localStorage.clear();
var types = [ "appointment", "contact", "note", "task" ];
for (var i = 0; i < types.length; i++) {
  var typ = types[i];
  var dat = fetching["data_" + typ];
  var len = dat.length;
  var lst = window.localStorage;
  for (var j = 0; j < len; j++) {
    var obj = dat[j];
    lst.setItem(typ + "_" + obj._id, JSON.stringify(obj));
  }
}
```

HTML5 introduces a set of DOM storage mechanisms, collectively referred to as *Web Storage* (or simply the Storage interface), which provide developers with a persistent client-side data storage mechanism beyond tried-and-true cookies. These mechanisms allow for a larger amount of data to be stored and to store it in a number of ways. Some of these mechanisms even use a true relational database to store data and allow querying operations against it. For our purposes in My Mobile

Organizer, we make use of the localStorage mechanism. This localStorage mechanism uses a simple key-value pair to store data, and it allows for a much larger volume of data than does cookies, butotherwise it works in the same way (the data is tied to a given domain, and so on).

> **Note**   The size limit for localStorage is browser-dependent and not explicitly defined by the W3C spec. The lowest limit of any current browseris 2.5MBfor Chrome, Opera, and Firefox, all the way up to 10MB with IE. It's also true that, in at least some browsers, the users themselves can manipulate this limit up or down (but few do in my experience). You therefore can think of 2.5MB as the maximum allowed,which will probably be a safe assumption 99 percent of the time across all current-day browsers.

You access localStorage by way of the `window.localStorage` object. Although it's not done in My Mobile Organizer (because the premise of the app requires it be running in a browseror on a mobile device that supports it), it's usually a good idea to ensure that `localStorage` is available before trying to use itbecause in recentbutnotridiculouslyold browsers, it may well not be. A simple way to do this is as follows:

```
function supports_html5_storage() {
  try {
    return 'localStorage' in window && window['localStorage'] !== null;
  } catch (e) {
    return false;
  }
}
```

Call this function before trying to use `localStorage`, and ensure it doesn't return `false`; then you're good to go.

The `localStorage` object presents a number of methods for you to use. The first method, `clear()`, does exactly what you'd think it does: it clears all stored data tied to the current domain. That is, therefore, the first thing the callback function does since the next step will be to populate the data with the fresh data from the server.

That population occurs within the loop, which iterates once for each entity type, as listed in the `types` array. A reference to the data stored in the `fetching.data_*` members is dynamically calculated based on the `type`. The data returned by the server, as you'll see in Chapters 7 and 8, are arrays, so the code begins to iterate over that array in the inner loop. For each element in the array, a call to the `setItem()` method of `window.localStorage` is made, and the next item in the array is converted to a string of JSON and stored. Each item is keyed by type_id, where typeis appointment, contact, note, or task, and whereidis the ID of the item as returned by the server. (Again, as you'll see in later chapters, that's guaranteed to be a unique numeric ID, so every element stored in localStorage will have a unique ID too.)

The type has to be part of the key because there's no way to group the data you store in localStorage. It's just one big collection of values each referenced by a given key. More importantly, because of that, there's no way to query localStorage as you would a database only, say, to get a list of notes out of localStorage. However, with a key in that form, we can at least pull just the notes, for example, out of the overall collection of data by iterating through it, assuming we have it in JavaScript variables, something you'll see done later in this chapter.

> **Tip**   You'll notice in this loop that things like `window.localStorage`, `fetching.data_*`, the length of the data array, and so on, are referenced by variables defined within the loops. This is a great habit to get into, especially when you're dealing with a loop.
>
> The reason for this is that it cuts down on scope chain lookups. For example, referencing `window.localStorage` means that JavaScript has to find the `window` object and then find the `localStorage` property of this object. However, the variable lst already points to that, which cuts down on the lookup time. The same is true of accessing the global-scoped `fetching.data_*` arrays, which is slower than using the reference to them stored in the `dat` variable.
>
> Of course, if the volume of data is small, then the number of iterations in the loop will be small too, and it probably won't matter much. (Even when it does matter, it typically does so only in aggregate, which is why you should think of this more when loops are involved). However, in a case where the loop iterates many times, you will start to see a difference. I encourage you to use this "trick" any time loops are involved, and you may find a nice little boost in JavaScript performance as a reward!

Jumping back a bit, if the code finds that any of the data arrays aren't populated, then it is assumed that connectivity failed. In that case, `showConnectivityMsg()` is called to tell the user what happened. ()

Finally, when all this work is done, it's time to make the UI available to the user.

```
fetching = null;

$.mobile.loading("hide");
```

In addition, the `fetching` structure is set to `null` so that it can be garbage-collected. There's no sense letting it continue to take up memory when we're actually done with it at this point.

Now, remember that what we just examined is the callback for some Ajax calls. These lines are actually the next bit of code encountered:

```
$.ajax({ url : ajaxURLPrefix + "/appointment" })
.done(function(inResponse) { completeLoad("appointment", inResponse); })
.fail(function(inXHR, inStatus) { completeLoad("appointment", null); });
```

There is one of these statements for each of contacts, notes, and tasks as well, but because they are all the same, aside from the entity type being changed, we'll just look at one.

The `$.ajax()` function is provided by jQuery to make Ajax calls. Although it has many different options available, what is probably its simplest form is used here. All we have to do is pass to this method an object that provides information about the call, most importantly the URL to call, which is formed by taking the `ajaxURLPrefix` previously described and appending the entity type. In Chapter 7, we'll talk about these RESTful URLs in detail, but for now it's not terribly important, other than to realize that each entity has its own URL.

In addition to the first argument, we also have to pass some callback functions. In fact, I lied when I said this was the simplest possible form of a $.ajax() call. An even simpler one would be supplying no callback functions at all! That's perfectly valid, and it may make sense in some cases (perhaps just to ping the server to ensure that a session doesn't time out, for example). Here, though, we're very much interested in the outcome of the call, so the done() method is called (using the chain calling mechanism that jQuery has made popular), and it is provided a function. This anonymous function does nothing but call the function referenced by the variable completeLoad that we just looked at, passing it the entity type and, naturally, the response from the server. This is that indirection I hinted at earlier: it allows us to tell completeLoad what entity type was retrieved. Without this, we would have had to include that information in the data returned by the server or somehow keep track of that between the Ajax call and the callback firing. There are certainly other ways to pull this off, and none of them is particularly complex, but I thought this was the simplest.

When an Ajax call fails, we need to deal with that as well, and the fail() method is perfect for this as it allows us, like with the done callback, to specify a handler for a failed request. We again feed it a reference to a function, and again it's an anonymous function calling completeLoad. This time, though, notice that the response from the server will always be null. As you'll recall, completeLoad uses this to set the flags and determine when network connectivity wasn't available.

Keep It Local: Getting Data from Local Storage

Any time the user flips to a different entity page or when they add or remove an item, the list view for that entity type is re-created. As part of that, the list of entities of a given type needs to be retrieved. In the previous section, I mentioned that with localStorage working the way it does, the only way to get all of the items of a given type is to read all of the stored data and just pull out the types we need based on what their key starts with. Populating the list view is where this comes into play, and it's the getAllFromLocalStorage() function that plays a primary role in doing this.

```
function getAllFromLocalStorage(inType) {

  var items = [ ];

  var lst = window.localStorage;
  for (var itemKey in lst) {
    if (itemKey.indexOf(inType) == 0) {
var sObj = lst.getItem(itemKey);
      items.push(JSON.parse(sObj));
    }
  }
```

There's not really a lot to it, as you can see. It begins with iterating over all the items in window.localStorage, as referenced by the lst variable. With every loop iteration, the key of the next item is retrieved into the itemKey variable. Then that value is checked to see whether it contains the type passed in (which is a string, either appointment, contact, plan, or note). If it's found, then we call the getItem() method of the window.localStorage object to get the item itself. The item is in the form of a JSON string, so we pass that to JSON.parse() to get a true object from it, which we then push onto the items array.

Once that loop completes, we have all of the items of the specified type. The next step is to sort that data so that it displays in a prescribed order.

```
items.sort(function(a, b) {
  switch (inType) {
    case "contact":
      return a.lastName > b.lastName;
    break;
    case "appointment": case "note": case "task":
      return a.title > b.title;
    break;
  }
});
```

```
return items;
```

A plain old JavaScript sort() method call is made on the items array that uses a custom function. The function sorts based on the entity type and all, but contacts use the same field to sort on: title.

Finally, the items array is returned to the caller, and our work here is done.

A List Above: Showing a List View

If the user selects the List View menu option on any entity page, the showListView() function is called.

```
function showListView(inType) {

  updateID = null;
  document.getElementById(inType + "EntryForm").reset();

  $("#" + inType + "Entry").hide("fast");
  $("#" + inType + "List").show("fast");
  $("#" + inType + "Menu" ).popup("close");

}
```

The first step is to get a reference to the entry view of the specified entity (which you'll recall is passed in by the event handler attached to the List View menu item) and then use its hide() method to hide it. The argument to that method is the duration the hide should take, which allows you to have a little bit of animation. Typically, this value is in milliseconds, but you can optionally pass the string fast or slow to indicate a value of 200 or 600 milliseconds, respectively, as you can see in the code snippet.

Next, a reference to the list view is obtained, and it is shown again, this time using the fast string.

After that, the menu itself needs to be closed, since obviously it will be open at this point, or the user couldn't have triggered this function call! Since JQM will enhance the <div> to create the menu pop-up using the pop-upplug-in, the way in which we can access the methods of that plug-in is by calling the popup() method. The values you can pass to this method depend on what the plug-in supports and what you're trying to do. In this case, the simple string close closes the pop-up. You can also pass opento it if you want to open a pop-upprogrammatically, as well as reposition, if you want to move an already opened pop-up somewhere else on the screen.

The final two steps are to clear the updateID variable so that the user is free to select a new item for editing or creating a new item, and the code won't be confused in the latter case thinking that it's an edit operation. Finally, the entry form is cleared for the current entity. This ensures a clean slate should the user choose to create a new item.

> **Note**   jQuery is not used to clear the form because sometimes, with very simple things like this, it's best to avoid using jQuery at all. Although it wouldn't make any differencein this case, why incur that extra overhead when JavaScript provides what we need and without being much more complex? Even if you're a huge jQuery proponent, it's still best to consider whether you really need to use it or notin each situation, not only for performance reasons but also for code maintenance. Remember, the next person who has to work on this code may not know jQuery as well as you do! In addition, it's important to realize that the form is cleared only after the entry view is hidden. This avoids having the user seeing the clear occur, which wouldn't look so hot. This too is a good practice: Don't let the user see things occur that might confuse them if they don't actually need to see them.

Saving Is Good: The doSave() Function

It wouldn't do much good to let the user enter data for an entity and then not save it, would it? In light of that fairly obvious statement, the doSave() function exists to save the entered data when the user clicks the Save button.

```
function doSave(inType) {

  if (!validations["check_" + inType](inType)) {
    $("#infoDialogHeader").html("Error");
    $("#infoDialogContent").html(
      "Please provide values for all required fields"
    );
    $.mobile.changePage($("#infoDialog"), { role : "dialog" });
    return;
  }
```

The first thing that needs to happen is to validate what the user entered to make sure that all of the required fields have been filled in. To do this, the validations object is used. This is something you'll look at in the upcoming section "Everyone Needs Validation: Validating a Form Before Saving." In short, that object contains four methods—one for each entity type. Each of these methods is named check_XXX, where XXX is an entity type. This allows us to call the correct methoddynamically based on inType passed in to doSave(). If thatmethod call returns false, then the entry form isn't valid; the info dialog is shown to let the user know this and the save is aborted.

If the form is valid, though, the next step is to scrim the screen.

```
$.mobile.loading("show");
```

This way, the user can't interact with anything while the save request goes out to the server. This avoids any unintended problems due to the user's actions somehowconflicting with the Ajax request. For example, perhaps they change screens, and then the request comes back and the callback code tries to execute. If that code makes bad assumptions about the user being on the same page they were on when the request began, then errors could occur. Putting up the scrim ensures that this can't happen.

Next we'll flip the screen back to the list view of the current entity page. This way, once the save completes, the user will see the list updated to include the new item immediately.

```
$("#" + inType + "Entry").hide();
$("#" + inType + "List").show();
$("#" + inType + "Menu" ).popup("close");
```

The next step is to figure out the URL that the Ajax request will go to and what HTTP method will be used. Remember, doSave() will be called whether the user is adding a new item or whether they're editing an existing item. When adding an item, the HTTP method used is POST, which is typically the method used in a RESTful API to indicate adding a resource. In the case of an edit, PUT will be used instead.

```
var httpMethod = "post";
var uid = "";
if (updateID) {
  httpMethod = "put";
  uid = "/" + updateID;
}
```

Therefore, if there is a value in the updateID global variable, which it obtained when the user tapped an item in the list as a result of the call to the viewEditItem() function (you'll see this near the end of this chapter), then it's an update and therefore a PUT request. Otherwise, it's a POST request by default. The uid variable is also defined at this point, and it is simply the updateID with a forwardslash in front of it, since this will be used to build the URL in just a few lines.

Before that, though, we need to get the data that is going to be sent to the server. The getFormAsJSON() function does that for us.

```
var frmData = getFormAsJSON(inType);
updateID = null;
document.getElementById(inType + "EntryForm").reset();
```

This function returns a string of JSON that contains all of the data the user entered. This is the next function we'll review, so don't worry, you'll see how that's done shortly! For now, it's enough to know that you get a string of JSON back from it.

The entry form is then reset for cleanliness, since we have its data now, and then it's time to make the actual Ajax request to the server.

```
$.ajax({
  url : ajaxURLPrefix + "/" + inType + uid, type : httpMethod,
  contentType: "application/json", data : frmData
})
```

Our friendly neighborhood $.ajax() function is used, and the URL called is constructed as part of that call. The ajaxURLPrefix starts the URL as always, followed by the entity type as specified by inType and then the uid value that we built earlier. The httpMethod variable tells the function what HTTP method to use, and the data passed to the server is specified by the data attribute of the configuration object passed to $.ajax(). The contentType is also set to correctly indicate JSON so that the browser and server handle it properly.

Don't be too concerned with the actual URLs at this point, as that's a topic we'll get into when we discuss the server in later chapters. This is how the URLs are called, how the server functions are executed in other words, but the particulars of why the URLs are constructed this way is a topic we'll get to in later chapters.

If the request is successful, the callback function passed to the done() method of the $.ajax() object is called.

```
.done(function(inResponse) {
  frmData = frmData.slice(0, frmData.length - 1);
  frmData = frmData + ",\"__v\":\"0\",\"_id\":\"" + inResponse + "\"}";
  window.localStorage.setItem(inType + "_" + inResponse, frmData);
  populateList(inType);
  $.mobile.loading("hide");
  $("#infoDialogHeader").html("Success");
  $("#infoDialogContent").html("Save to server complete");
  $.mobile.changePage($("#infoDialog"), { role : "dialog" });
})
```

The first step is to add the created item to localStorage. To do this, we need to take the string of JSON we just sent to the server, stored in frmData, and add a __v and an _id field to it so that it matches what was stored on the server. The response from the server is the ID of the newlycreated resource only, not the resource itself, so we can't just store what the server returned. Therefore, we have to "shave off" the closing brace of the JSON. In other words, if we created a note, the JSON sent to the server would be something like the following:

```
{ title : "My Note", text : "My note text" }
```

The JavaScript string object's slice() method is used to get rid of that closing brace. Once that's done, we can do straight sting concatenation to add the __v and _id fields using the ID returned by the server as the value for _id. (Because this app doesn't use __v, the value doesn't really matter; zero just happens to match what the server creates). After that, frmData is saved to localStorage under a key formed by concatenating inType with the returned ID, separated by an underscore.

After the item is saved, the populateList() function is called. As you'll see a little later in this chapter, this is responsible for redrawing the entity list on the current page with the updated data, including the new item. Finally, the scrim is removed via the call to $.mobile.loading("hide");, and an info dialog is shown to the server to let them know the save was completed.

Now, if anything goes wrong, another function, as passed to the `fail()` method called on the `$.ajax()` object, will execute.

```
.fail(function(inXHR, inStatus) {
  $.mobile.loading("hide");
  $("#infoDialogHeader").html("Error");
  $("#infoDialogContent").html(inStatus);
  $.mobile.changePage($("#infoDialog"), { role : "dialog" });
});
```

All that we do in this case is hide the scrim and alert the user to the failure, including showing the `inStatus` message that indicates some small level of detail about the failure (usually an HTTP 500).

A Form in Sheep's Clothing: Getting a Form's Data as JSON

As part of the `doSave()` function, you saw that the `getFormAsJSON()` function is called in order to get the entity data that is sent to the server. This function is as follows:

```
function getFormAsJSON(inType) {

  var frmData = $("#" + inType + "EntryForm").serializeArray();
  var frmObj = { };
  for (var i = 0; i < frmData.length; i++) {
    var fld = frmData[i];
    frmObj[fld.name] = fld.value;
  }
  return JSON.stringify(frmObj);

}
```

Since what is sent to the server is a string of JSON representing an object that contains the form's data, we need to create that JSON string now. To do this, we're going to create an intermediary object that we'll then hand off to `JSON.stringify()` to get the JSON string to send.

The first step is to get a reference to the appropriate entity entry formpassed in, as specified by `inType`, using jQuery, of course. The `serializeArray()` method is then called on the retrieved form object. This is a method with which jQuery enhances the form and returns to us an array of objects. Each object in that array is one field of the form, and each object has two attributes: `name` and `value`. We then iterate that array, and for each object in it, an attribute is added to the intermediary object referenced by `frmObj`. The `name` attribute of the form field object becomes the name of the `frmObj`attribute, and the value is self-explanatory.

Once the loop completes, the completelyformed `frmObj` is passed to `JSON.stringify()`. The end result is that a string of JSON, representing an object where each attribute of it maps to a form field with the current value of that field stored in it, is returned to the caller. It is then sent along to the server eitherforthe add or update operation.

Everyone Needs Validation: Validating a Form Before Saving

As part of the process of saving an entity, a little bit of validation of the entered data needs to be performed. This amounts to nothing more than ensuring that all of the required fields are populated. Of course, in keeping with the overall paradigm throughout this code, we want to make the code do this as generically as possible. This is one place, though, where we necessarily have to get a bit specific.

Here, though, we do something a little different: rather than a "naked" function in global scope, as everything else in main.js is, instead we have an object named validations defined.

```
var validations = {
```

Within this object will be a series of functions, which are termed *methods*, as is customary for a function enclosed within an object. Each method is named using this standardized form: check_XXX, where XXX is an entity type.

For example, the first such function is check_appointment().

```
check_appointment : function() {
  if (isBlank("appointmentTitle")) { return false; }
  if (isBlank("appointmentDate")) { return false; }
  return true;
},
```

As you can see, all the function does is call isBlank(), passing it the ID of a required field on the appointment entry form, two of them in the case of the appointment entry form. If isBlank() returns true, then false is returned from check_appointment() because the output of this method, or any of the methods of the validations object, indicates whether a given form is valid (true) or not (false).

Similarly, the check_contact() method handles the contact entry form validations.

```
check_contact : function() {
  if (isBlank("contactFirstName")) { return false; }
  if (isBlank("contactLastName")) { return false; }
  return true;
},
```

Yep, the note entry form gets its own method as well.

```
check_note : function() {
  if (isBlank("noteTitle")) { return false; }
  if (isBlank("noteText")) { return false; }
  return true;
},
```

We wouldn't want to leave the task entry form out in the cold, so it too has a method.

```
check_task : function() {
  if (isBlank("taskTitle")) { return false; }
  return true;
}
```

The doSave() method dynamically selects which of these methods to call based on the entity type. This means you could extend this app to support other types of entities, and all you'd need to do is add a new method for it to this validations object, following the same pattern.

When You Gotta Go: The doDelete() Function

As musician Billy Joel once so eloquently put it in the song "Say Goodbye to Hollywood," "So many faces in and out of my life, some will last, some will just be now and then." I've had many friends in my life, but, as Billy says, friends come and friends go.

Now how it this relevant to My Mobile Organizer? Simple: we need the ability to delete contacts, appointments, notes, and tasks!

The doDelete() function is what fulfills this need, and it's called when the user taps the Delete button on an entity entry screen.

```
function doDelete(inType) {

  $.mobile.loading("show");

  $("#" + inType + "Entry").hide();
  $("#" + inType + "List").show();
  $("#" + inType + "Menu" ).popup("close");
```

As with all operations requiring a call to the server, we begin by putting up the scrim to block the UI from further user interaction. Next we flip back to the list view for the current entity page, because that's where we're going to need to be after the delete is done anyway.

After that, we need to figure out the RESTful URL we'll be calling.

```
var uid = "/" + updateID;
```

The URL will be in the form ajaxURLPrefix/xxx/yyy, where ajaxURLPrefix is the value of that variable (as is true for all our Ajax calls), xxx is the entity type passed in to this function as the inType argument, and yyy is the unique ID of the entity to be deleted. That gives us a nice RESTful URL.

The next thing we want to do is clear the entry form.

```
updateID = null;
document.getElementById(inType + "EntryForm").reset();
```

Although we don't really need to do this because the form will be cleared when adding a new item or populated with data if another item is selected for editing, I prefer to clear it manually here just because I tend to be obsessive-compulsive about cleanliness like that! The code also clears the updateID variable, really for the same reason, since that would be overwritten, or cleared, when a new item is selected or added, respectively.

In any case, with that out of the way, it's time to make our Ajax call to the server to do the delete.

```
$.ajax({ url : ajaxURLPrefix + "/" + inType + uid, type : "delete" })
```

Since this is a RESTful API, the HTTP method is set to `delete` via the `type` attribute of the configuration object passed to `$.ajax()`. As you know, the `$.ajax()` function generally has a callback handler associated with it for handling successful requests, and that's next. (This is all one big statement, but I've broken it up on the page to better explore each piece separately.)

```
.done(function(inResponse) {
  window.localStorage.removeItem(inType + "_" + inResponse);
  populateList(inType);
  $.mobile.loading("hide");
  $("#infoDialogHeader").html("Success");
  $("#infoDialogContent").html("Delete from server complete");
  $.mobile.changePage($("#infoDialog"), { role : "dialog" });
})
```

Once the response comes back from the server, we need to get rid of the entity from our localStorage data cache too. The `removeItem()`function allows us to do that. We pass to it the appropriate key value for the item, which you'll recall is in the form `type_ID`, and it's removed.

That doesn't update the screen, however, so we need to call the `populateList()` function next to take care of that. Since that function rereads the data from localStorage, that's effectively all we need to do here, other than showing an info dialog to let the user know the delete was successful.

Now, if the Ajax request fails for any reason, we need to handle that too.

```
.fail(function(inXHR, inStatus) {
  $.mobile.loading("hide");
  $("#infoDialogHeader").html("Error");
  $("#infoDialogContent").html(inStatus);
  $.mobile.changePage($("#infoDialog"), { role : "dialog" });
});
```

In this case, the item needs to remain in localStorage, so we skip the `removeItem()` call. Also, since the list doesn't need to change, there's no call to `populateList()` to be done either. An info dialog is shown once more so that the user knows what's going on, and the `inStatus` variable passed to the `fail()` callback is shown so that they get some degree of detail on what failure occurred.

Your Page Is Showing: The pageShowHandler() Function

As you'll recall from when we looked at `index.html`, every time the user flips to an entity page, the `pageshow` event fires. This results in a call to `pageShowHandler()` in order to do some initial setup work. Now it's time to see what that setup work actually is!

```
function pageShowHandler(inType) {

  if (!pageVisited[inType]) {

    $.mobile.loading("show");

    populateList(inType);
```

```
  if (!networkAvailable) {
    $("#" + inType + "NewLink").remove();
    $("#" + inType + "SaveButton").button("disable");
  }

  pageVisited[inType] = true;
  $.mobile.loading("hide");

}

}
```

First, this code only ever executes on the first time the user visits this page. Assuming that's the case, then first the scrim is shown via a call to $.mobile.loading("show");, as we've previously discussed. Next, a call to populateList() is made that takes care of initially loading the list of entities. We'll be looking at that function next. Before we do, however, a few more tasks need to be accomplished.

If the networkAvailable flag is false, meaning network connectivity has not been detected, then the New link on the entity page's menu is removed so that the user cannot add a new item. The remove() method is one that jQuery gives us, which allows us to remove matching elements from the DOM, whether one or many (as is typical of jQuery methods). In addition to that, the Save button is disabled so that they won't be able to save any changes to existing items.

Finally, the pageVisited flag for this entity type is set so that this code won't execute again, and the scrim is hidden so that users can get on with their business.

Hey, I didn't say it was a *lot*of work, now did I?

An Empty List Is a Dull List: The populateList() Function

Now it's time to look at the code that is responsible for putting items in the list view on an entity page. In the previouschapter, you saw the markup for that list, and it really wasn't much to see: just an empty <ul> with a few JQM-specific data-* attributes to configure the listview widget that JQM would create in its place. However, that doesn't explain how the list of items gets there. The populateList() function, on the other hand, very much does!

This function is called from three different places: doSave(), doDelete(), and pageShowHandler(). In other words, the list of entities on the current page will be updated any time we add a new item or delete an existing item or when the page is visited (for the first time, as you'll recall from looking at the pageShowHandler() function).

The populateList() function begins unassumingly enough, as follows:

```
function populateList(inType, inFilterField, inFilterValue) {

  var ul = $("#" + inType + "ListUL");
  ul.children().remove();
```

The first step is to clear the list. This will have an effect only after adding or deleting an item, because there's nothing to clear when called from pageShowHandler(). Nonetheless, it certainly does no harm in that there's no need for any sort of logic to differentiate these cases. Clearing a listview widget really means removing all the items from the underlying <ul> that constitutes its data. To do that, we ask jQuery to get a reference to it, and since all the listview widgets on all four entity pages are named in a consistent way, we can dynamically construct the appropriate ID easily enough using the inType value passed in to this function. Once we have that reference in hand, it's a simple matter of getting a reference to the collection of children of the <ul> (the <li> elements, in other words) by calling the children() method. Finally, that collection has a remove() method that allows us to remove items. Conveniently, while you can remove individual items with this method by passing a selector, if you pass no selector, then all of the elements are removed from its parent. Therefore, that's all we do here!

> **Tip** The only reason I didn't use chaining and wrote $("#"+inType+"ListUL").children().remove(); was that the reference to the <ul> element will be reused shortly. It's always a good practice to avoid extra DOM lookups when you can, whether using jQuery or not, just to keep performance as high as possible.

Now with the list cleared, it's time to repopulate the list with current data. This will naturally include any item that was just added or deleted, so the first step is to get all of the data for this entity type.

```
var items = getAllFromLocalStorage(inType);
```

With that collection in hand in the form of an array, we now need to create an <li> for each entity and each item in that array and insert it into the <ul> underlying the listview widget.

```
var len = items.length;
for (var i = 0; i < len; i++) {
  var item = items[i];
  if (inFilterField && inFilterValue &&
    item[inFilterField] != inFilterValue
  ) {
    continue;
  }
  var liText = "";
  if (inType == "contact") {
    liText = item.lastName + ", " + item.firstName;
  } else {
    liText = item.title;
  }
  ul.append(
    "<li onclick=\"viewEditItem('" + inType + "', '" + item._id + "');\"" +
    "id=\"" + item._id + "\">" + liText + "</li>"
  );
}
```

We begin to iterate over the array, and we pull out each item into the uncreativelynamed variable `item`. Now we have to do a bit of filtering. This function accepts two arguments:`inFilterField` and `inFilterValue`. This allows us to filter the items by any field. The logic is simple: if there's a field and a value passed in and if this item doesn't have the specified value in the specified field, then we skip this item and `continue` the loop.

If it matches or if no filter criteria are supplied (which equates to the caller wanting all items), then the next step is to build a snippet of HTML for a new `<li>` element and append it as a child of the `<ul>` underlying the `listview` widget. The only real kink in the works here is that for contacts, the list items show "last name, first name." All other lists show the title of the item, be it an appointment, note, or task. So, a quick bit of logic deals with that, and we wind up with the text that the user will see on the screen for this item in the variable `liText`, whether from the item's `title` field or the combination of `lastName` and `firstName` fields.

Once we have the text, the `append()` method that jQuery adds to the referenced `<ul>` element from before allows us to insert a new DOM node. We simply pass to it the HTML for the item, a `<li>` in this case, and jQuery takes care of adding it for us. The new `<li>` element will have an `onClick` handler attached to it that results in a call to `viewEditItem()`, which we'll see later, that sets up the screen for editing the selected item. This function accepts an entity type and the unique ID of the item, as stored in the `_id` field of the item. The ID of the `<li>` is also set to this unique server-generated ID, just in case it's needed later. (It actually isn't, but I like to put IDs on DOM nodes, even if I merely *suspect*that I may need to address it directly down the road, just to save time later.)

Once all of the `<li>`elements are added to the `<ul>`, there's one thing that needs to be done.

```
ul.listview("refresh");
```

JQM needs to be told that the underlying `<ul>` for the `listview` widget has changed and that it needs to be re-created and redrawn on the screen. As with JQM button widgets, which provide a `button()` method to send method invocation requests to the button, a `listview` widget provides a `listview()` method for that same purpose. The `refresh` method is one of only two that the `listview` supports. (The other is `childPages`, which returns a jQuery object that contains all of the immediate child pages when dealing with nested lists).

Once that call completes, the list on the screen will be updated with whatever changes just occurred, if any, and the user can go about their business.

Time to Create: The New Menu Item Handler

Handling the New menu item on a page menu is about as easy as handling the click event for the List View item. In fact, you'll notice quite a lot of similarity between the two pieces of code.

```
function newItem(inType) {

  updateID = null;
  document.getElementById(inType + "EntryForm").reset();
```

```
$("#" + inType + "Entry").show("fast");
$("#" + inType + "List").hide("fast");
$("#" + inType + "Menu" ).popup("close");

$("#" + inType + "DeleteButton").button("disable");

}
```

There are really only two differences between this and showListView(). First, in this case, the entry view for the entity, as specified by inType, is shown, while the list view is hidden. This is exactly opposite of showListView(), which is only logical.

The other difference is that here we need to disable the Delete button, since it doesn't make sense to delete a new item.

> **Note**   There are actually three differences: the third is that the order here is a little different from in showListView(). There the entry form clear was done after the visibility switch, but here it's done beforehand. This isfor the same reason as described when discussingshowListView(): doing the clear first avoids having the user see it occur. To their eyes, it's a clean switch; in other words, the form is empty as soon as they see it.

Change Is Inevitable: Editing an Existing Item

As you saw as part of the populateList() function, when the user taps an item in a list of entities, the viewEditItem() function is called. The basic purpose of this function is to flip to the entry view for the given entity type and populate the form there with the data for the selected entity so that the user can edit it. Let's see how this magic is accomplished.

```
function viewEditItem(inType, inID) {

  updateID = inID;
```

First, the ID of the item being edited is recorded in the updateID global variable. We'll need this later when the Save button is tapped.

Next, we need to get the data for the selected entity.

```
var itemData = JSON.parse(window.localStorage.getItem(inType + "_" + inID));
for (fld in itemData) {
  if (fld != "_id" && fld != "__v") {
    $("#" + inType + "EntryForm [name=" + fld + "]").val(itemData[fld]);
  }
}
```

Recall that the entities are kept in localStorage, and they are keyed with a value in the form type_ID. Therefore, we use the inID passed in, construct that key value, and look up the item in window.localStorage() using the getItem() method. This will return to us a string in the form of JSON, so we feed that to JSON.parse() to get a real object out of it. This keeps us from having to write any nasty string parsing logic; it's much easier to work with the fields of a real object.

In fact, dealing with the fields of the real object is precisely the next step! The fields are iterated over in order to populate the appropriate edit form field for each. However, there is one minor issue to be dealt with, and that is that the object, which will have come from the server during the initial data load, will contain two fields that the user cannot edit, namely, _id and __v. The _id field is the generated ID that the server creates when the entity was saved. The __v field, as you'll see when we look at the server-side code, is a version field that MongoDB, our persistent storage mechanism underneath it all, attaches to every object. This __v field can be ignored entirely for the purpose of this application, and, along with _id, we need to skip it in this particular situation.

If the next field isn't one of those, however, then we need to populate the form field. To do this, we need to use jQuery to get a reference to it. The way we do this is to use a CSS attribute selector in the form ofxxxEntryForm [name=yyy], where xxx is the entity type and yyy is the field's name. Note that the field'sname is used and *not* the field's ID. This relates to the possibility (and the reality, as it happens!) that a field in one form might have the same name as the field in another (even though they may have different IDs). By using a selector in this form, we narrow down the scope of where jQuery looks for the field to the specific form and then of course to the field with the specified name attribute.

Once jQuery gives us that reference, we chain a call to the val() method it adds to set the value. The value to which to set the form field is found using a simple array notation lookup into the itemData object created earlier from the retrieved JSON string (see, it really *is* easier to deal with a real object!).

Once all of the form fields have been populated, it's time to flip to the entry view for the entity.

```
$("#" + inType + "Entry").show();
$("#" + inType + "List").hide();
$("#" + inType + "Menu" ).popup("close");
```

Of course, part of that task is to hide the list view, and to be safe, we'll ensure the menu pop-up is closed as well. (That really shouldn't ever be necessary, but it does no harm to be sure.)

Finally, there's only one thing left to do.

```
$("#" + inType + "DeleteButton").button("enable");
```

The user can delete an item in addition to editing it, of course, so the Delete button is enabled. jQuery provides the reference to it and the button() method that JQM provides, which you've seen used a number of times before, and this is how we accomplish that.

Clear Your Mind: The clearData() Function

The function to clear all of the data that is present on the About panel is as trivial to implement on the JavaScript side as it was on the markup side. Naturally, it's the clearData() function that does this.

```
function clearData() {

  $.mobile.loading("show");
```

First the screen scrim is shown, which we always do when calling the server. Speaking of which, here's the code that calls the server:

```
$.ajax({ url : ajaxURLPrefix + "/clear" })
```

The jQuery $.ajax() method again allows us to call the server. This time, there's no dynamic URL based on entity type to deal with, but we still need to construct the URL using the ajaxURLPrefix, adding /clear to it.

> **Note**   Verbs are always interesting in the REST world because they don't really fit the model exactly. There's quite a bit of debate about how best to handle things such as this clear operation, a search, a login request, and so forth. The basic principle of REST is to not even think about URLs because they should really be automatic—in a sense they define themselves, once you decide what resources your API deals with. However, a verb like this clear operation doesn't deal with resources *per se*, or more precisely, it deals with many of them. So, what's the answer on verbs? Well, I take this simple approach: although a GET isn't supposed to produce any side-effect on the server, I'm going to do it anyway because it's the least amount of work since $.ajax() does a GET by default.

I've actually broken down the single $.ajax() statement here because it also has a done() handler defined:

```
.done(function(inResponse) {
  window.localStorage.clear();
  $.mobile.loading("hide");
  $("#infoDialogHeader").html("Operation succeeded");
  $("#infoDialogContent").html("Data cleared");
  $.mobile.changePage($("#infoDialog"), { role : "dialog" });
})
```

When a successful response comes back, we know that the server-side data is not cleared. That leaves the client-side cache to deal with, and that's what the window.localStorage.clear() call addresses. Once that's done, there are just some UI tasks to accomplish, namely, to remove the scrim so that the screen is available to user again and to show the user an info dialog letting them know that the data has been cleared. We use the same info dialog mechanism used previously to do this.

Of course, there's the possibility that the clear request to the server failed for some reason, whether it's network connectivity going down or some error on the server. Therefore, there's a `fail()` handle defined as well.

```
.fail(function(inXHR, inStatus) {
  $.mobile.loading("hide");
  $("#infoDialogHeader").html("Operation failed");
  $("#infoDialogContent").html("Data not cleared");
  $.mobile.changePage($("#infoDialog"), { role : "dialog" });
});
```

In this case, the only thing we need to do is to show the info dialog. We're not going to clear the local data cache if we're not sure the server clear worked. Therefore, this turns out to be a straightforward handler indeed.

A Needed Utility: Checking Whether a Form Field Is Empty

The last bit of code in `main.js` is the `isBlank()` function that is used by the methods of the validations object. As its name implies, it tells the caller if a specified form field is "blank" (but what that term means can be tricky!).

```
function isBlank(inID) {

  var fld = $("#" + inID).val();

  if (fld === null) {
    return true;
  } else if (fld === undefined) {
    return true;
  } else if (fld === "") {
    return true;
  }

  return false;

}
```

First, jQuery is used to get a reference to the form field. Then, the `val()` method, another jQuery convenience method that it adds automatically to the object returned by `$()`, is used to get the value.

Next, the code covers three possibilities: the field wasn't found, the value was `null`, or the value was empty. In all three cases, we want to tell the caller the field was blank. If execution falls through the `if` block, then the field isn't blank and `false` is returned.

Summary

In this chapter, you saw the JavaScript that makes up the client portion of My Mobile Organizer. You also saw how Ajax is used to retrieve data from the server and how that data is stored in localStorage. You then saw how items are created and edited and how Ajax is again used to replicate the changes to the server. You learned how to work programmatically with a number of JQM widgets, such as pop-ups and pages, as well as deal with forms and their data.

In the next chapter, we'll begin to explore the serverside of the My Mobile Organizer equation by looking at the first technology that will allow us to build the service layer the client uses, namely, Node.js.

Part 2

The Server

See, Meg, things always work out if you just do whatever you want without thinking about the consequences.

—Peter Griffin

Education is when you read the fine print. Experience is what you get if you don't.

—Pete Seeger

Mistakes are the portals of discovery.

—James Joyce

Once we accept our limits, we go beyond them.

—Albert Einstein

Think? Why think! We have computers to do that for us.

—Jean Rostand

Chapter 5

Introducing Node.js

With the client portion of My Mobile Organizer out of the way, it's now time to turn our attention to writing the server-side component. We need a place to persist our data "in the cloud," as it's called these days, because storing it on the client isn't the way to go if we want to share that data, something that My Mobile Organizer allows. (When data is stored on the cloud, of course, you can access it from multiple devices if you're inclined to do so.)

In this chapter, we'll begin exploring the back end that the client app uses. In the previous two chapters, you saw calls being made to that remote API exposed by the server component. Now it's time to pull back the curtain and meet the wizard making all the magic that happens back there!

Writing Servers Is Hard

There are tons of possible choices for developing a server back end, both free and commercial. Some are big and complex and robust, while others are small and relatively simple though effective. There's no shortage of options, all with their particular pluses and minuses.

Java is perhaps the most popular these days, and that's almost certainly more true in the business world than anywhere else. Java is, at this point, a well-known quantity. It is stable and robust, and it performs well (all things being equal) on the newest hardware. There are many Java developers whose knowledge you can draw upon. Also, a strong talent pool is clearly an important consideration in the business world where the lifetime of an application is usually measured in years.

That's not meant to short shrift the competition, though. Certainly, Microsoft technologies, led by its NET platform, are extremely popular. PHP is another big player. There are lots of others too, such as Ruby On Rails, and even good old-fashioned C-based CGI scripts aren't entirely unheard of even today!

An interesting transformation has been occurring over the past few years, however, and I would argue that it has been led primarily by mobile technologies, that is, *server agnosticism*. In other words, the idea has become very popular indeed that by using a simplistic interface, a server back end can be written using virtually any technology.

None of this, however, makes the job of writing a server application any *easier*! It's still a somewhat specialized talent, and it becomes an even more difficult task to do well when you have to consider things such as high-volume response handling and top-notch performance. Performance, particularly in the mobile space, is of primary concern because the devices that you're dealing with tend to be resource-constrained—yes, even in this day of super-powered smartphones! You need a back end that responds almost instantaneously to all requests and one that can continue to do so even under high load.

Another consideration that often comes into play is the number of technologies involved that a developer needs to know to be effective. On the client side, assuming you're a fan of web technologies and not going the native app route, you're primarily dealing with HTML, CSS, and JavaScript. Then, when you hit the server side, you're now talking about an entirely different set of technologies, whether it's Java (which only *looks* like JavaScript superficially), PHP, Ruby, or C#. Finding developers who know all of this well and who can be effective on both sides of the network equation can be difficult.

There is an answer, of course, and I'm not spoiling any surprise here by telling you that I'm referring to Node.js!

Node.js (and JavaScript) to the Rescue!

Ryan Dahl. That cat has some talent, I tell ya! Ryan is the creator of a fantastic piece of software called Node.js, or just plain Node, for short. (I find myself not being able to drop the .js most of the time, as it's really one of the key aspects of it.) Ryan first presented Node.js at the European JSConf conference in 2009, and it was quickly recognized as a potential game-changer, as evidenced by the standing ovation his presentation received.

Node.js is a platform for running (largely server-side) code that is high-performance and capable of handling tons of load with ease. It is based on the most widely used language on the planet today: JavaScript. It is extremely easy to get started with and understand Node.js, yet it puts tremendous power in the hands of developers.

It's no wonder that so many large players and sites have adopted Node.js to one degree or another. And these aren't minor outfits either; we're talking about names you certainly know, including DuckDuckGo, eBay, LinkedIn, Microsoft, Walmart, and Yahoo.

So, why have these companies, and countless more, jumped on the Node.js bandwagon? The following are a few of the reasons that float to the top.

Node.js is, first and foremost, a runtime for JavaScript code. You can run JavaScript code that interacts with the local file system, databases that call out to remote systems, and lots more—all within Node.js. At its most basic level, that's all Node.js really is.

However, what really sets Node.js apart from other runtimes, and what it's primarily known for, is its role as a server. Now to be clear, Node.js isn't in and of itself a server—you can't just start up Node.js and make HTTP requests to it from a web browser, for example. It won't do anything in response to your requests by default.

No, to use Node.js as a web server, for example, you have to write some (very simple and concise) code that then runs inside Node.js. Yes, you effectively write your own web server and app server, if you want to split hairs (or potentially FTP, Telnet, or any other type of server you might want).

That's a very odd thing to do as a developer, to say the least, and it does sound daunting! To be sure, it would be if you tried to write a web server from scratch, especially if you want it to do more than just serve static content files.

However, because of the way Node.js implements this capability, it winds up being about as simple as things can get. You'll be seeing this for yourself in just a few pages. Always remember, though, acting as a server is just one capability that Node.js provides as a JavaScript runtime, and it can provide this functionality only if you, as a developer, feed it the code it needs to do so!

Performance

Node.js uses Google's popular and highly tuned V8 JavaScript engine to execute. This same engine powers Chrome, Google's much-loved web browser—a browser that is always at or near the top of the JavaScript benchmark charts. If you think JavaScript is a slow, interpreted scripting language, then you haven't been paying attention to what Google has been able to achieve with V8.

Node.js, by extension, benefits from this work. As long as you don't write bad code (something no technology can yet fix!), you'll find that Node.js performs at fantastic levels. You no longer need to resort to more low-level and difficult programming to get the performance you need!

High Volume

In a sense an extension to performance, load-handling capacity is another major concern in writing high-volume servers. Node.js can handle a tremendous amount of concurrent requests, or *load*. It does this by putting the notion of event-driven asynchronous programming at its very core.

As you get a bit further along in this chapter and start working with some Node.js code, you'll see that nearly everything you do with Node.js is asynchronous in nature. Need to read some data from a database? You'll be dealing with a nonblocking API where you supply callbacks for everything. What about reading files off a file system? It's the same answer: asynchronous nonblocking APIs. From the ground up, Node.js works this way, and if it's a concept with which you're unfamiliar, don't worry, because you will be mastering it very shortly!

The benefit to this approach is that no one request or execution thread will block the whole server... well, generally speaking anyway. As I said, you can write bad code even with Node.js that will lead to nothing but heartache, but it's a lot harder to do with Node.js because its underlying architecture is geared toward avoiding such situations. The result is that Node.js can handle a lot more load than most other technologies, all else being equal (meaning, primarily, hardware).

End-to-End Technological Consistency

JavaScript everywhere is the mantra and overriding goal of using Node.js as is developing rich Internet applications (RIAs) on client machines. While JavaScript on the client is something that most developers are comfortable with nowadays, the idea of writing a server application in JavaScript is still seen by many developers as some sort of unholy demon let loose from the gates of Hell. To be sure, the idea of JavaScript on the server isn't a new one; Netscape provided this feature in the 1990s if you wanted it. However, speaking from painful experience, I can tell you that you *didn't* want it!

The story is vastly different now. Developers know JavaScript quite well, and many even like it. In fact, some of us downright love it! It can perform extremely well when done right, and it can even perform some tricks because of built-in flexibility that other languages can only dream of.

Therefore, the big benefit of Node.js in many people's eyes is using the same well-known and proven technology, that is, the same language, on both sides of the Net-based application equation. No longer do developers have to do a mental context-switch when jumping between client work and server work. This makes them far more efficient over time. In fact, developers who perhaps otherwise couldn't work on one side of the fence or the other for lack of knowledge and experience now can effectively work on both the client and server parts and become key players on their teams.

Simplicity Is Not a Dirty Word!

The "JavaScript everywhere" concept certainly makes things simpler for developers. There is suddenly less you have to know to do your work. The notion of event-driven programming, while initially foreign to some developers, is an easy concept to wrap your head around. All of this combines to make Node.js simple, which is a good thing to be sure.

Another key aspect of this simplicity formula is the driving design goal of Node.js, which is keeping its core functionality to an absolute minimum and providing extended functionality by way of APIs that you can pick and choose from as needed. In addition, the design of those APIs is always done with simplicity in mind: the complexity exposed to developers by the APIs is always kept to a minimum.

In addition to all of this, getting, installing, and running Node.js are trivial exercises, regardless of your operating system preference. There are no complicated installs with all sorts of dependencies, nor is there a huge set of configuration files to mess with before you can bring up a server and handle requests. It's a five-minute exercise, depending on the speed of your Internet connection (and how fast you can type, as you'll see shortly!).

All of this makes working with Node.js so much simpler than many competing options, while providing you with top-notch performance and load handling capabilities. Moreover, it does so with a consistent technological underpinning as that which you develop your client applications.

That's Node.js in a nutshell. Next let's see about getting it onto your machine so that we can start playing with some code together.

Getting and Installing Node.js

Getting and installing Node.js couldn't be easier, and there's only one address to remember: `http://nodejs.org`. That's your one-stop shop for all things Node.js, beginning with, right on the front page, downloading it. Well, technically, the button you want is labeled Install, as you can see in Figure 5-1.

***Figure 5-1.** Whatever the label, you're certainly not going to miss it!*

The actual Download button will also work, but that will take you to the page you see in Figure 5-2, where you'll have to make some decisions on what to download. That's good to know, but that big Install button will provide you with what you need for whatever system you're running, so unless you have a reason to do otherwise, click that button.

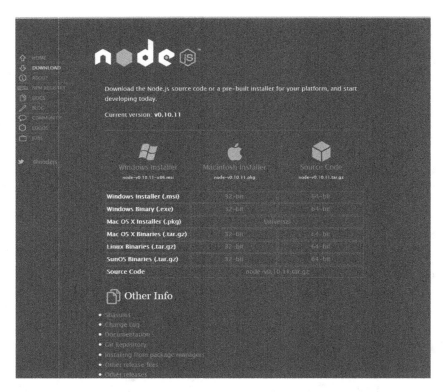

Figure 5-2. The download page provides more options, if you need them

The download will install in whatever fashion is appropriate for your system. For example, on Windows, Node.js provides a perfectly ordinary and straightforward installer that will walk you through the necessary (and extremely simple) steps. On Mac OS X, a typical install wizard will do the same.

> **Note**   On a *nix system, you can install from source if you want, as in build Node.js yourself. A few dependencies are required to do so, but they should be included with the source package, and Python should be all you need to build it. That being said, I suggest not building from source unless you have a good reason to do so. It's just easier to let the web site give you what you need in an executable form.

Once the install completes, you will be ready to play with Node.js. The installer should have added the Node.js directory to your path. As a first simple test, go to a command prompt and simply type **node** and press Enter. You should be greeted with a > prompt. Node.js is now listening for your commands in CLI mode. To test it, type the following:

```
console.log("test")
```

Press Enter, and you should be greeted with something like what you see in Figure 5-3, if running in Windows. (On Mac OS X or *nix, it should look substantially the same, accounting for platform differences.)

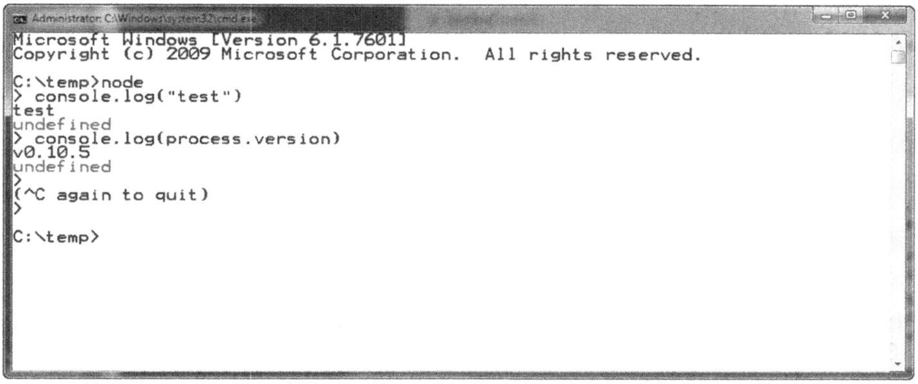

Figure 5-3. Say hello to my little friend, Node.js!

In Figure 5-3, you can see that I've actually executed a second command, `console.log(process.version)`. This shows the version of Node.js I'm running. It also demonstrates using a global object, `process`, which represents the Node.js execution process and provides numerous attributes and methods, of which `version` is one. This simple command also demonstrates a second global object, `console`. Its `log()` method is one you'll use a lot as you work with Node.js.

Interacting with Node.js in CLI mode is fine, but it's limited. What you *really* want to do is execute a saved JavaScript file using Node.js. As it happens, that's easy to do! Simply create a text file named `listing_05-01.js`, for example, and type the code in Listing 5-1 into it and save it.

Listing 5-1. A Quick Node.js Test

```
var a = 5;
var b = 3;
var c = a * b;
console.log(a + " * " + b + " = " + c);
```

To execute this file, assuming you are in the directory in which the file is located, you simply need to type this:

```
node listing_05-01.js
```

Press Enter after that, and you should be greeted with an execution, such as the one you see in Figure 5-4 (in which I've also displayed the JavaScript file to be executed).

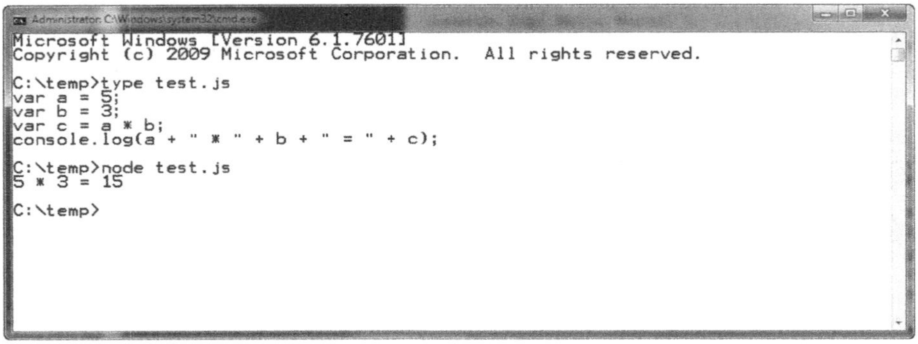

Figure 5-4. Yep, Node.js executes files too!

Now, clearly this little bit of code is unexceptional, but it *does* demonstrate that Node.js can execute plain old JavaScript just fine. You can experiment a bit here if you like, and you will see that Node.js should execute any basic, plain old JavaScript that you care to throw at it.

Even if that were all Node.js did, it would be pretty cool and useful for many things. Of course, that's *far* from all that Node.js can do! We're here to talk about writing server software, and Node.js makes that a trivial exercise indeed.

My First Node.js Server

When I say that Node.js makes writing server software trivial, that may well be the understatement of the year! Perhaps the simplest example (that actually does something anyway) is what you can see in Listing 5-2.

Listing 5-2. A Simple Web Server in Node.js

```
var http = require("http");
var server = http.createServer(function (inRequest, inResponse) {
  inResponse.writeHead(200, { "Content-Type" : "text/plain"} );
  inResponse.end("Hello from my first Node.js server!");
});
server.listen(80, "127.0.0.1");
```

Type that into a file, save it as listing_05-02.js, and then launch it from a command line like the following:

```
node listing_05-02.js
```

> **Tip**   You may have to add sudo before that on a Mac or other *nix machine for it to work. This is a generic comment that applies throughout this chapter and, in fact, to the rest of the book any time you're executing something from a command prompt.

Now fire up your favorite web browser, and visit `http://127.0.01`. You'll be greeted with the text "Hello from my first Node.js server!" If that isn't a little bit amazing to you, then you've probably seen the Flying Spaghetti Monster[1] travel one too many times around your neighborhood and have been totally desensitized to the amazing!

Obviously, this is a very simplistic example. For one thing, no matter what the request is, the response will always be the same. This would make for a workable implementation of ping perhaps, but not a whole lot more. Writing a more robust server takes more than that, as you'll see over the next few chapters. Nevertheless, underneath it all is really not much more than in this example.

So, what exactly is going on in that simple example? Quite a bit actually, and most of it is key to how Node.js works. The first concept is the idea of importing modules. The concept of modules in Node.js is an implementation of the modules specification defined by the CommonJS project (`http://commonjs.org`). The purpose of this project is to define a "standard library" for JavaScript outside of the browser in much the same way that the standard library for C is defined. The modules specification is one of the first things the project created, and it specifies how JavaScript code should be organized and modularized. Essentially, the modules specification says that a module in JavaScript should be its own scope; that is, each JavaScript source file is a module and has its own scope. If you declare a "global" variable in a module, it won't actually be added to a global scope because there essentially *is* no global scope. This is very different from a web browser where everything ultimately belongs to global scope, whether directly or as part of another object that itself is in global scope.

In Node.js, a module usually maps to a specific JavaScript source file. If you create `main.js`, for example, and it `require()`s `account.js`, what you wind up with is two completely separate scopes: one for `main.js` and one for `account.js`, each considered a module. Therefore, if you define a variable abc in each, there will be no conflict; both variables will exist, quite possibly with separate values, and each will be accessible only to code in the file in which it is declared.

In our example code, `http` is a module. However, in this case, it is one of the core Node.js modules, and, as such, it is compiled directly into the Node.js binary. Therefore, you won't find a separate JavaScript file for it in the Node.js installation directory. This is true of all of the Node.js core modules, and so to import any of them, you just `require()` them by name. (We'll be looking at other modules later in this chapter.)

For any other modules, whether you create them yourself or they are from a third party, you import them in the same way as long as they are in the same directory as the file that is importing them. For example, to import the file `account.js` in the same directory, you simply `require("account")`. You can drop the `.js` extension, or you can include it; it will work either way. In addition, you can provide a path, whether absolute or relative, to the file (and you can again drop or include `.js` extension as you desire). Also note that when you're importing modules that are in JavaScript files that are part

---

[1]The Flying Spaghetti Monster, or FSM for short, is the deity at the head of Pastafarianism, a religious movement (generally understood to be a parody religion, although some would argue that statement) whose adherents tend to take a, shall we say, lighthearted, view of mainstream religions. The FSM is usually depicted quite literally as a ball of spaghetti (and meatballs, never forget the meatballs!) with two stalk eyes on top who can fly (well, he's a god, *of course* he can fly!). I don't mean this reference as a judgment on any religion, Pastafarianism or otherwise, but merely to illustrate that if you actually saw the FSM flying around in real life, then I think we would *all* agree it would be a pretty amazing thing!

of your application, you should prefix the module name with forward slashes to indicate that the module is in the same directory as the file importing it. (You can also specify a subdirectory in this manner.)

The require() function returns an object that is essentially the API provided by the module. This object can include methods, attributes, or whatever you want. In fact, it could conceivably be just a variable with some data—an array perhaps.

More times than not, though, it will be an object with some methods and attributes. In the case of http in our example, one of the methods the object returned is createServer(). This method creates a web server instance and returns a reference to it. The argument you pass to this method is a function that serves as a request listener, that is, the function executed any time a request is made to the server.

Creating a web server alone won't actually do anything. It won't respond to requests until we do a little more work. The createServer() method returns a reference to the web server instance, which contains the method listen(). That method accepts a port number on which the server should listen and, optionally, the hostname on which to listen. In the example, the standard HTTP port 80 is specified, along with the standard location machine address 127.0.0.1. Once we call this method, the server will begin listening for requests, and for each request that comes in, it will call the anonymous function passed to createServer().

This callback function receives two arguments, inRequest and inResponse, which are objects representing the HTTP request and response, respectively. In this simple example, all this callback function does is first to write an HTTP header to the response object specifying a good outcome via an HTTP 200 response code. We also pass, as the second argument to writeHead(), an object that defines response headers. In this case, the Content-Type header is set to text/plain to indicate a simple text response. Finally, the end() method is called on the response object, passing the response we want to send back. This completes the handling of a given request.

As you can see, creating a server with Node.js is exceedingly simple, in its most basic form at least. Now let's talk a bit about the underlying structure that you can see demonstrated even in this simple example, namely, the asynchronous and event-driven nature of Node.js.

Asynchronous, Nonblocking, Event-Driven Programming Is King

Let's begin by defining event-driven programming. Simply put, *event-driven programming* is a style of programming where the program responds to significant events as they happen, rather than simply executing a series of instructions as quickly as it can. Those events are frequently user-generated, things such as clicking buttons or expanding sections on a web page. Other types of events are systematic, such as a response being received from a remote server because of a request for data being made by a client system.

All types of events are dealt with by means of a "callback function." All this means is that when you are writing a program, you tell the runtime environment that whenever event A happens, whatever that may be, then it should call function B in response. The function can then handle the event in whatever way is appropriate.

This event-driven style is what's referred to as *asynchronous programming* because the statements aren't necessarily executed in the order that they appear in the code in a linear way. Think about any code you've ever written. Usually, when a line of code is encountered, the runtime environment executes it and waits for it to complete. Even if that statement results in a call to a remote system, for example, the next line of code will not execute until that call comes back. Such a statement is termed a *blocking* statement because program execution beyond that statement is blocked until it completes, no matter how long it takes.

The asynchronous, event-driven model of programming is nonblocking by contrast. No single statement will ever block execution of the next line of code. Even if a given statement takes an hour to complete, the rest of the program will continue at the same time that statement does its work (or, more precisely, it waits on some resource to complete its work on the behalf of the statement), and only when that work is done will some callback function be called.

Clearly, this paradigm can be difficult to work with! For example, it is frequently true that the program *can't* meaningfully continue until that long-running statement finishes. Perhaps you're getting data from a database, for example, that you'll use to populate a table on a web page. If you were to such write code like this...

```
callServer();
populateTable();
```

...then you'll find that things don't work as expected if `callServer()` takes a couple of seconds to complete. The call to `populateTable()` will in all probability have no data yet to use, and you'll wind up with a blank table.

Instead, you need to do something like this:

```
callServer(populateTable);
```

In this case, `populateTable()` is a callback that will be called only when `callServer()` completes, however long that takes. The rest of the program can continue in the meantime, though. That's the proper approach in the asynchronous world: callbacks become the star of the show! This is nothing new if you've done Ajax development, of course, or even any sort of web development. Have you ever attached a function to a button using the `onClick` attribute? That's asynchronous programming. Likewise, that's event-driven programming using callbacks.

This paradigm allows for tremendous load handling capabilities because a second request, in the case of a web server, for instance, does not need to wait on a subsequent request to be finished. Instead, the server can begin processing the second request and go back to finish the first when some callback occurs. The server is never blocked from at least beginning to handle other requests.

This is the model at the core of Node.js, and it is what provides it most of its power. Node.js is based, internally, around the concept of an *event loop*. All this means is that there is an infinite loop running in a single process that continually looks at what events have occurred and what callbacks need to be executed. It deals with queuing all events automatically, and it just keeps calling the appropriate callbacks as fast as it can. As a developer using Node.js, you don't really need to know this, though. You just need to know that your callbacks will be called when events occur that trigger them, all as quickly as possible.

This has some tangential benefits that are quite big, most importantly, that you are guaranteed only to ever have a single callback execute at any given time because Node.js has a single event loop running at any given time. This means you never have to be concerned with any sort of concurrent programming, synchronization, and all that sort of jazz. Your code becomes considerably simpler as a result. Moreover, a given callback event handler will always run to completion and not be interrupted by another. This again makes your life a lot simpler!

This all works because of two key points about JavaScript.

- Functions are first-class citizens.

- JavaScript supports closures.

The first point means you can do things like this in JavaScript:

```
var f = function() {
  console.log("Hello!");
};
execF(f);
function execF(inF) {
  inF();
}
```

A function can be the value of a variable just like a number, string, array, or many other things. Because of this, you can pass functions around to other functions, just like any other value. (You're actually passing a reference, not the function itself, but that frankly doesn't matter in practice.) You can even dynamically execute a function, as shown in execF(). You can pass a reference to any function you want to execF(), and it will execute it just fine by way of the inF argument.

The other part of the equation is closures. Let's ask ourselves, what happens if execF() has to make a call to a remote system? Ignore for a moment how you might do that, but it should be obvious that the amount of time that it will take will vary each time you call execF(). It might even fail if network connectivity is down. What if we only want the function passed in to execF() to be called once that response comes back? We can do that, and without specifically storing inF in between!

The reason is that every statement executed in JavaScript has a *context*. The context is, in practice, the collection of variables available at the time the statement is executed. This happens all of the time without you realizing it: a given statement has access to all of the global variables that exist at the time it executes. In effect, global scope is the closure around the statement. We don't generally think of it that way, but it actually is the case.

A closure, however, becomes more obvious in the case of asynchronous programming. Let's create an admittedly contrived example.

```
function testme() {
  var sGreeting = "All done!";
  (function() {
    console.log(sGreeting);
  })();
}
testme();
```

Now, if you execute this with Node.js, you'll see the output "All done!" Take a look at that code for a minute, though...what's going on?

Inside the `testme()` function, a function is declared, but a reference to it is not stored. That makes it an anonymous function, because it has no name. That function definition is wrapped in parentheses and then is immediately called. However, remember that a variable declared inside a function using the `var` keyword is not accessible outside of that function. Thus, the question then becomes how exactly is that anonymous function able to access the variable `sGreeting`?

Does it simply always have access to its enclosing function, meaning `testme()` here, and everything inside of it? In other languages, the answer would be yes, but in JavaScript, it's a no. Instead, what happens is that the anonymous function forms a closure around all of the variables available at the time it's defined, which in this case means `sGreeting`. When that function is executed, it will, as if by magic, have access to `sGreeting`.

Now here's where the asynchronous part comes into play: what would happen if that anonymous function were executed as a callback to some remote call? In that case, being asynchronous, execution would have continued after the statement that makes this call, which means that the `testme()` function would have ended. More importantly, the variable `sGreeting` would no longer exist. Yet, despite that, the anonymous function would still display "All done!" when it is executed.

Err, how exactly?

The answer is the closure formed around the anonymous function. It remembers the state of the environment at the time it was declared, so any variables that existed at the time will still be available to it, even if those variables no longer exist anywhere else.

The reason this is so handy is that you don't need to stash stuff in global scope and worry about collisions. Imagine if you had such a callback function that handled multiple simultaneous requests. If each has its own set of input data and you still need that data after the asynchronous call, how would you keep track of it? How would you ensure that each callback uses only the data from the appropriate request? Sure, you could imagine schemes to do this I'm sure, but a closure is by far the easiest answer.

Between functions being first-class citizens and closures, the event-driven, nonblocking asynchronous style of programming can be implemented in JavaScript, and that all combines to make Node.js very powerful while minimizing complexity. You'll definitely be seeing these concepts in action over the course of the next three chapters.

The Core API

Before we get to that, though, let's look at some of the core modules that Node.js ships with and the API they all combine to form. The following is in no way, shape, or form an exhaustive look at all of the core modules Node.js ships with. I'm going to cherry-pick a few that I believe will be of most value to you more times than not. That being said, you should absolutely spend a few minutes looking through the API documentation on the Node.js web site to see what else there is.

Global

The first module isn't really a module *per se*, but instead it is a collection of objects that are made available to all modules, so it in effect *acts* like a global scope.

Before we get to that, though, let's talk briefly about scope in Node.js modules.

In contrast to JavaScript in a browser, Node.js doesn't really have a global scope. When you declare a variable, it is scoped to the current module only. To make something global, you have to attach it to a special GLOBAL object. For example, you can write this:

```
GLOBAL.myName = "Frank";
```

Now you can access GLOBAL.myName from any module you load, whether it is yours or not. This is the only way to share data across modules. Well, sort of. There is, in fact, another way, and it's what makes modules tick and allows the Node.js core modules to present an API to you. This other method is to export things from modules. For example, let's say you have the file MyModule.js.

```
function sayHi() {
  console.log("Hello!");
}
exports.sayHi = sayHi;
```

Now, if you include this module in another module, you'll be able to access the sayHi() function because it's been exported. The object returned as a result of Node.js loading this module has had that function added to it. You can therefore do this:

```
var m = require("MyModule");
m.sayHi();
```

None of this actually tells you what's available in the global namespace, though. Here's some of what you'll find there:

- ▨ console: You've seen this a bunch of times already. It's the object that allows you to write output to the console during program execution. The most commonly used method it presents is log(), but there are also info(), error(), and warn(), allowing you to log output at varying severity levels. The console object also has a dir() method, which can print an object and all its attributes—extremely handy for debugging. If you've ever used Firebug in Firefox, then the console object should be quite familiar to you.

- ▦ process: The process object represents the Node.js process itself, and it allows you to do things such as get the current working directory by calling the cwd() method on it, exit Node.js execution by calling its exit() method, or get the version of Node.js by reading the version attribute. You can even tell what processor architecture and platform your code is running on by interrogating the arch and platform attributes, respectively. You can see how much memory your program is using by calling the memoryUsage() method.

- ▦ require(): Remember, in JavaScript, functions are proper objects, so the require() function that you've seen a number of times is available in the global namespace, as is setTimeout(), clearTimeout(), setInterval(), and clearInterval(), all of which are JavaScript mainstays.

File System

The File System module, which is technically in the fs module, contains tons of functions for working with files. With it, you can read files, as shown in Listing 5-3.

Listing 5-3. Reading a Text File Synchronously

```
var fs = require("fs");

console.log(fs.readFileSync("testfile.txt", "ascii"));
```

Assuming testfile.txt is in the same directory, its content will be displayed on the console. You'll notice that the fs.readFileSync() method seems to, by its name, imply that, contrary to most of Node.js, this call is synchronous and, hence, blocking. In fact, it is. Sometimes you really do need the program to wait until the file is completely read before continuing. However, at other times, probably most of the time in fact, you'll want to do it asynchronously. The fs module has you covered, as Listing 5-4 demonstrates.

Listing 5-4. Asynchronously Reading testfile.txt

```
var fs = require("fs");

fs.readFile("testfile.txt", "ascii", function(err, dat) {
  if (err) {
    console.log("Error!");
  } else {
    console.log(dat);
  }
});
```

Naturally, you can write files just as easily. Take a look at Listing 5-5 to see how.

Listing 5-5. Yep, We Can Write Files Too!

```
var fs = require("fs");

fs.writeFile("outfile.txt", "I was written by Node.js", function (err) {
  if (err) {
    console.log("Errro1");
  } else {
    console.log("File written, reading back...");
    fs.readFile("outfile.txt", "ascii", function(err, dat) {
      if (err) {
        console.log("Error!");
      } else {
        console.log(dat);
      }
    });
  }
});
```

This example actually demonstrates something else that is common in Node.js code: nested callbacks. Here, the callback function for the `writeFile()` call makes an asynchronous call to `readFile()`, which therefore needs a callback function. It's not uncommon to see a series of nested asynchronous calls like this in Node.js code. Arguably, it isn't the prettiest way to write such code. Most people prefer having stand-alone callback functions that are then used, like those shown in Listing 5-6.

Listing 5-6. Avoiding Nested Callback Functions

```
var fs = require("fs");

var callback1 = function(err) {
  if (err) {
    console.log("Errro1");
  } else {
    console.log("File written, reading back...");
    fs.readFile("outfile.txt", "ascii", callback2);
  }
};

var callback2 = function(err, dat) {
  if (err) {
    console.log("Error!");
  } else {
    console.log(dat);
  }
};

fs.writeFile("outfile.txt", "I was written by Node.js", callback1);
```

Listing 5-5 and Listing 5-6 are functionally equivalent, but they differ in style. Which style you prefer is more or less a personal preference. I tend to do a mixture: I'll nest if it's only one or two levels deep, but if it's much more than that, I start thinking about stand-alone functions. That's just me, though.

OS

The os module provides a few simple operating system and environment-related functions. Some of these are actually echoed in the global namespace, but they are available here as well. Listing 5-7 shows some of them in action.

Listing 5-7. Some Examples of Using the os Module

```
var os = require("os");

console.log("\nTemporary directory .. " + os.tmpdir());
console.log("\nEndianness .......... " +
  os.endianness() == "LE" ? "Low-endian" : "High-endian"
);
console.log("\nHost name ........... " + os.hostname());
console.log("\nOS type ............. " + os.type());
console.log("\nOS release .......... " + os.release());
console.log("\nTotal system memory .. " + os.totalmem());
console.log("\nCPU information ...... " + JSON.stringify(os.cpus()));
console.log("\nNIC infoormation ..... " +
  JSON.stringify(os.networkInterfaces())
);
```

When I execute this on my PC, the result is as shown in Figure 5-5.

Figure 5-5. Getting some system information with Node.js and the os module

Also shown by this example is the JSON object, which is available intrinsically in JavaScript, at least in the version that Node.js uses. This object has two main purposes: creating objects from JSON using the JSON.parse() method and converting objects to JSON using the JSON.stringify() method. The latter comes in handy in order to display the CPU and NIC information. If we attempted simply to append the output of the os.cpus() or os.networkInterfaces() method, you'd find that the output is simply [object Object], which is the default toString() implementation for JavaScript objects, and it is also not very helpful! Displaying JSON is quite a bit more helpful, and it is easy to accomplish with JSON.stringify().

Util

The utilities module, or util, as you'll actually require() when you use it, has a couple of handy utility-type functions in it. Listing 5-8 shows a couple of them in action.

Listing 5-8. A Few of the Functions Available in the util Module

```
var util = require("util");

console.log(util.format("%d:%d%s", 6, 54, "am"));
util.log("I am a timestamped message");
var o = { firstName : "John", lastName : "Sheridan" };
console.log(util.inspect(o, { colors : true }));
var a = [ 1, 2, 3 ];
console.log(util.isArray(a));
console.log(util.isDate(a));
```

The format() method allows you to format an arbitrary number of arguments using a C printf-like format specification. The %d placeholder is for numbers, and %s is for strings, among others; the arguments that follow the specification are inserted for those placeholders. The output from that line in this example would be "6:54am," and of course you could pass variables as the arguments, which is really when this method would come into play. (It also allows you to specify a variable for the format specification itself, if you want.)

The log() method is similar to console.log(), except that it will include a timestamp before the logged message.

The inspect() method acts a lot like console.dir(), but it offers a number of options. You can optionally send an object as the second argument to set some settings, among them, colors. When true, the output will be color-coded using ANSI color codes. You can also define how deep into the object graph of the object you're logging by setting the depth attribute. This means that if the object you want to inspect() contains references to other objects and potentially those objects have references to yet more objects, you can determine how far down this chain you want to display. The showHidden option, when true, allows you to see the nonenumerable properties of the object as well.

The isArray() and isDate() methods do precisely what their names imply: they return true if the object passed to them is an array or date object, respectively. In the example, isArray() returns true while isDate() returns false. While not the largest module around, what it provides can be very handy indeed!

DNS

The dns module allows you to look up IP addresses for domain names and to resolve domain names to IP addresses. Listing 5-9 shows an example of both.

Listing 5-9. Using the dns Module

```
var dns = require("dns");

dns.lookup("www.apress.com", function(inError, inAddress) {
  if (inError) {
    console.log("Error: " + inError);
  } else {
    console.log(
      "Address for www.apress.com = " + JSON.stringify(inAddress)
    );
```

```
  dns.reverse(inAddress, function(inError, inDomains) {
    if (inError) {
      console.log("Error: " + inError);
    } else {
      console.log(
        "Domain for IP " + inAddress + " = " + JSON.stringify(inDomains)
      );
    }
  });
  }
});
```

The code first looks up the IP address for www.apress.com and then attempts to find the domain name for the returned IP address. The code is quite straightforward, as are all good Node.js core API functions!

I hope that this small collection of examples has whet your appetite for what is built in to Node.js. You'll see a few more modules in use in the upcoming chapters that go into the server code, including things like the http module, querystring module, and url module, all of which help perform various functions that a typical web server would need to perform. Of course, the core modules are not all that are available to you, as you're about to find out!

Extensibility via Packages and Package Manager

In addition to the core API and the modules that constitute it, Node.js allows you to import tons of third-party modules that extend its functionality greatly. These modules can provide things such as database functionality, HTML parsing, frameworks for creating web applications more easily, and packet analysis, to name a few.

Another module that is of great importance is Node Package Manager (NPM). NPM manifests as a command-line tool, npm. This tool used to be separate from Node.js, but it now comes with it so that you no longer have to install npm separately. In short, npm is your gateway to installing modules. However, before using npm, you need to understand the concept of global and local module modes.

If you look in the directory where Node.js was installed, which will be dependent on your operating system and possibly by choices made during installation, you'll see a directory named node_modules. As its name implies, this is where modules are stored. By default, you should see a single module there: npm. This folder represents global modules, that is, modules available to all programs that are run with Node.js. You can also install modules in local mode, which boils down to nothing more than a node_modules directory, under the directory in which your project is stored.

Now let's play with npm a little. There is a module available named request, which allows you to make HTTP requests to other servers from your Node.js programs. I can hear you exclaim: "That's a handy capability to have! I want it!" That's easy enough: drop to a command prompt and execute the following (with sudo, if applicable):

```
npm install -g request
```

You'll be greeted with output that looks something like Figure 5-6.

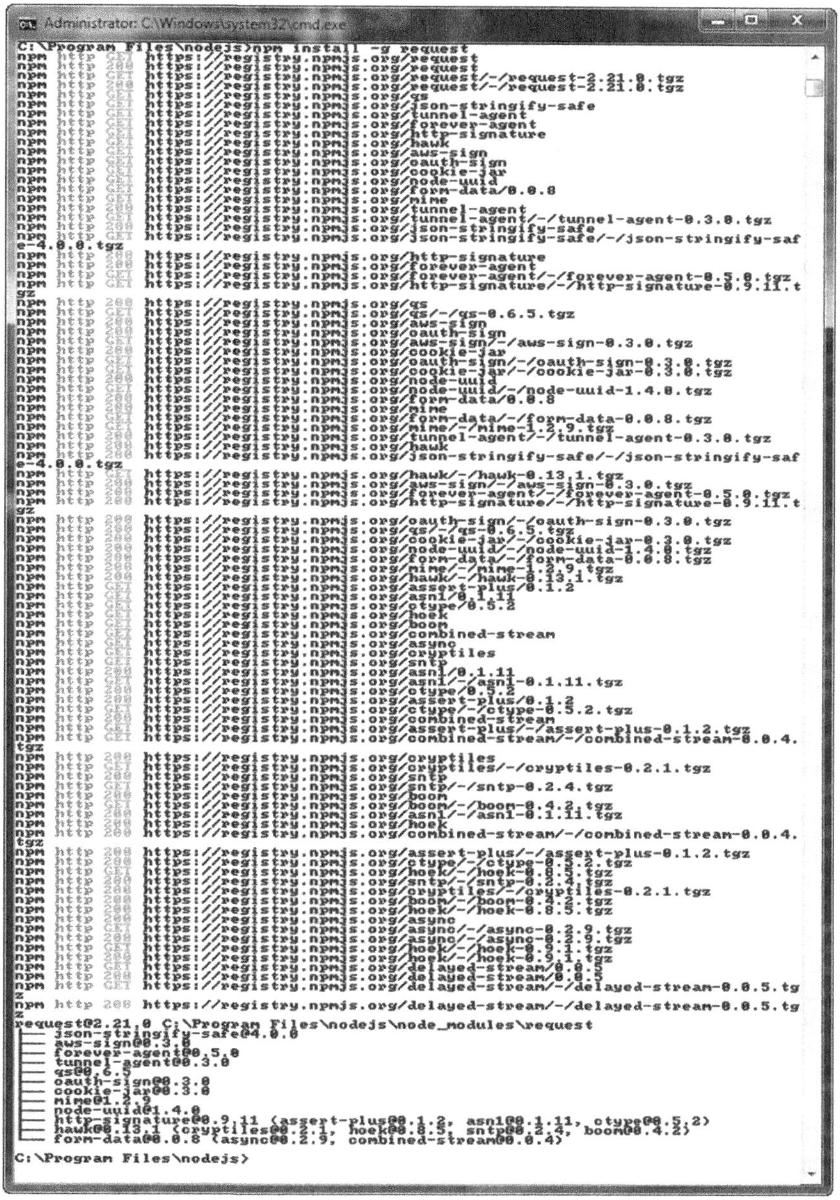

Figure 5-6. Using npm to install the request package

Now, if you look in that node_modules directory again, you'll see that there is suddenly a request directory underneath it containing some JavaScript files and other materials related to the module. Now, in your programs, you can do this:

```
var r = require("request");
```

The –g command-line switch is the key to putting the module in the global node_modules directory. However, if you simply drop that switch and execute the command again, you'll find that a node_modules directory is created in your current directory. The request module will be placed there instead. This is local mode.

In general, local mode is preferred because you can then, on a project-by-project basis, determine what modules are used and what versions are used, since projects can use different versions at times.

Speaking of versions, there's a handy npm command that you'll want to know.

```
npm update
```

This command will update all the modules in the current directory to the latest version in the npm repository online.

> **Tip** You can browse the repository by hitting the NPM Registry link on the Node.js web site.

Two more commands that you may find useful are as follows:

```
npm list
```

As you probably can guess, this lists all of the modules available in the repository. Finally, you can get information about a given module with this:

```
npm view XXX
```

Replace XXX with the name of the module about which you want information (request, for example), and you'll see a JSON dump with a ton of information on the module. Overall, it's probably easier to browse the NPM Registry on the Node.js web site, but either way should get you the information you need.

You should also be aware that npm takes care of module dependencies for you. For example, if module A depends on module B and you try to install module A, you'll find that module B is installed as well.

An extension of this dependency mechanism is that Node.js allows you to define some metadata about your application by including a package.json file in the root of your application. Among other things, you can list the dependencies your application has, like so:

```
{ "name" : "My First Node.js Application",
  "version" : "1.0",
  "dependencies" : {
    "request" : ">0.1.0",
    "sax" : "*"
  }
}
```

This says that your application requires the `request` module, any version greater than 0.1.0, and the `sax` module (for XML parsing), where any version is acceptable. The nice thing about this is that when someone wants your application, you can give them just the code of your application and not the modules on which it depends. Then all they need to do is to go to a command prompt in the root directory of the application and execute the following:

```
npm install
```

The `package.json` file will be parsed, and the modules it depends on are downloaded. The person can then execute your application without worry!

The `npm` command supports a number of other options and functions, but these are the ones you're likely to need most of the time.

The last point to make about loading modules is that there is a hierarchy that Node.js uses to locate modules. First, the core modules that ship with Node.js have precedence. So if you are trying to include a module named `http`, for example, and you `require("http")`, you will be importing the core `http` module, not your custom `http` module that you might be trying to import. You'll need either to name the module differently or to provide a full path to it to disambiguate the one you want.

If you try to import a module that isn't a core module, Node.js will first look in the global `node_modules` directory under the Node.js install directory. If it can't find the module there, it next will look in the `node_modules` directory local to the file trying to import the module. If it can't find it there, then it will look for a `node_modules` directory in the parent directory. Node.js will continue to go up the directory hierarchy in this way until it finds the module or hits the file system root. If the module cannot be located in this manner, then the program will end with an error on start-up.

Summary

In this chapter, you looked at Node.js and began to get a feel for what it is, how it works, and what it can do. You looked at some basic Node.js code for creating a web server, and you saw some of the core APIs available to your Node.js applications. We talked about the event-driven programming model that pervades Node.js development and how that helps ensure good performance and concurrent request handling. Of course, you saw how to get started with Node.js, where to find it online, and how to install it.

In the next chapter, we'll look at another server technology that plays exceptionally well with Node.js, namely, MongoDB, which will be used to build out the data storage requirements of the server component of My Mobile Organizer.

Chapter 6

Introducing MongoDB

Data storage. Most apps need it, and My Mobile Organizer is no exception. We're talking beyond the localStorage you saw in previous chapters. That covered the client-side offline data cache, but we need something more persistent on the server side as the authoritative data store.

There's no shortage of options, all of which are available in the world of Node.js. You could go with plain old text files and simply read and write them directly on the local file system. There are relational database connectors available so that you could go with something like MySQL or Oracle.

Those options, however, have (at least) one downside in common: rigidity. With text files, you'll need to adhere to some specific format and write the code to generate and parse that format carefully. It's easy to break something when you need to change the format later to expand on it. With a relational database, you're working with tables and rows and specific data formats, so your data model has to fit into those constraints.

To be sure, all of that is really no big deal. After all, we're programmers; we've been dealing with that stuff for decades! This isn't the past, or even the present, though; this is the future! Hmmm, that doesn't seem quite right. In any case, isn't there another choice—maybe one that even has a whole movement named after it by its adherents?

Funny you should ask.

NoSQL: Or, How I Learned to Stop Worrying and Love Flexibility

In a classic relational database management system (RDBMS), you have tables, perhaps like the one shown in Figure 6-1.

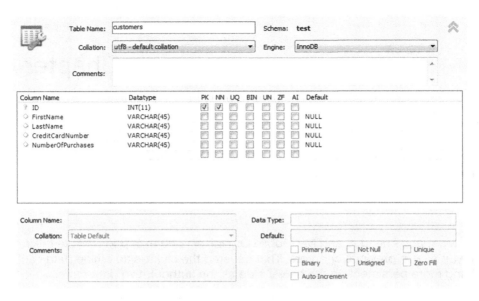

Figure 6-1. *A simple relational table in MySQL (although it could be any RDBMS)*

If you want to get the list of customers in that table, the magic of the Structured Query Language (SQL) allows us to write a query like so:

```
select * from test.customers
```

This results in a list such as the one shown in Figure 6-2.

ID	First Name	Last Name	Credit Card Number	Number Of Purchases
111	Bill	Lumberg	1872836475	12
123	Janet	Reynolds	9989182732	3
341	Alex	Walberg	9080706065	4
456	Mike	Brown	1910283746	8
554	Sally	Rider	1112225637	2
767	Miranda	Jackson	5095874645	1
789	Christine	Watson	1162273384	17

Figure 6-2. *A list of all customers, thanks to SQL*

Now that's straightforward and highly useful and, I bet, nothing new to you. We can perform all sorts of fancy query tricks beyond this, such as only showing customers with ten or more purchases.

```
select * from customers where NumberOfPurchases >= 10
```

This is the bread-and-butter of much programming these days, certainly in the business world.

The problem, as some see it anyway, is that each row in that table has a rigidly defined structure. Each row, which logically represents a customer, has a unique ID, a first name, a last name, a credit card number (don't get any ideas; they're bogus!), and a number of purchases (which really isn't the best database design, but that's neither here nor there for this discussion). If you need to add attributes later, say, a middle name, you can add a column to the table, but now all of the existing items will have blank or null values in that field (assuming you allow blank or null values) unless you do some extra work. While adding a column is usually a benign enough change, sometimes it's a more complex situation than that, and you can easily break things, especially where table relationships are involved.

Speaking of relationships, that's the other aspect of an RDBMS, which is, pardon the pun, key. For example, it's nice that we can see how many purchases Janet Reynolds has made with that simple query, but this doesn't tell us anything about the orders themselves. To deal with that, you'll typically create another table, named `orders` probably, with a structure like that shown in Figure 6-3.

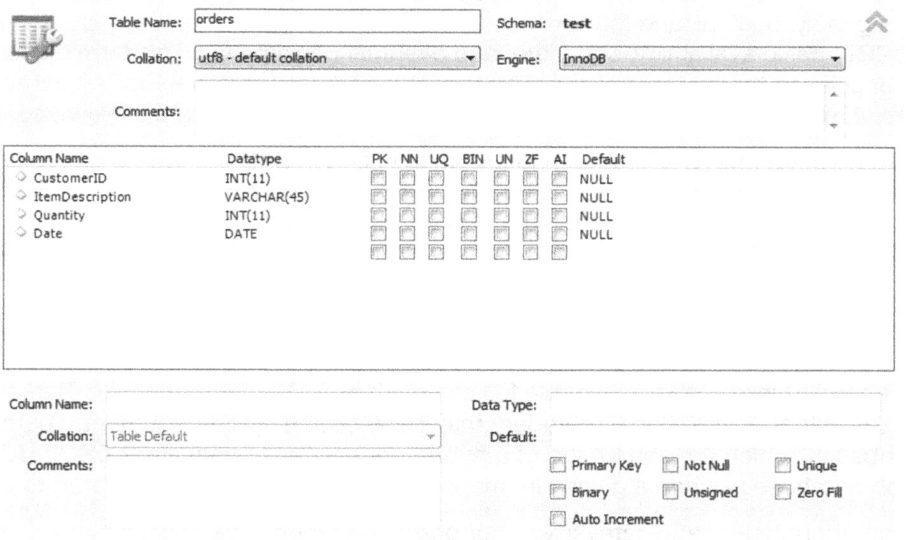

Figure 6-3. Our new orders table

Now, if we want to get a list of orders for Janet Reynolds and we want to include Janet's information on each row too, we can a query like so:

```
select * from test.customers, test.orders where test.customers.id = test.orders.customerid
```

The result is shown in Figure 6-4.

ID	FirstName	LastName	CreditCardNumber	NumberOfPurchases	CustomerID	ItemDescription	Quantity	Date
123	Janet	Reynolds	9989182732	3	123	Kitchen Table	1	2013-01-01
123	Janet	Reynolds	9989182732	3	123	Chair	4	2013-01-01
123	Janet	Reynolds	9989182732	3	123	Toaster	2	2013-01-01

Figure 6-4. A simple join query

This is a basic SQL join between the two tables based on their relationship, namely, the fact that the `CustomerID` field in the `orders` table is a foreign key into the `customers` table on its `ID` field.

SQL is a very powerful language, and a relational database is appropriate for all sorts of use cases. Underneath it all is the concept of *ACID*, an acronym for atomicity, consistency, isolation, and durability. ACID describes the ability of the RDBMS to ensure that the data is always in a consistent state at the end of every operation. This is accomplished by many hard rules that you must follow, which results in nothing that might violate ACID being allowed.

While ACID is likely what you want in a banking application, for example, there are some situations where it isn't, arguably, optimal, and that's where the NoSQL concept comes into play. The BASE model underpins NoSQL: basic availability, soft state, and eventual consistency. This term leads you into a lot of computer science theory such as the CAP theorem and horizontal versus vertical scaling, but for developers, it more or less boils down to the idea that the persistent data store loosens the rules.

For a start, you no longer have to create a rigid database schema. There are no tables at all to define, so you don't have to specify what attributes a customer has, for example, by creating columns in a table for each. Instead, you store a value for a given key in the database, and that value can be almost anything. There actually are a number of different possible "values" for a given key, but they all boil down to some form of binary data.

You could literally store an image, such as a GIF file. It's simply mapped to a unique key, and that key, among other mechanisms, can retrieve it. You can also store a document, which is just a binary object that is encoded in some recognizable format, such as XML, JSON, or PDF. This object is still mapped to a key, although additional metadata may be encoded in the document. There are also columnar databases, which are something of a hybrid between relational and NoSQL databases. Finally, a graph database is when a given key maps to a collection of objects related to one another.

The bottom line, though, is that whatever you happen to be storing; it's always mapped to a unique key value. That is, pardon the pun again, the *key*! Because of this, there are no SQL queries to write. You look things up by specific key values or iterate over a collection of objects.

That being said, it *is* still in fact possible to query a NoSQL database if what you're storing is structured in some way. If you're storing JSON documents, for example, you might have a customer document like so:

```
{ FirstName : "Jack", LastName : "Miller", CreditCardNumber : 123456789, NumberOfPurchases : 6 }
```

It would be possible to find only the document with a `LastName` of Miller. You don't give up those sorts of capabilities by going to NoSQL; it's just that you no longer have to write SQL queries. Now instead, and depending on which NoSQL implementation you use, you might write code more like this to find a customer with `FirstName` Jack:

```
var c = Customers.find({ FirstName : "Jack" });
```

Perhaps the more interesting part of all of this, however, is that the documents you store do not have to have any defined structure. While the document for Jack Miller might be what we just looked at, in the very same data store you might have a document like this:

```
{ ProductName : "KitchenTable", Price : "500.00" }
```

It is 100 percent OK to do this in a NoSQL world. This doesn't break querying, as any document that doesn't have an attribute on which you're querying will simply be ignored. By extension, you can change the structure of a document at any time. If you need to add a `MiddleName` field, for example, you simply do it. You can even choose to do it for only some documents. Yes, it's true that you have to write robust code that can handle these potential differences. That's not as hard as it may sound at first, though. This is because most NoSQL databases have the notion of versioning within them. For example, version 1 of your customer document may not include the `MiddleName` field, but version 2 may include it. Documents of different versions can exist in the same data store because the document contains its version number, so your code can branch accordingly when it's processing a document.

At this point, JSON is the most-used data storage format, and for good reason. NoSQL plays very well with JavaScript, as you're about to see. The common use of JSON is in no small part a main contributor to why this is the case. With that being said, let's turn our attention to one specific NoSQL implementation: MongoDB.

One Contender Among Many: MongoDB

MongoDB is an open source document-based NoSQL database implementation that was created in 2007 by a team of former DoubleClick programmers who later went on to found 10gen. They were developing a cloud-based application platform, conceptually similar to Google App Engine, Amazon EC2, or Microsoft Azure, and as part of that, they decided they needed a high-performance, highly available, and easily scalable data store.

As a result, MongoDB was born, its name taken from the character in the classic Mel Brooks comedy *Blazing Saddles*.

> **Note**   After the fact, the story changed a little bit to indicate that its name was taken from the word *huMONGOus*, but it's a matter of lore whether that was the original intent or not.

Unfortunately for 10gen, but fortunately for the rest of us, its application platform didn't do well, and, as a result, in 2009 MongoDB was ripped out of the platform and separately open sourced. This immediately opened the floodgates, and MongoDB took off in no time.

MongoDB has a number of points in its favor.

- Documents stored in MongoDB map nicely to programming language data types, specifically those found in JavaScript, making them easy to work with.
- A document itself can have other documents, or arrays of documents, embedded within it, which reduces the need to do joins, as you would have in a relational database.

- The fact that there is no well-defined schema to which documents must adhere means that MongoDB makes polymorphic behavior easy to achieve.

- A number of factors make MongoDB perform very well, including its ability to be embedded within larger applications. The ability to include keys from embedded documents in indexes makes queries lightning-fast, and an optional streaming write mode means reduced I/O blocking.

- MongoDB supports the notion of replicated servers with automatic master failover, meaning that if your primary MongoDB server goes down, your application can easily use a replicated version to ensure the availability of your data store.

- The notion of sharding is supported, which is an approach to distributing data automatically across machines to enhance I/O.

- The "eventually consistent" read model that MongoDB employs can also be distributed across clustered machines. This helps enhance the scalability of the data store.

All of these points result in MongoDB being a very good choice for a cloud-based computing infrastructure, while simultaneously being very easy for developers to work with.

The Document Store Model

Part of what makes MongoDB so easy to work with is its document-based storage model. At a high level, any MongoDB installation consists of one or more databases. Each database then consists of one or more collections of documents. You can think of a collection in a similar way to how you think of a table in a relational database, except that they need not all share a similar structure and they are always accessible by a key value. (The document is the value in the key-value pair, in other words.) Even the data type of a given field in two documents can be different, but the documents can still be members of the same collection in the same database.

This is because MongoDB doesn't require you to define specifically what a document is. You simply store a document in a collection, regardless of its structure. If you have a lot of relational database experience, I'm sure that sounds like utter chaos! To be sure, you can absolutely mess things up and make it exactly that. However, in practice, with just a little bit of care, you can avoid any nasty side effects. By doing so, you'll gain a tremendous amount of flexibility and shortened development time, in addition to all of the performance and scalability benefits that MongoDB offers automatically.

Now let's get out of the realm of theory and get MongoDB up and running so that we can play around with it a bit!

Getting and Installing MongoDB

Before you go any further, head over to www.mongodb.org and hit the Downloads link. You'll be greeted with the table you see in Figure 6-5.

	OS X 64-bit	Linux 32-bit note	Linux 64-bit	Windows 32-bit note	Windows 64-bit	Solaris 64-bit	Source
Production Release (Recommended)							
2.4.4 6/4/2013 Changelog Release Notes	download	download	download	download	download *2008R2+	download	tgz zip
2.4.5-rc0 6/24/2013 Changelog Release Notes	download	download	download	download	download *2008R2+	download	tgz zip
Nightly Changelog	download	download	download	download	download *2008R2+	download	tgz zip
Previous Release							
2.2.4 4/2/2013 Changelog Release Notes	download	download	download	download	download *2008R2+	download	tgz zip
2.2.5-rc0 6/20/2013 Changelog Release Notes	download	download	download	download	download *2008R2+	download	tgz zip
Nightly Changelog	download	download	download	download	download *2008R2+	download	tgz zip

Figure 6-5. Choose the red pill…, or blue…, or green, purple, orange, mauve…

Choose the installation option appropriate for your system and download it. Extract the archive you downloaded to a location where you'd like MongoDB to be "installed," and… well, actually, you're done! There is no installation *per se*, although for nomenclature purposes, I'll refer to the directory you extracted MongoDB to as the "installation directory."

> **Tip**   The MongoDB web site has a neat feature that allows you to play with a MongoDB installation online. Simply click the Try It Out link at the top of the page, and you'll find yourself at a MongoDB command prompt (which I'll be discussing two sections from now). There, you can create collections, add and remove documents, query for documents, and so on. It's a nifty way to start playing with MongoDB without even going through the (minimal) trouble of downloading and extracting an archive.

There is actually one last step you'll need to do, and that's to give MongoDB a directory to use in which to store its data. If you're installing on a Windows machine, all you need to do is create the directory c:\data\db. MongoDB will use that location by default. Yes, you can of course put it where you like, but then you'll need to tell MongoDB where it is specifically. That isn't hard, of course, but we're being lazy here...err, that is, *efficient*...so use the default location for now. If you're a Unix/Linux/OS X user, create that directory as /data/db.

Up-and-Running MongoDB

Once you have MongoDB downloaded and extracted and you have a suitable data directory created, the next step is to start the MongoDB server. To do so, go to a command prompt, and navigate to the bin subdirectory in the MongoDB installation directory. Once there, execute mongod (or /mongod for you Unix, Linux, or Mac folks). When you do, you should see output similar to Figure 6-6 (operating system differences excepted, of course).

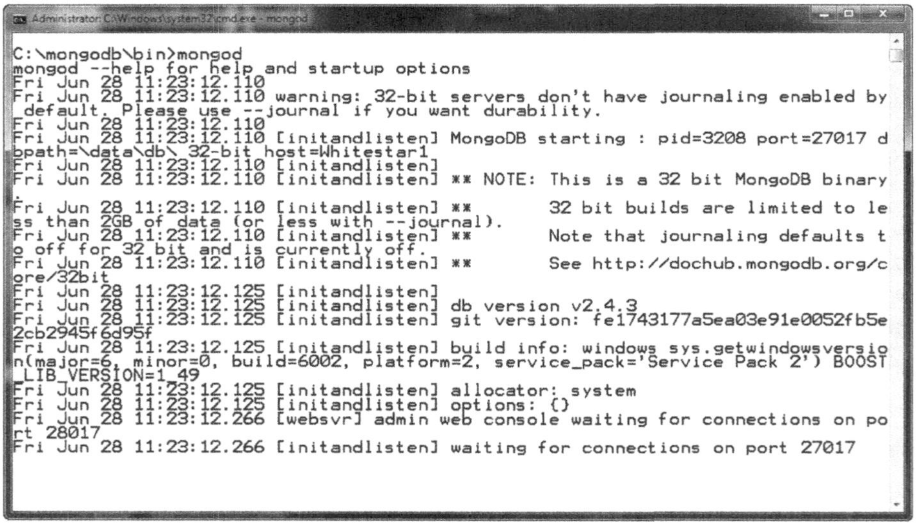

Figure 6-6. MongoDB, up and running!

As long as you didn't see any errors, you should now have a MongoDB server up and running! You're now ready to start playing around with it using the command-line shell application.

Command-Line "Database" Administration

To start the MongoDB shell, while still in the bin subdirectory, simply execute the mongo command. You should wind up with something that looks like Figure 6-7.

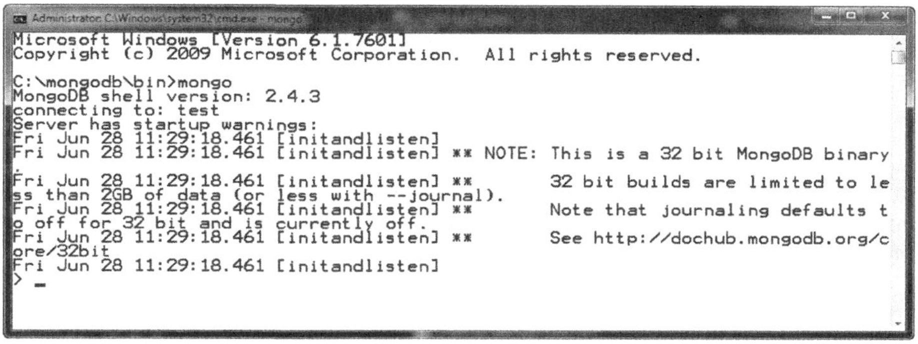

Figure 6-7. The shell: she's alive and connected, captain!

> **Tip**   You'll need a new command prompt window here, since the previous one you used to launch MongoDB is blocked while the server is running. To stop the server, simply press Ctrl+C or Ctrl+Z, depending on your operating system.

If you glance back at the other command prompt window where the server is running, you should now also see some new information about an accepted connection. That's the shell application connected to the server.

So, what can you do in this shell exactly? Lots of things! First, let's see what databases are available to us by typing this command and hitting Enter.

```
show dbs
```

This will list all the available databases on this server. After a clean installation, you should see just one: `local`. It will also show you how much space each database is currently using.

Now there's a little bit of an oddity here in that there is actually another database that doesn't show up at first, named `test`. In fact, you are initially using that database without even knowing it!

At any time, you can determine what database you're in with this command:

```
db
```

If you do that immediately after starting the shell, you'll see `test` displayed. This means any operations you perform, unless and until you switch to another database, will be targeted to the `test` database, even though it doesn't yet show up when you list the databases.

You switch to a database at any time with the `use` command.

```
use test
```

Interestingly, if you list databases again at this point, `test` will now show up! I think this may just be a little quirk in the shell, but it's nothing to get hung up about.

I can hear you asking, "What about creating a database?" That's logically the first administrative task you'd want to perform. The short answer is that you don't explicitly create a database! Instead, there are two steps you need to perform to effectively "create" a database. First, issue this command:

```
use XXX
```

where XXX is the name of the database you'd like to create. For the sake of this example, let's use `example` as the name of the database. Issue that command now, assuming you are following along and trying all this as you go.

What this really means is that you can switch to a database that doesn't exist yet and MongoDB will not complain. The thing about it is that this step alone won't create the database because there is a second step you have to do, and that is to insert some data into the database. It's only at that point that the database actually comes into existence.

So, how do you insert data? The first step is to create some data to insert, and that's done with the magic of JavaScript! Enter the following command and hit Enter:

```
p1 = { firstName : "John", lastName : "King", age : 23 };
```

Then enter this command and hit Enter:

```
p2 = { firstName : "Melissa", lastName : "Jordan", age : 19 };
```

Now two JavaScript variables, p1 and p2, are in memory. That doesn't actually put anything into our example database, though; it just gives us some JavaScript objects that we *can* insert. To insert those objects into the database, we need two more commands.

```
db.people.insert(p1);
db.people.insert(p2);
```

Hit Enter after each of those commands. If you watch the console of the MongoDB server, which should appear in the window in which you launched MongoDB, you'll see a bunch of log messages fly by when you execute these commands, indicating that the data was saved. Still, we should probably confirm that. So, first let's see what collections are in this database with the following command:

```
show collections
```

You should see two collections listed, `people` and `system.indexes`. The `people` collection is the one in which we're interested, since it was created as a result of our two inserts. (`system.indexes` is a collection MongoDB uses behind the scenes, so we can ignore it for our purposes here.)

Good, it looks like our inserts were successful. We now have a real, materialized database, and it even has a collection in it. Presumably, that collection has two documents in it representing the two JavaScript objects created. Let's confirm that too with a simple query.

```
db.people.find()
```

Do that, and you should see that the objects that were inserted are read back to you on the console, as shown in Figure 6-8.

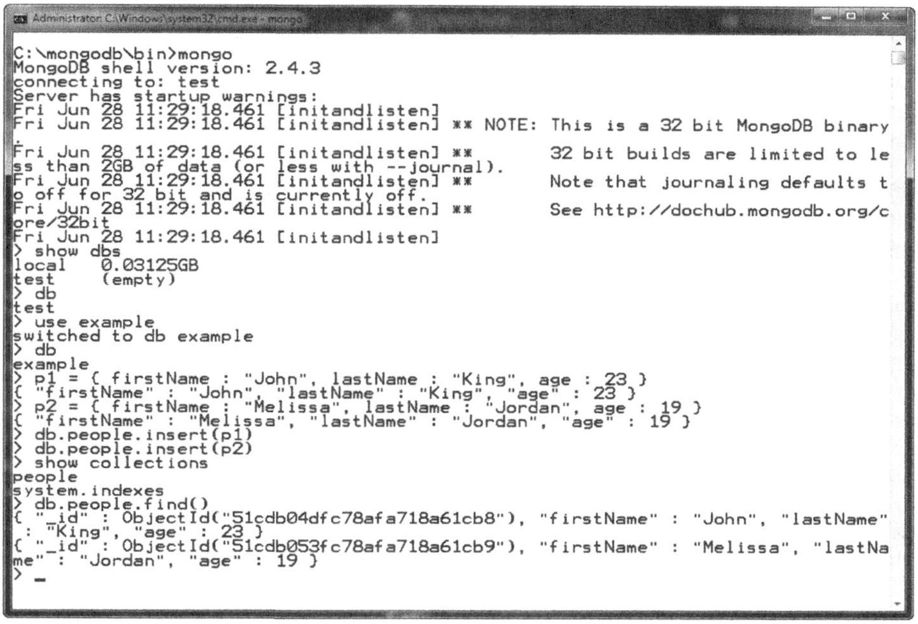

Figure 6-8. Soylent MongoDB is…people!

In case it's not obvious at this point, the MongoDB shell is effectively a JavaScript interpreter. The db object that is used here to do inserts and queries is just that: a JavaScript object. As such, it has properties and methods that can be used to perform all sorts of operations. At any time, you can use the help command from the shell prompt to see some other things that you can do. Some of the other commands you'll discover that you can execute from that help information include the following:

- db.help(): Executes the help() method of the db objects, which lists help information about most of the methods of the db object available to you

- db.XXX.help(): Executes the help() method of a collection object, where XXX is the name of a collection in the current database (people, for example), which lists help information about most of the methods that you can execute on that collection

- help admin: Shows help for administrative tasks that you can perform such as spawning programs, shows memory usage information, and manipulates files in directories

There's much more that you can do, and the help command will allow you to discover those things. However, at the end of the day, playing around in the MongoDB shell isn't what we're here to do. We need to create a server application for My Mobile Organizer to use that includes data storage in MongoDB. So, surely there must be a way to work with MongoDB from Node.js, right? Of course there is!

MongoDB in the World of Node.js: Mongoose

As you discovered in the previous chapter, one of the most powerful aspects of Node.js is its ability to be extended by the use of modules. This is the mechanism used to bring MongoDB support to Node.js. While there are a few alternative modules, the one that rises to the top is Mongoose.

With Mongoose, which you can find at `http://mongoosejs.com`, you are dealing with a simplified object-modeling framework that abstracts away some of the potentially messy details of working with MongoDB from Node.js code. With Mongoose, you write code that looks like this:

```
// Import Mongoose into our application
var mongoose = require("mongoose");

// Connect to the example database on the MongoDB server running locally
mongoose.connect("mongodb://localhost/example");
// Create a Person model
var Person = mongoose.model(
"Person",
mongoose.schema({
firstName : String, lastName : String, age : Number
  })
);

// Create two people (which are instances of Person)
var p1 = new Person({
firstName : "John", lastName : "King", age : 23
});
var p2 = new Person({
firstName : "Melissa", lastName : "Jordan", age : 19
});

// Save our people to the database
p1.save();
p2.save();

// Retrieve a person from the database
Person.find({ firstName : "Melissa" }, function(person) {
console.log(person);
});
```

That is, essentially, the Mongoose-based equivalent code to what we did in the MongoDB shell application earlier. In short, we begin by creating an object model. This model begins with a schema that describes a given type of model object, a person in this case, and then the creation of a model object based on that schema. Here we wind up with a `Person` class from which we can then create instances of using the specified data for our two people. Any object of type `Person` automatically has a number of methods, one of which is `save()`, which of course saves the object to the database. We can then use the `find()` method, passing it an attribute and value to match to get a specific object. This code runs in Node.js, so we know that it will have an asynchronous form to it. That's why we supply a callback function to the `find()` method, which gets called once the object is retrieved.

That's jumping ahead a bit, though! Let's step back and see how to get Mongoose installed first.

Installing Mongoose

You already know how, don't you? Why yes, you do.

```
npm install mongoose
```

Yep, that's all it takes! The Node.js module system will grab Mongoose out of the cloud and install it into the directory from which you run that command, presumably your application project directory. Once that's done, you're off to the races. We can now look at some specific functionality that becomes available to you when this is complete.

Connecting to the Data Store

Connecting to the database you saw in the previous example simply boils down to one line of code.

```
mongoose.connect("mongodb://localhost/example");
```

In simplest terms, that's all it takes. You pass the URI to the database to which you're connecting, which can use the mongodb protocol in the case of a local server or a proper host name if it's on a remote machine. Optionally, after the URI, you can pass additional arguments.

- Database name. (Alternatively, you can just append it to the URI, as I've done here; either way will work.)
- Port.
- An options object, which can include attributes such as user for username, pass for password, and auth for authentication options. (Yes, you can apply user-level security to your databases if you like.) You also have the option of specifying server information and database name here too if you prefer.

The final argument you can pass to the connect() method is a callback function that will be called when either the connection is successfully opened or an error occurs.

Defining Schemas and Models

Everything you do with Mongoose begins with the notion of a schema. A *schema* is a description of a collection in a database, and it defines the structure of the documents stored in that collection. Defining a schema is a simple matter.

```
var MySchema = new Schema({
fieldA : String,
fieldB : String,
fieldC : [{ fieldC1 : String, fieldC2 : Date }],
fieldD : { type : Date, default : Date.now },
fieldE : Boolean,
fieldF : {
fieldF1 : Number,
fieldF2 : Number
  }
});
```

A number of interesting things are on display here. First, each field that you define has a specific type. MongoDB offers the following schema types:

- String
- Number
- Date
- Buffer
- Boolean
- Mixed
- ObjectId
- Array

In addition to a type, you can also specify a default value for a field, as in `fieldD`, which takes the time when an object of this type is created as its value.

Notice too that a field can be a composite of multiple values, as in the case of `fieldC` and `fieldF`. In the case of `fieldC`, it's in the form of an array, whereas `fieldF` is an object.

Once you have a schema defined, you then need to create a model based on it. A *model* is really nothing but a constructor function created from a schema. Later, you create documents by creating instances of a model. To create a model, you just do the following:

```
var MyModel = mongoose.model("MyModel", MySchema);
```

The first argument is a name for the model that is used going forward by Mongoose. It becomes the collection in which documents of this type will be stored. The second argument is a reference to the schema object. In the earlier example, I put the schema definition inline with the model creation. That's perfectly valid syntactically, and you may choose to write your code that way, but it's purely a stylistic choice. Of course, if you think you may need to do something with the schema object later, then you'll want to write it as you see here, as a separate object reference.

With the model created, you can begin creating documents based on it.

```
var m = new MyModel({
fieldA : "aaa", fieldB : "bbb", fieldC : ["ccc", new Date() ],
fieldE : true, fieldF : { fieldF1 : 123, fieldF2 : 456 }
});
```

> **Tip** Note that `fieldD` is not populated because it has a default value, the only field that does. While you won't get an error if you don't supply values for fields that don't have defined defaults, you may have unexpected results later. In general, I suggest you always explicitly populate any field that doesn't have a default value defined.

The variable m points to a Mongoose `Document` object. This object presents you with an API for manipulating that document, including saving, retrieving, and querying.

Saving Documents to the Store

Saving a document is simply a call to the save() method.

```
m.save();
```

Notice that you don't need to specify the database or collection. Obviously, the database is whatever database to which you're currently connected, and the collection is an intrinsic property of the schema and model definition, so there's no need to specify that either. You don't need to do anything else, although you almost certainly will. More specifically, you'll usually want to include a callback function as the second argument.

```
m.save(function(err, obj) {
if (err) {
// Handle error
} else {
// Do something for a successful save
  }
});
```

The err argument passed in to the anonymous function passed to save() will contain information about the error, and obj will contain the object that was being saved. If err is null, then no error occurred. That's how you can handle both errors and successful saves in the same function.

You can also update an existing document easily. One way to do that is first to retrieve the document, make the appropriate changes, and then call save() again. Mongoose will handle that just fine. An easier way, though, is this:

```
MyModel.findByIdAndUpdate(id, {
fieldA : "new_value", fieldB : "another_new_value"
}, null, function(err, obj) {
// Handle success or failure
});
```

The previous snippet retrieves the document specified by the id variable, applies the values from the object passed as the second argument, and then saves it to the database, calling the callback when the operation completes, whether successfully or not. The null as the third argument is an object that allows you to specify various options, including the following:

- new: When set to true, the modified object is returned to the callback; when false, the original object is returned.

- upsert: When true, the object will be created if it doesn't already exist. (You can do all of your saves in this way if you want, just be sure that you always specify all of the fields that don't have defaults in all situations.)

- select: This specifies which fields of the document to return.

Retrieving Documents from the Store

Every document you save is assigned a unique ID. You don't need to do anything special for this to occur. This is the key of the document, and it is how you fetch a specific document.

```
var d = MyMode.findById("51cdb04dfc78afa718a61cb8");
```

Now you almost certainly would never hard-code an ID like that, since you wouldn't actually know the ID before you save a document, but this is just to illustrate the idea. Incidentally, any time you retrieve a document, you can do this to get the ID.

```
var id = d._id;
```

That _id field is always available to you, even though you don't explicitly include it in the schema or model anywhere. You should also take care never to override this value in your code, or you'll almost certainly cause damage to your stored data (and MongoDB may well refuse to save an object without error if that field has been modified).

That's fine if you know the specific ID you want. However, what if instead you want to retrieve all the documents in a collection? That's easy enough.

```
MyMode.find(null, null, null, function(err, objs) {
// Do something
});
```

The first argument to find() is an object whose attributes are fields in the documents that you want to retrieve and the values you want to match. So, if you only wanted documents where fieldA has a value of abc, you would pass { fieldA : "abc" } as the first argument to find(). Passing null means that there are no match conditions, and you want all objects of this type. The second argument to find() allows you to specify which fields you want returned. So, if you want only fieldA and fieldB in the returned object, pass "fieldA fieldB" as the value instead of null, which causes all fields to be returned. The third argument to find() allows you to specify options for the retrieval. This allows for things like sorting of the results.

The fourth argument to find() is the callback that will be called when the data is retrieved. The objs argument passed to the callback is an array of Document objects that you can do with whatever you need to.

More Mongoose Methods

Many more Mongoose methods are available for manipulating data stored in a MongoDB database. You'll see more of them over the next two chapters, but I highly encourage you to spend some time going through the Mongoose API documentation because there is absolutely more there that isn't covered in this book. The preceding was just meant to give you a brief overview of what's possible and to let you see at least the basics in action as part of My Mobile Organizer.

To be sure, what you'll see in the next two chapters, coupled with what you've already seen in this chapter, is enough to do probably most of what you'll ever need to do with Mongoose. That being said, there's much more it *can* do. By all means, get to know this great tool as much as you can; it will make you a more effective developer!

Summary

In this chapter, you were introduced to the NoSQL concept and MongoDB, a specific implementation of that concept. You learned about the document storage model that MongoDB provides, and you saw how to get the database installed and running. You learned how to interact with that server from the MongoDB shell application, and you saw how to get Mongoose installed in a Node.js application. Finally, you saw some examples of using Mongoose and MongoDB from Node.js code.

In the next chapter, we'll begin to put all of the puzzle pieces together from this and the previous chapter, and we will start to code the server side of My Mobile Organizer. We'll begin by creating the web server, which will handle the REST interactions from the client application before we look at creating a data access object (DAO) to handle the data storage needs of the application.

Chapter 7

Writing the Server with Node.js and MongoDB, Part I

Are you ready to kick this pig? Over the past two chapters, you were introduced to Node.js and MongoDB, and you received the foundation of knowledge that you need to build My Mobile Organizer. Now it's time to do just that!

There's just one more thing you need to know before we get down and dirty with some server-side code, and that's what this REST stuff is all about. I've mentioned it a number of times in the preceding chapters, but now is the time to really look at it and see what all the fuss is about.

Don't worry, though. You've been waiting patiently for some actual code long enough, and this won't take very long. Soon we'll be swimming in code!

The World of REST

Representational State Transfer (REST) is essentially a set of principles that when combined describe how common standards, HTTP specifically, can be used to define a remote system interface in a client-server system. (Although REST in theory can work over other protocols, in practice it is rarely used with anything but HTTP.) REST is a programming and operating system–neutral architecture (a set of best practices really or a pattern even) that allows you to create a web-based API in a de facto, standard way. In fact, the World Wide Web is an implementation of the REST architectural style.

The underlying concept is that of resources. In the REST world, a *resource* is nearly any abstract concept that coherently and meaningfully can be represented in a form that can be transmitted over HTTP. A bank account, a user record, a product description, or a student list for a class described in JSON, XML, or even plain-text document form are all valid examples of resources. This document form represents the state of an object, whether it's the current state (typically when a client retrieves the resources from a server) or an updated state (typically the new version of a resource a client sends to a server for storage). The client initiates a state transition by requesting a representation of a resource from a server or sending a new representation to the server for storage. When this design is used, the API presented to clients is said to be RESTful.

Perhaps the primary benefit of REST is its simplicity and reduction of overhead in nearly every way. Rather than complex XML messages that must be created and parsed on both sides of the conversation, simpler data formats, most notably JSON, are used. These formats are easier to create and consume (though at the cost of less rigidity, which is sometimes a problem in terms of validation).

Three components go into the idea of REST. One is the matter of URLs and how you use them to address a given resource or collection of resources. The other is HTTP methods and their meaning. The third is the data format representation of an addressed resource against which you are performing an action. Let's look at each of these concerns individually.

URLs for Fun and Profit

Simply put, a URL allows you to identify a thing, or set of things, with which you want to interact. In the REST world, a URL identifies a resource or a collection of resources. Of course you know all about URLs, because you use them every day in your browser. You also know about resources, even if you don't realize that you do, because a web page itself is a type of resource.

With REST, your URLs will nearly always refer to nouns. For example, let's say your web site is www.mysite.com. Given that, the URL www.mysite.com/users refers to the collection of users available on your site. The /users portion is the resource in which you're interested. If you were using such a RESTful API, you would expect to get back a list of users and some data about them.

What if instead you want to retrieve information about a specific user with the username billg? The URL in that case might be as follows:

www.mysite.com/users/billg

Note that, unlike the more typical URLs you see associated with web pages, you aren't using query string parameters.

www.mysite.com?user=billg

Instead of something like that, the parts of the URL serve the same purpose. The important thing to note here is that we don't deal with verbs in the URL. In other words, you don't write this:

www.mysite.com/users/add

add is a verb, which makes this a non-RESTful URL. Only nouns go into the URL. The verbs, the action to perform on the specified resource, are determined by the method.

> **Note**   Although I've shown it here, when you see a RESTful API described, you will usually see it shown without the domain name: just /users, /users/billg, or /users/add, for example. The domain name is still necessary, of course, to ensure that the reference to the specific resource is unique across the entire Internet.

Giving Methods Meaning

HTTP methods are the set of values valid in an HTTP method header attribute. When you launch www.google.com in your browser, for example, you are making an HTTP GET request, where GET is the method. If you were to sniff the traffic, as I've done in Figure 7-1, you could see the requests and the GET method associated with them (the initial request is for www.google.com; the subsequent requests are for the resources that page then loads).

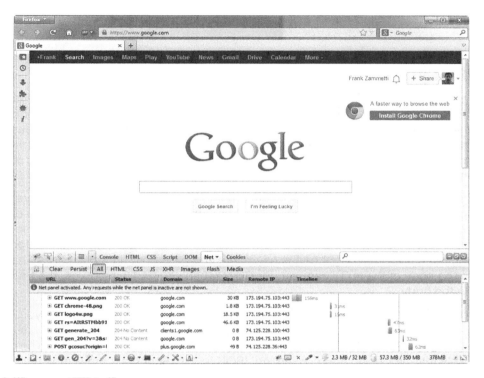

Figure 7-1. Sniffing some HTTP traffic

With a RESTful interface, the most common HTTP methods, namely, GET, POST, PUT, and DELETE, are given specific meanings.

- *GET*: Retrieves a resource (or resources). GET is the only method considered "safe," meaning it doesn't result in a data change on the server.

- *POST*: Creates a new resource (unsafe).

- *PUT*: Updates an existing resource (unsafe).

- *DELETE*: Deletes an existing resource (unsafe).

Now if you go out on the Web and look up *REST*, you may see some different meanings for these methods, specifically for POST and PUT. Sometimes you'll see it stated that PUT is for both create and updates while POST is essentially for multiple updates. Sometimes you'll also see it said that you should use POST for both. Another school of thought is that POST should be for things that don't precisely fit the REST model, like a user login request. Any of these approaches are valid because they still adhere to the underlying REST principle of URLs addressing resources, HTTP methods describing actions, and a representation of the current state of an object.

> **Note** In my experience, using POST for creates and PUT for updates is quite common. It makes sense to me, so I've gone with that approach in My Mobile Organizer. If you see it a different way, though, that's no problem—you're still doing REST, and that's the main point!

Data Format Smackdown

Speaking of current state, the third part of the REST trifecta is that of state and representing that state. When we talk about *state*, we mean either the current state of a given resource or the future state of it. When you make a GET request, assuming that you accept the meanings I specified earlier, you are requesting the current state of the resource. When you POST, PUT, or DELETE the resource, the method refers to what the client is saying the *future* state of the resource should be *after* the operation completes.

When you perform a GET or DELETE, all of the information required to perform the operation is specified as part of the URL and HTTP header. The method is in the header, and the resource is in the URL, whether it refers to a collection of resources (perhaps /users) or a single resource (maybe /users/billg). When you perform a PUT or POST, there will usually be more information to be transmitted. For a user, that might be the username and password. In those cases, the data is transmitted in the body of the HTTP request. Similarly, when you GET a resource, the transmitted state is also in the body.

What form does the data you transmit to the server, or the data the server returns to you, have to be in? The short answer is it can be in any format that can be transmitted via HTTP, and it will still be valid REST. However, JSON is by far the most common state representation format. The reason for this is most likely that producing and consuming JSON in JavaScript in a browser is trivial, and this is what most RESTful APIs are accessed from. JSON is inherently a simple data format that, even if you had to write code to produce it by hand, is extremely easy to deal with. It's simpler than XML, and it doesn't require a unique XML-based language, such as SOAP.

The downside to JSON is that it isn't very rigid with regard to data types and even structure. While there have been attempts to produce something along the lines of XML schemas for JSON, the idea being that you can validate a JSON document against its schema, they haven't met with much success. In part, this is because JSON is extremely flexible, and that flexibility is attractive when coupled with its simplicity.

> **Note** It's not uncommon to see RESTful APIs that allow you to choose your data representation format. Sometimes this is done via a header, while at other times it is done by using a different URL for JSON versus XML or others. Naturally, that adds to the complexity of developing the interface, so you have to weigh the benefits versus the costs.

Whether you use JSON or not, any HTTP request, whether going to or coming from the server, should specify the Content/Type header so that the receiver of the state representation knows how to handle it. Sometimes this handling will be automated, or it will happen without you specifically coding for it because of the library you used to make your remote calls.

There is considerable debate about what the response for the various HTTP methods should be for methods other than GET (which is self-evident). When you DELETE a resource, what should be returned? Some say that the resource deleted should be returned, while others say that some sort of simple indicator that the operation was successful should be displayed. Similarly, when you POST a new resource, do you get back the unique resource identifier that you would use to GET the resource? Alternatively, are you echoed back a copy of the resource you sent in? Perhaps just a simple "OK" identifier would suffice? You'll see the choice that I made in the next chapter, but it's ultimately a question you'll need to answer for yourself because, like the meaning of the HTTP methods, there is no "one-size-fits-all" answer.

The final aspect to think about is that of HTTP response codes. Setting an appropriate response code on the server for your clients is a key component to making the interaction as smooth as possible. Once again, you can come up with some different meanings and still be doing valid REST. There is somewhat less debate, however, on what the meanings of various response codes should be and how they should be used. The following list summarizes probably the most common usages today:

- *200 – OK*: This response code indicates a successful operation. Usually this would be used when you DELETE a resource or PUT changes to a resource.

- *201 – CREATED*: This response code is frequently used for POST creation of a new resource (sometimes 200 is used for this, though).

- *400 – BAD REQUEST*: This response code is usually used to indicate that the data format sent when PUT updating or POST creating a resource was invalid or malformed in some way. 500 is frequently used instead of this.

- *401 – UNAUTHORIZED*: This response code is used to indicate that you need to authenticate before performing the requested operation.

- *405 – METHOD NOT ALLOWED*: This response code is used when the requested HTTP method isn't supported. (For example, perhaps in a read-only interface, you wouldn't support POST or PUT.) 500 is frequently used instead of this.

- *500 – INTERNAL SERVER ERROR*: This response code is generally used when some sort of error occurs that is not covered by the previous scenarios. Some APIs use this in place of 400 and 405 (but less frequently in place of 401).

Code Preliminaries

With the discussion of REST out of the way, we can now get into some code!

The code of our server, which lives in the main.js file (not to be confused with main.js for the client side as they're two different files), contains all of the actual server code. That, in addition to the DAO.js file covered in the next chapter, makes up the entirety of the server side of My Mobile Organizer. In the source bundle, you'll also find a run.bat file that you can use to start the server.

> **Note**   I'm a Windows person, so I didn't include a shell script for all of you *nix folks—I know you're smart
> enough to handle it on your own, so I'm not worried. Just remember to launch MongoDB first, or the server
> won't start properly. Once MongoDB is up and running, simply launch Node.js and pass it `main.js` as a
> command-line argument. From there you should be good to go.

Here Comes the Code: First, A Few Imports

The first bit of code in `main.js` contains some imports of modules that the code needs.

```
var http = require("http");
var DAO = require("./DAO");
```

The `http` module contains all of the code Node.js needs to construct an HTTP server, once we give
it the appropriate kick in the pants and tell it how we want it built. The DAO object is the subject of the
next chapter, but in short, it's where all the code that accesses MongoDB lives. Note the difference
in the requirements, though: `http` is a locally installed module, while DAO is actually `DAO.js` in the
same directory as `main.js`. This is consistent with the previous discussion of module imports and
how you reference them and how Node.js searches for modules.

One Global to Rule Them All

In keeping with the idea of modular code, you generally want to have as few global variables as
possible. While the module system of Node.js means that variables declared in one source file are
local to that source file, they are still global to all the functions and objects in that particular source
file. Even in that context, the idea of "global scope pollution" can come into play, so even in this case
it's a good idea to keep "free-floating variables" to a minimum. That being said, there are clearly times
when that's the right answer. One such case is the `reqID` variable, which is defined next in `main.js`.

```
var reqID = 1;
```

The `reqID` variable is used for logging purposes. Each request that comes in will have one or more
log messages in the console window (meaning the terminal window on a Unix, Linux, or Mac system,
or the command prompt window on a Windows machine from which you launch Node.js) associated
with it, but because of the asynchronous nature of Node.js, the log messages could be mixed. For
example, if you have multiple Ajax requests come in at the same time, a situation that you'll recall
does occur when the app starts up when the initial data retrieval is done, then the log messages
can get all mixed up because their order isn't deterministic. Moreover, the calls to MongoDB are
asynchronous, so even if there was only one Ajax request at a time, you still might have a situation
where the log messages look all out of whack.

To help combat this, every log message will have a unique ID prepended to it so that even if
the messages appear out of order in the console, you can still tie together which messages are
associated with which requests. It's not a perfect system, but it's better than you'd have without
it. Since `reqID` will be needed in a number of functions throughout this module (yes, `main.js` *is* a
module as far as Node.js is concerned), it makes sense to make it global to the module.

Kicking It Off

With our imports and lone global variable out of the way, the code can now begin. However, in the interest of making it easier to explain, the first chunk of code we'll look at is actually the *last* piece of code you find in main.js. From a logical standpoint, it makes sense to look at this first, even though it has to come after all of the other code in order to avoid forward reference problems.

```
var server = http.createServer(serverCore);
server.listen("80", "127.0.0.1");
console.log("\nApp available at http://127.0.0.1:80\n");
```

I've said many times how simple Node.js makes things, but isn't it still a little shocking? I know it is to me! Two lines of code is all that it takes: http.createServer() is the main one, using that imported http module to create a web server. A reference to a function, serverCore(), is passed to it, and this is what we'll be focusing on in the next section. Once that's done, we tell the server to listen on port 80 and use the local loopback address (either or both of which you can change, of course, as appropriate for your machine), and the server is started. A log statement reminds us how to access the server, and that's that!

> **Note** I looked for a good, clean way to determine the port and IP used automatically so that the log statement wouldn't have to be changed when the values in the call to listen() changed. It appears that to do it in a way that will work on both Windows and *nix is tricky, so I didn't bother. If you want to e-mail me a simple solution, though, I'll name my dog's next puppy after you!

Core Server Processing, Part I

The callback function the server will use, serverCore(), is where the main work of handling requests is done. Well, to be precise, it's where *half* of that work is done, as you'll see.

```
function serverCore(req, resp) {

  try {
```

This is a typical callback that is fed to the http.createServer() method and that accepts a request and a response object as arguments, abbreviated to req and resp to save my fingers a little typing. Everything done here is wrapped in a try...catch block so that the server doesn't go down if failures occur.

```
reqID = reqID + 1;
```

For every request that comes in, reqID gets incremented. This way, every request is guaranteed to have a unique ID associated with it. The ID shown in the console is actually a combination of the time the request hits this function and reqID, because just the time alone wouldn't be sufficient to guarantee uniqueness. While it's highly unlikely that there would be two requests handled at the same time as expressed in milliseconds, it can't be entirely ruled out. However, when reqID is appended to the time, it ensures it.

```
var dataObj = {
  id : new Date().getTime() + reqID, req : req, resp : resp,
  data : null, ident : null
};
```

Next we declare a variable `dataObj` that contains a number of fields. This object will be passed around between any methods that need information about the request being serviced. This is just a convenience so that the code deals only with a single object throughout. The `id` field is of course the unique ID of the request as mentioned, constructed from the combination of the current time and `reqID`. The `req` and `resp` fields are simply the request and response objects passed in to `serverCore()`. The `data` field is an object that is constructed from the body of the incoming response. This will be the state representation of one of our four entity types (appointment, contact, note, or task) from the client. Finally, `ident` is an identifier that tells us what type of entity is being dealt with. This is taken from the URL, so for `/contact`, for example, the value of `ident` will simply be `contact` (once we do some further work in this function, that is).

```
console.log(dataObj.id + ": " + req.method + " " + req.url);
```

An initial logging statement is next, which records the HTTP method and requested URL in its entirety. This is useful information when debugging, for sure, so you can see whether what was requested matches what you expect from the client.

A Special Case: OPTIONS

Continuing with `serverCore()`, we hit some logic next that handles one particular "special" case.

```
if (req.method == "OPTIONS") {
  resp.writeHead(
    200, {
      "Content-Type" : "text/plain",
      "Access-Control-Allow-Origin" : "*",
      "Access-Control-Allow-Methods" : "GET,POST,PUT,DELETE,OPTIONS",
      "Access-Control-Max-Age" : "1000",
      "Access-Control-Allow-Headers" :
        "origin,x-csrftoken,content-type,accept"
    }
  );
  resp.end("");
  return;
}
```

OPTIONS is another HTTP method that isn't used all that often but that is used when running this application on a desktop machine using Firefox. If the client portion of My Mobile Organizer is run in Firefox, then it actually sends an OPTIONS request before a PUT or POST. This has to do with the same-origin policy that cross-domain Ajax requests are and aren't allowed to make. In short, Firefox (and why it's the only browser that does this I'm not sure) sends OPTIONS first, essentially, to see whether it's allowed to make the request. The server needs to respond with the `Access-Control-Allow-Origin:*` header, which triggers Firefox sending the originally desired

POST or PUT. In addition, I've found that the other headers you see here need to be set for things to work in all cases. They further define what methods are allowed cross-origin, the headers that are allowed, and the maximum number of seconds the response to this preflight request can be cached without sending another preflight request.

The bottom line is that if the method of the request is OPTIONS, which is determined easily by checking the `method` attribute of the `req` object, we immediately want to cut this request short and return an empty response with all of the appropriate headers set. The method `resp.writeHead()` allows us to pass an object where each attribute is the name of a header, along with its value. Then a call to `resp.end("")`; concludes the response, and we return from `serverCore()` right then and there, knowing a POST or PUT is coming our way shortly.

None of this is too complicated, but it covers one particular situation that needs to be dealt with if you want to have an easy time developing an application like this on a desktop using Firefox, as I do.

Handling GET and DELETE Requests

Having dealt with that one special case, we can get to the business of handling the usual cases, beginning with GET, PUT, and DELETE requests, as the server must do in order to be a proper REST service provider as per the discussion in the opening section of this chapter.

```
if (req.method != "POST") {
  dataObj.ident = req.url.substr(req.url.lastIndexOf("/") + 1);
}
```

When the method isn't POST, we need to determine the ID of the resource that's being manipulated. Remember, this doesn't matter for POST because in that case we're adding a new entity, a new resource in REST parlance, and that ID will be generated as a side effect of the item being added to the database later in the DAO code. Therefore, we look for the last / in the URL and take everything to the right of it. That's the ID we want.

At this point, though, we might not actually have an ID because the request could be to get an entire collection, meaning that the request might have been /user and not /user/12345, for example. The IDs are all 24-digit hexadecimal values, so we need to validate whatever we have here, if it's not `null`.

```
if (dataObj.ident != null) {
  dataObj.ident = dataObj.ident.match(/^[a-f0-9]{24}$/i);
}
```

If it *is* `null`, then the request was for a collection and the validation doesn't need to be performed. A little bit of regex magic easily validates the value. The result of this is that the value of `dataObj.ident` is now guaranteed to be either `null` or a valid ID value in all cases. Well, not *all* cases technically: if the request was malformed in some way, then we might not have a valid ID, but that's actually OK because the requested resource simply will not be found later, and no error will occur, which is the key point.

The next step applies only if the request type is GET or DELETE.

```
if (req.method == "GET" || req.method == "DELETE") {

  serverCorePart2(dataObj);
```

For these two methods, we have everything we need, which is just the ID of the entity. So, serverCorePart2() is called, passing along the dataObj. This will continue processing the request. The code there is common to all request types, but there's still some work to do for POST and PUT, and that's why the core serving processing is broken up between these two functions.

Handling POST and PUT Requests

For POST and PUT, we have to get the body content before continuing.

```
} else if (req.method == "POST" || req.method == "PUT") {

  var body = "";
  req.on("data", function (inData) {
    body += inData;
  });
```

Getting the body content is an asynchronous operation, like most I/O operations in Node.js land, so we have a callback situation to deal with. An event handler for the data event is hooked to the request object using its on() method, and the body variable is built up as the content streams in.

Next we have to do something when all of the body content is received, and the end event is perfect for that.

```
req.on("end", function() {
  if (body == null) {
    body = "";
  }
  dataObj.data = JSON.parse(body);
  serverCorePart2(dataObj);
});
```

A quick check is done to ensure that the variable body isn't null, since that would cause an error in the next line, which is to parse the body variable and produce an object from the assumed JSON string that's in it now using the common JSON.parse() function. That object is stored in dataObj.data, and then that same serverCorePart2() function is called, passing dataObj along to it.

So, whether the request method was POST, PUT, DELETE, or GET, we'll wind up in serverCorePart2(). The only difference is that for POST and PUT, dataObj.data will have an object constructed from the JSON data passed in with the request. Before we can look at that function, though, there's a little more work to be done here in serverCore(), namely, dealing with errors and exceptions.

Handling Unknown Methods and Exceptions

If an HTTP method, other than the four for which the code is explicitly designed to address (plus OPTIONS as the "special" fifth method) is received, we reject the request.

```
} else {

  console.log(dataObj.id + ": Unsupported method: " + req.method);
  completeResponse(
    dataObj, 405, "text", "Unsupported method: " + req.method
  );

}
```

The `completeResponse()` function that we'll see shortly is called to, well, *complete* any response. In this case, we'll be returning an HTTP 405 status, METHOD NOT ALLOWED, so the caller has a clue about why their request wasn't fulfilled. A little bit of logging is done too so that we can see what method was requested in order to keep those damned, dirty hacker hands off of us.[1]

Finally, we have to deal with the unexpected: exceptions.

```
} catch (e) {
  console.log(dataObj.id + ": Exception processing request (part 1): " + e);
  completeResponse(dataObj, 500, "text", "Exception: " + e);
}

};
```

Some simple logging and a call to `completeResponse()` are all it takes, returning an HTTP 500 response code. The exception will be returned to the client, which may or may not be what you want a REST API to do. That's entirely a design decision, which is up to you. As a learning exercise, it's easier to see the exception information in the browser, if nothing else, rather than having to track it down in the console log messages.

Core Server Processing, Part II

The second half of the server core processing code is rather simple, and it begins much like the first half in `serverCore()` did.

```
function serverCorePart2(dataObj) {

  try {
```

Once again, we'll wrap everything in `try...catch` to avoid the server going down if problems occur, but this time note that `dataObj` is the only argument passed in. The `serverCore()` function is a callback that Node.js's `http` module uses, while `serverCorePart2()` is something I dreamed up, so the method signature was up to me too.

Next we'll do some quick logging for debug purposes.

```
console.log(dataObj.id + ": ident: " + dataObj.ident);
console.log(dataObj.id + ": data: " + JSON.stringify(dataObj.data));
```

---

[1]Yep, that was a forced *Planet of the Apes* reference! Or a *Big Bang Theory* reference for you kids who don't know Charlton Heston but do know Howard Wolowitz and remember the "The Spaghetti Catalyst" episode.

The parsed body object hasn't been logged before, so it's important to do so now. The dataObj.ident was sort of logged previously by virtue of logging the URL, but that was just incidentally, and this is the first chance to ensure that the parsing code didn't mess up in serverCore(), since it wasn't logged back there, so it's good to log here too.

Next we have a big honkin' if block.

```
var opType = "";
if (dataObj.req.url.toLowerCase().indexOf("/appointment") != -1) {
  opType = "appointment";
} else if (dataObj.req.url.toLowerCase().indexOf("/contact") != -1) {
  opType = "contact";
} else if (dataObj.req.url.toLowerCase().indexOf("/note") != -1) {
  opType = "note";
} else if (dataObj.req.url.toLowerCase().indexOf("/task") != -1) {
  opType = "task";
} else if (dataObj.req.url.toLowerCase().indexOf("/clear") != -1) {
  opType = "clear";
```

The purpose of this logic is to make the code after this generic. As you'll see, that code will call methods on the DAO object dynamically. To do that, though, we need to know the entity type that is being dealt with so that those methods know what entity type they are dealing with. However, it's not just entity types that are possible here: the UI also has that pesky Clear All button, and we need to code for that as well.

Of course, if we don't recognize the requested operation, we'll abort with a 403 response code.

```
} else {
  console.log(dataObj.id + ": Unsupported operation: " + dataObj.req.url);
  completeResponse(
    dataObj, 403, "text", "Unsupported operation: " + dataObj.req.url
  );
  return;
}
```

Assuming that the execution gets past that if block, then it's time for that dynamic DAO call code I mentioned.

```
if (opType == "clear") {
  DAO.CLEAR_DATA(dataObj);
} else if (dataObj.ident == null && dataObj.req.method == "GET") {
  DAO.GET_ALL(opType, dataObj);
} else {
  DAO[dataObj.req.method](opType, dataObj);
}
```

In the case of the opType clear, it's not really dynamic at all; the CLEAR_DATA() method is explicitly called.

For GET requests where no ident value is present, that corresponds to getting an entire collection, all contacts, for example. In that case, again it's not really dynamic: the GET_ALL() method is called, passing in the opType, which remember in this case will be one of our four entity types.

Finally, when an ident is given, that's where it gets dynamic; the HTTP method is used to determine the DAO method to call. Yes, there are literally methods named GET(), PUT(), POST(), and DELETE() in the DAO. Once again, opType and dataObj are passed to them so that they can do their work. Note that there aren't separate get_contacts() versus get_notes() methods; there's just a single GET() method. That's where opType comes into play; it's what tells those methods what type of entity to deal with.

As in serverCore(), the final step is to deal with any exceptions that might occur.

```
} catch (e) {
  console.log(dataObj.id + ": Exception processing request (part 2): " + e);
  completeResponse(dataObj, 500, "text", "Exception: " + e);
}
```

An HTTP 500 response code is again sent, along with some exception information. It's probably not going to help the user any, but it's helpful for developers.

> **Tip**   If I haven't said this before, I'll say again it now: returning "naked" exception information to a UI is bad UX. Don't do it—under pain of death! Make those errors that are seen by the user very friendly. (It's OK to have a "Click here for details" button that leads to technical details, though, which I recommend.)

Completing Responses

The final function to look at in main.js is the completeResponse() function that you've seen called a number of times.

```
completeResponse = function(dataObj, statusCode, contentType, content) {

  var ct = "text/plain";
  if (contentType == "json") {
    ct = "application/json";
  }
  dataObj.resp.writeHead(
    statusCode, { "Content-Type" : ct, "Access-Control-Allow-Origin" : "*" }
  );
  dataObj.resp.end(content);

}
```

It accepts a couple of arguments.

- dataObj: That's our friendly neighborhood dataObj, which is used to pass around everything needed to process a given request and that contains all of our request information. Most significantly, in this case, that means the response object.

- statusCode: This is the HTTP response status code.

- contentType: The value of this is assumed to be either text or json. If text, nothing really happens because the default value text/plain will be used. But it makes the rest of the code clearer to see text passed in. However, in the case of json, the default is overridden with the more appropriate application/json header value.

- content: This, of course, is the actual content to return to the client.

Once the content type is determined, we have some headers to write, using the `resp.writeHeader()` method. Only two are necessary now, though: the `Content-Type` header and the `Access-Control-Allow-Origin` header discussed earlier. This ensures that cross-domain Ajax continues to work as we expect.

Finally, the response is completed with a call to `resp.end()` and the content written out.

Mocking Testing from the Command Line

The last thing I'll discuss before we wrap up this chapter is the notion of testing. One of the benefits of a RESTful interface is that it's rather easy to test. There are thousands of tools from which you can choose, ranging from the extremely simple to the very sophisticated. Some are free, and some cost money, but all will do the job.

In keeping with the theme of simplicity provided by this stack that we've been exploring, I'm going to suggest one of the most basic ways to do at least some basic level of testing: the ubiquitous cURL command-line tool.

cURL is a program, available on virtually all operating systems, that allows you to make HTTP/HTTPS requests with just a simple command-line interface. Technically, cURL is a project that is comprised of a library, which other programs can use, and the command-line tool. The distinction doesn't really matter for our purposes here, because our interest is in the command-line tool. Most importantly, the tool makes it easy to script semi-automated tests.

The source package for this book includes the Windows version of cURL (`curl.exe`), and on most *nix systems, the tool either is already present (this is true on a Mac, for example) or is easily fetched via apt-get. Note that the actual executable will almost certainly be called `curl`, not `cURL`, as *nix systems are case-sensitive. This is the case on a Mac, for example.

Once you have cURL available, you can begin making arbitrary HTTP requests to any URL you like. For example, let's grab the simple page at my site, `zammetti.com`. Figure 7-2 shows what this interaction looks like.

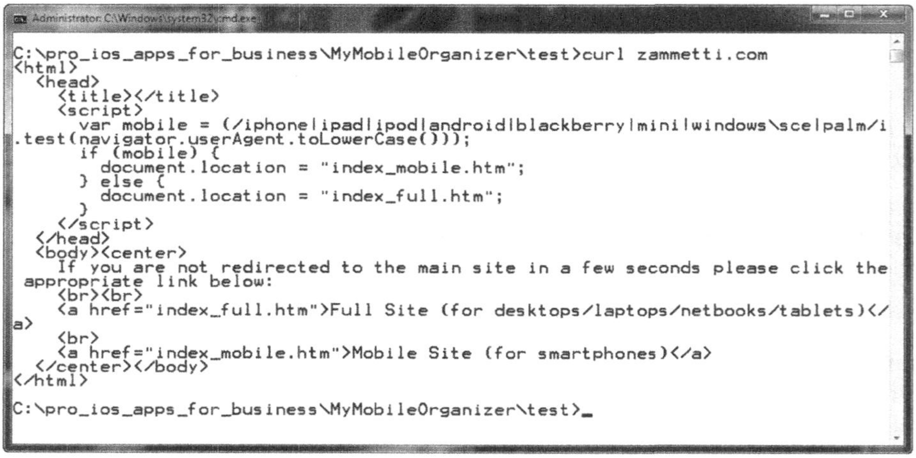

Figure 7-2. The `zammetti.com` page retrieved via the default GET operation of cURL

As you can see, the HTML document at that location is fetched by cURL when executing in its simplest form, meaning when you pass no command-line arguments. cURL does a basic GET request of the specified URL and dumps the response to the console and nothing more.

Of course, cURL provides a *ton* of command-line options, which allow you to do all sorts of things, such as most importantly for us, submit data. This isn't meant to be a tutorial on the intricacies of cURL, but there are just a handful of options that you need in order to use cURL as a rudimentary test tool. These options are as follows:

-#: This isn't actually necessary, but it's nice. It adds some progress information as the requested operation is performed.

-v: This displays verbose fetching information. Figure 7-3 shows this information.

Figure 7-3. Verbose logging of the GET of zammetti.com

-X: This allows you to specify the HTTP method to use for the request.

-H: This allows you to specify headers to be sent along with the request.

-d: This allows you to send data in the body of the request. Usually, you specify a file name as the value of this argument.

With these simple options, I build the `test.bat` file (included in the source package, of course), which allows you to run a test of all operations for a given entity. It provides a simple interface whereby you simply execute the following:

```
test XXX
```

Here, XXX is one of the four entity types (appointment, contact, note, or task). The script will then execute eight total test operations in turn.

1. Two POST requests to test entity creation

2. A GET request using the ID of the last created item to test the retrieval of a specific item

3. Another GET request without an ID to test getting all of the entities in the collection

4. A PUT request to test updating an item

5. Another GET to ensure that the update was successful

6. A DELETE to test item removal

7. A final GET to ensure that the item was removed

Even if you aren't a DOS batch file guru, I don't think you'll have much trouble understanding what's going on in this code. You can judge for yourself, though, by looking at Listing 7-1.

Listing 7-1. A Simple DOS Batch File Acting as a Rudimentary RESTful API Test Script

```
@echo off
cls

IF "%1" == "" GOTO BLANK

del response.txt

echo ------------------------------------------------------------------------
echo Testing %1 create (POST)...
echo ------------------------------------------------------------------------
curl -# -v -X POST http://127.0.0.1:80/%1 -H "Content-Type:application/json" -d @%1_create.json -o
response.txt
curl -# -v -X POST http://127.0.0.1:80/%1 -H "Content-Type:application/json" -d @%1_create.json -o
response.txt

SET /p ident= < response.txt

echo.
echo.
echo ------------------------------------------------------------------------
echo Testing %1 read (GET)...
echo ------------------------------------------------------------------------
curl -# -v -X GET http://127.0.0.1:80/%1/%ident%
```

```
echo.
echo.
echo -------------------------------------------------------------------------
echo Testing %1 get all...
echo -------------------------------------------------------------------------
curl -# -v -X GET http://127.0.0.1:80/%1

echo.
echo.
echo -------------------------------------------------------------------------
echo Testing %1 update (PUT)...
echo -------------------------------------------------------------------------
curl -# -v -X PUT http://127.0.0.1:80/%1/%ident% -H "Content-Type:application/json" -d
@%1_update.json
curl -# -v -X GET http://127.0.0.1:80/%1/%ident%

echo.
echo.
echo -------------------------------------------------------------------------
echo Testing %1 delete (DELETE)...
echo -------------------------------------------------------------------------
curl -# -v -X DELETE http://127.0.0.1:80/%1/%ident%
curl -# -v -X GET http://127.0.0.1:80/%1/%ident%

GOTO DONE

:BLANK
echo Must specify appointment, contact, note or task

:DONE
```

The %1 token is replaced by whatever argument is on the command line, which is expected to be one of the four entity types. That's how this single script can be used for any entity type without any sort of branching logic involved. The response.txt file is created by each of the first two POST requests and the value written to it (the second simply overwrites the first), which is the response from the server, namely, the ID of the item created. (You will see the code that does this in the next chapter.) This value, which will always be for the second item created, is then retrieved into the variable ident and used for the other operations that act on a specific entity. Again, this is all to ensure that the script is generic and that it works for all entity types and without any user interaction beyond launching it.

The outcome of running this script is shown in Figure 7-4, Figure 7-5, and Figure 7-6. These three figures represent a single execution of the script for the note entity. However, the resulting output was too big to fit into one screenshot, so look at all three of them in order, and you'll have the complete picture of what happened during that run.

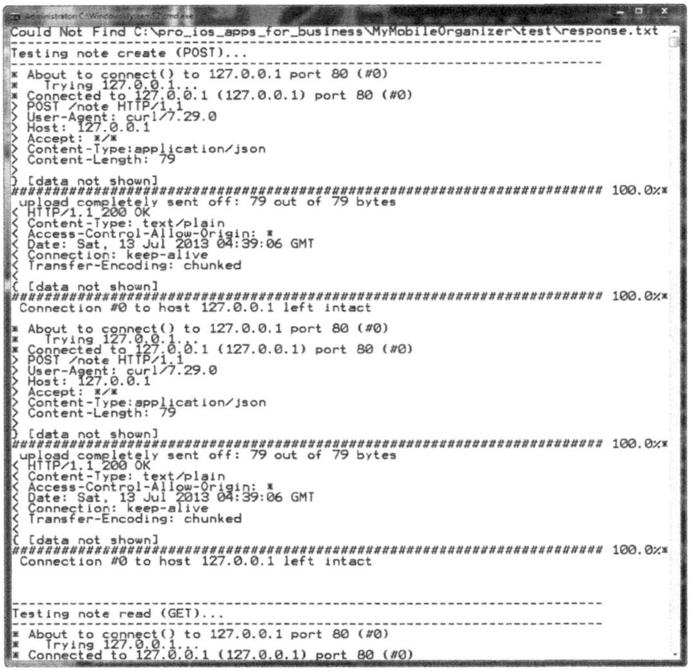

Figure 7-4. Test script run, part 1

Figure 7-5. Test script run, part 2

Figure 7-6. *Test script run, part 3*

There is no automated verification of each step because that's a much more involved task to implement. (That's where a more capable, "proper" test tool might come into play.) However, the output is certainly good enough for a manual review and to make sure everything looks good. In this case, it does, proving that, at a fundamental level, the API for working with notes is functioning as expected, all without involving the real client app.

It's a simple but effective way to test a RESTful API, especially one built on Node.js. It's simple to get such an API up and running, as you saw in this chapter, and testing it can be just as easy!

Summary

In this chapter, you built, well, an actual server! Using Node.js, you constructed a program that presents a RESTful API for the mobile side of My Mobile Organizer. You learned how to deal with POST data as well as GET, DELETE, and PUT requests. You saw how to construct your Node.js code in a logical manner, which allows for easy extensibility later. You also saw that it doesn't take much code to accomplish our goals with this technology stack at your disposal.

You also observed how to use a common command-line tool to test the API without having to worry about writing the client-side code to call it. This allows for semi-automated testing after you make changes to confirm that you didn't break anything.

In the next chapter, we'll complete the server code by constructing the DAO code that talks to our MongoDB database. Once that's done, My Mobile Organizer is done!

Chapter 8

Writing the Server with Node.js and MongoDB, Part II

Building the server in Chapter 7 wasn't too difficult, I'm sure you'll agree, but it's only half of the equation. Responding to requests properly is fine, but it doesn't help us actually work with data—as you'll recall, there was no code in the previous chapter that dealt with that.

In this chapter, we'll look at the code that takes care of working with data and acts as a service that the server code in main.js uses, namely, the code in the DAO.js file. This will be a relatively small chapter because the amount of code to look at is not that great, but that's a consequence of using Node.js and Mongoose, and, at the end of the day, it is a Very Good Thing.

A Data Access Object for All Seasons

The concept of a data access object (DAO) is to abstract away from your main application code the code that accesses your persistent data store. The purpose of this is to allow you to swap out persistent stores and have to touch the smallest amount of code possible. It also helps separate your concerns a bit: you can focus on creating a solid data access API separate from your application code, much as you create a server-side API for your mobile client code to use. Reducing coupling between these layers is a key component of keeping your design flexible and tolerant of changes. It's also just a good, clean way to organize your code in most developers' opinions, mine included.

In this case, we have the DAO.js file that houses all of the code that works with MongoDB. This module presents the data access API the client code uses. The DAO.js file starts like so:

```
var mongoose = require("mongoose");
```

The mongoose module is what we'll use to access MongoDB, as discussed in Chapter 6, so the first thing to do is to import that module. The next step is to define the schemas that will be stored in the database. To keep the code clean, I've placed all four of the schemas that will be created, one for each entity type, into an object aptly named schemas. The first part of this defines the appointment schema.

```
var schemas = {
  appointment : mongoose.Schema({
    category : "string", title : "string", description : "string",
    location : "string", date : "date", allDay : "boolean",
    startTimeHour : "number", startTimeMinute : "number",
    startTimeMeridiem : "string", endTimeHour : "number",
    endTimeMinute : "number", endTimeMeridiem : "string"
  }),
```

In this way, the code can access schemas.appointment, which makes it more self-documenting and helps minimize any possibility of name conflicts. All of the fields for an appointment are present, of course, defined with their types, as described in Chapter 6.

Next a schema for contacts is added.

```
  contact : mongoose.Schema({
    category : "string", firstName : "string", lastName : "string",
    address1 : "string", address1Type : "string",
    address2 : "string", address2Type : "string",
    phone1 : "string", phone1Type : "string",
    phone2 : "string", phone2Type : "string",
    eMail : "string"
  }),
```

> **Note**   Keep in mind that what's being described here is one big object: schemas. I've simply broken out
> each schema definition inside that object's definition to make it a littler clearer as you read through it.

The schema for notes is next, and it's the smallest of the bunch. (Ideally that doesn't doom it to a life of therapy!)

```
  note : mongoose.Schema({
    category : "string", title : "string", text : "string"
  }),
```

Last, but not least, the task schema is defined.

```
  task : mongoose.Schema({
    category : "string", title : "string", text : "string",
    completed : "boolean", priority : "number", dueDate : "date"
  })
};
```

With the schemas defined, we can go ahead and define the models based on them. As with the schemas object, I've created one object, models, to hold all of the models, so again, models.appointment can be written any time the code needs to access the model for appointments.

```
var models = {
  appointment : mongoose.model("appointment", schemas.appointment),
  contact : mongoose.model("contact", schemas.contact),
  note : mongoose.model("note", schemas.note),
  task : mongoose.model("task", schemas.task)
}
```

Once the models are defined, the next step is connecting to the database.

```
mongoose.connect("localhost", "MyMobileOrganizer");
```

The code assumes that the MongoDB instance that the app will use is running on the same machine as the server. Of course, you can change this to an IP address or hostname if you want to run it somewhere else. The database name that the app uses is specified as MyMobileOrganizer, and recall that MongoDB will create that database the first time it's used, so there's no initialization tasks that we need to accomplish and no SQL creation scripts or anything like that to run before this code executes.

However, it's important to realize that, in the case where MongoDB is not running at the time that the mongoose.connect() command executes, then the server will die upon start-up. The reason for this is because that line of code is not in a function. This means it will execute immediately upon DAO.js being imported in main.js. This is true because the interpreter underlying Node.js always evaluates such module-level code immediately any time a module is loaded. That seems like a fair design to me, since if the server isn't up, there's not a heck of a lot it will be able to do anyway, so there's no point in it continuing to run at that point. The run.bat file takes care of running MongoDB before launching the server, although you can do the steps manually if you prefer.

Object Creation: POST Requests

A *POST request* corresponds to a request from the client to create a new entity. When such a request hits the server, the server code in main.js parses the incoming request, creates an object from the JSON found in the request body, and then calls the DAO's POST() function to fulfill the request. Without entities being created, it wouldn't make much sense to talk about updates, deletes, or retrievals, so let's look at this POST() function first.

ON PROPER LAYER SEPARATION

In one way, this is actually a terrible DAO design from an architectural standpoint because there is some leakage of the HTTP layer into the DAO by virtue of the method names here matching HTTP methods. The DAO is a separate architectural layer from the HTTP server layer housed in main.js, and as such, the DAO shouldn't really know anything about the HTTP layer. In fact, it should be callable from a non-HTTP client if you wanted to as well. While it actually can be that, the fact that the methods of the DAO are named after HTTP methods represents a bit of "uncleanliness" in terms of the design.

If you're an architectural purist, this hurts your brain a bit—it hurts mine a bit to be sure! However, it's one of those cases where designing for perfection stands in opposition to designing for simplicity. It is, in my mind anyway, simpler to have the methods named this way because it makes the code in main.js more generic. Do you remember that dynamic method call structure that uses the HTTP method to determine the DAO method to call? That little bit of reduced coding is, to me, worth a little bit of architectural "ugliness."

It's a fine line but one that every developer has to walk, trying to find the right balance. I think if you start from a place of designing for perfection and then back off from that when necessary (or reasonable anyway), then you'll wind up with a solid design. Any warts that may exist, which these method names arguably are, will not only be on purpose but won't be anything too major, nine times out of ten, and they will just be something that you can debate with other developers over a tall, cold one![1]

```
function POST(opType, dataObj) {

  console.log(dataObj.id + ": DAO.POST() - CREATE : " + opType);

  var obj = new models[opType](dataObj.data);
  console.log(dataObj.id + ": obj: " + JSON.stringify(obj));
  obj.save(function (inError, inObj) {
    if (inError) {
      throw "Error: " + JSON.stringify(inError);
    } else {
      console.log(dataObj.id + ": Success: " + inObj._id);
      completeResponse(dataObj, 200, "text", "" + inObj._id);
    }
  });

}
```

All of the DAO functions, save for the CLEAR_DATA() function, have the same signature. They receive an opType that tells them what entity is being dealt with, and they receive dataObj, which is the dataObj you saw in main.js containing the request and response objects, which were created by parsing the POST body (when applicable) and ident of the entity to deal with (again, when applicable). Notice first that there is no branching logic based on opType. Everything is done in a dynamic fashion, such as accessing the appropriate model object using bracket notation, so that the code that executes is the same for all entity types. This keeps the function short and sweet, and it allows for easily adding new entity types later if you want without having to modify the DAO code at all.

When doing a creation, the first step is to create an object using the appropriate database model object for the opType specified. That's what the first line does. The dataObj.data object is what the client passed in, and the data from it is transferred into the object created from the model. Once we have that object, we log it for debugging purposes.

Next, the save() method is called on that object. The save() method is provided by Mongoose by virtue of creating an object from a model. Doing this gives us all of the database methods we'll need in all of these DAO functions.

The save() method requires a callback function to call when the operation completes. Well, it doesn't require it *per se*, but you'll rarely call it without one. Here certainly, we need one. An error object is passed to the callback, if an error occurred, as well as the entity object that was created. The callback first checks whether an error occurred. If so, it is thrown as an exception, which will be caught in the main server code, and an error is returned to the client. If no error occurred,

---

[1]That's not an endorsement for alcohol necessarily! I in fact don't drink myself, so "a tall, cold one" to me is just a big bottle of Pepsi Max. Whatever works for you, I say.

then we need to fashion a proper response to the client. The completeResponse() function takes care of most of the details of that, as you already saw in the previous chapter. The code here just has to pass dataObj so that completeResponse() can do its work; plus, the HTTP response code to be set is passed (200 to indicate a good outcome here). The call to completeResponse() also passes the type of response (either text or json as discussed in the previous chapter) and the text of the reply, which is the ID of the newly created item in this case. Note that the _id field of the object is numeric, but we need to supply a string value, so adding an empty string to _id performs an implicit cast and ensures that everything works as expected in completeResponse().

It's a small function to be sure, but that's the point of Mongoose; such powerful code is almost trivial to write!

Object Retrieval: GET Requests

With the ability to create entity objects out of the way, being able to retrieve them is the next logical operation to implement. There are, in fact, two versions of the retrieval function that need to be implemented. We'll start with GET(), which retrieves a single entity by ID.

```
function GET(opType, dataObj) {

  console.log(dataObj.id + ": DAO.GET() READ : " + opType);

  models[opType].findById(dataObj.ident,
    function (inError, inObj) {
      if (inError) {
        throw "Error: " + JSON.stringify(inError);
      } else {
        if (inObj == null) {
          console.log(dataObj.id + ": Object not found");
          completeResponse(dataObj, 404, "json", "");
        } else {
          console.log(dataObj.id + ": Success: " + JSON.stringify(inObj));
          completeResponse(dataObj, 200, "json", JSON.stringify(inObj));
        }
      }
    }
  );

}
```

It's another small function that begins by calling the findById() method of the appropriate model object, once again done via bracket notation based on the value of opType. The dataObj.ident field provides the unique ID the caller is requesting. As with save() in the POST() function, the findById() method takes as its argument a callback function, and this callback function, as with the one for POST(), is passed an error object and the entity object that was retrieved.

Therefore, the first step is again to see whether an error occurred and, if one has, to throw an exception. JSON.stringify() gives us a plain-text version of the error object to pass back ultimately to the client.

If no error occurred, though, the first else block is entered. Here there's some logic to perform: if the object is null, then fairly obviously, I think, this means that the requested entity wasn't found. Note that this is a different case than an error: not finding the object is *not* considered an error condition. But, we do still have to handle it specially, which in this case means calling completeResponse() and telling it to return an HTTP 404 response code. That response code is the ubiquitous NOT FOUND response, so it makes perfect sense in this case. An empty string is the actual content of the response that will be returned, so the client will need to check for this response code if it wants to handle this case, not examine the response text. The way the client portion of My Mobile Organizer is written, though, means that not finding an entity can never really happen, so this branch is not necessary technically. However, it's a logical branch and allows for easier extension of the app down the road, so it's worth doing.

If the object is found, the final else branch is triggered, and there, aside from some simple logging, the only task left is to let completeResponse() finish things. Once again, JSON.stringify() is used to generate a JSON version of the object returned. This JSON string is the response body that the client will parse and work with.

Object Retrieval Redux: Get All Requests

The other retrieval operation that needs to be available in the DAO's API is the ability to get all objects of a given entity type from the database, since that's something the client app does when it starts. The GET_ALL() function supplies this capability.

```
function GET_ALL(opType, dataObj) {

  console.log(dataObj.id + ": DAO.POST(): " + opType);

  var opts = { sort : { } };
  switch (opType) {
    case "contact":
      opts.sort.lastName = 1;
    break;
    case "appointment": case "note": case "task":
      opts.sort.title = 1;
    break;
  }

  models[opType].find(null, null, opts, function (inError, inObjs) {
    if (inError) {
      throw "Error: " + JSON.stringify(inError);
    } else {
      console.log(dataObj.id + ": Success: " + JSON.stringify(inObjs));
      completeResponse(dataObj, 200, "json", JSON.stringify(inObjs));
    }
  });

}
```

First, some options are set up that will be passed to the find() method, as discussed previously in Chapter 6, which is responsible for the retrieval. Here the options are set up to sort the results. In fact, this isn't necessary. More precisely, this sort order will be rendered invalid once the items are stored to localStorage on the client because storage and retrieval in localStorage are nondeterministic with regard to ordering. However, I thought this is something you'd want to see how to do since it's so common, so there you have it! An object with a sort attribute is created, and then the sort attribute has an attribute added to it named after the field of the object to sort by. The value of that inner attribute is set to 1 to indicate to Mongoose that we want the results sorted by that field. For the appointment, note, and task entities, the title field is the sort field; for contacts, it is lastName instead.

Once that object is ready, the call to find() is made. The first argument to find() allows you to specify conditions that must be met, in essence, the search criteria. Here that's not needed, so null is passed. The second argument allows you to specify which fields you want returned in the objects, and again, null is passed to indicate that we want them all. The third option is for specifying options, including the previously determined sort order. The final argument is a callback, just like all of the model object methods we've seen previously.

Once again, a quick check for an error is done, and an exception is thrown if found. Otherwise, completeResponse() is used to return the returns, which at this point would be an array. Thus, JSON.stringify() once again converts that object to a JSON string representation for the client to use.

Object Updates: PUT Requests

With creates and retrievals out of the way, it's time to move on to updates. The PUT() function is where that functionality is implemented.

```
function PUT(opType, dataObj) {

  console.log(dataObj.id + ": DAO.PUT() UPDATE : " + opType);

  models[opType].findByIdAndUpdate(dataObj.ident, dataObj.data, { },
    function (inError, inObj) {
      if (inError) {
        throw "Error: " + JSON.stringify(inError);
      } else {
        console.log(dataObj.id + ": Success");
        completeResponse(dataObj, 200, "text", "" + inObj._id);
      }
    }
  );

}
```

As you can see, it is substantially like the others before it in form. The findByIdAndUpdate() method that Mongoose provides on the model object makes this an easy operation to perform when you have a specific ID, which of course we do by way of the dataObj.ident field. Mongoose will take care of determining which fields have actually changed in the target object; we just have to pass the new data to it as the second argument. The third argument is an object that specifies any options that we may want, which in this case is none, so an empty object is passed in. A response is generated by a call to completeResponse() when the operation is successful, and the _id of the object is returned. Or, an exception is thrown if anything goes wrong. The reason for throwing an exception here is to account for any situation that isn't expected to happen during normal program execution. In those cases, throwing the exception results in the exception handling code in main.js dealing with it, and that ensures that there is consistency in how any actual errors are handled. As a matter of design, exceptions should generally be thrown for such unexpected situations; otherwise, the code should generate a known response.

Object Deletion: DELETE Requests

Like the update operation implemented in the PUT() function, the delete operation in the DELETE() function is simple, thanks to Mongoose.

```
function DELETE(opType, dataObj) {

  console.log(dataObj.id + ": DAO.DELETE() DELETE: " + opType);

  models[opType].findByIdAndRemove(dataObj.ident,
    function (inError, inObj) {
      if (inError) {
        throw "Error: " + JSON.stringify(inError);
      } else {
        console.log(dataObj.id + ": Success");
        completeResponse(dataObj, 200, "text", "" + inObj._id);
      }
    }
  );

}
```

I could, of course, have written the code first to retrieve the object and then to call its remove() method to delete it. Similarly, when doing an update, retrieving the object first and then calling save() on it is quite possible and, in some cases, would be a good way to write the code. However, Mongoose recognizes that these are common operations, and so its API provides the findByIdAndUpdate() method and the findByIdAndRemove() method used here to delete the requested object. The rest of this function is otherwise just like PUT() and POST() before it (and isn't much different from the two retrieval functions either).

The Special Case: Clearing All Data

The other operation that the DAO needs to provide is the ability to clear all data in the database, since the UI has that button on the About screen. This function is a bit different from the rest, as you can see for yourself:

```
function CLEAR_DATA(dataObj) {

  console.log(dataObj.id + ": DAO.CLEAR_DATA()");

  models.appointment.remove({}, function(inError) {
    if (inError) {
      throw "Error: " + JSON.stringify(inError);
    } else {
      models.contact.remove({}, function(inError) {
        if (inError) {
          throw "Error: " + JSON.stringify(inError);
        } else {
          models.note.remove({}, function(inError) {
            if (inError) {
              throw "Error: " + JSON.stringify(inError);
            } else {
              models.task.remove({}, function(inError) {
                if (inError) {
                  throw "Error: " + JSON.stringify(inError);
                } else {
                  console.log(dataObj.id + ": Success");
                  completeResponse(dataObj, 200, "text", "");
                }
              });
            }
          });
        }
      });
    }
  });

}
```

This is a case where the asynchronous nature of Node.js is a little bit of a hassle, if for no other reason than the code is arguably a bit convoluted. Each of the four collections, one for each entity that is in the database, is removed in turn. The remove() method on the model object with no options passed to it does that. (The empty object passed to it ensures that no filtering or anything like that is done, so all objects of that type are removed.) To try to make this flow more easily understood, here it is broken down into the steps accomplished:

1. In the callback for removing appointments, a removal of contacts is triggered.

2. In the callback for removing contacts, a removal of notes is triggered.

3. In the callback for removing notes, a removal of tasks is triggered.

4. In the callback for removing tasks, a response is finally returned to the client to indicate the operation was successful.

5. If an error occurs in any of the previous steps, an exception is thrown.

The nesting of code like this is typical in an asynchronous paradigm. However, there are alternatives. First you could have separate functions defined for each callback. To some people, that makes the code cleaner. It means jumping around source code a little more to follow the flow, though, so I tend to not prefer that model.

Mongoose provides an alternative. The code could be written this way:

```
models.appointment.remove({}).exec()
models.contact.remove({}).exec()
models.note.remove({}).exec()
models.task.remove({}).exec()
completeResponse(dataObj, 200, "text", "");
```

That code is certainly cleaner and easier to follow, but you give up the asynchronous approach entirely: if an error occurs anywhere along the way, the client will not be notified of it. In a sense, this code could actually be considered broken because of that. However, in cases where the operation doesn't *have* to succeed, something like this could be acceptable.

> **Tip**   If you Google *Node.js clean up asynchronous code*, or something similar, you'll find hundreds of articles about various approaches to avoiding "callback hell," as it's often called. I encourage you to learn about the various approaches. My opinion is that each of them has validity in some circumstances, and they are good tools to have in your toolbox. You'll probably find that nesting callbacks needs to happen sometimes, though; it is, by and large, just part of the whole Node.js paradigm.

Don't Forget Those Exports!

Any time you have a Node.js source file that you want to turn into a proper module, you need to export functions so that external code can use them. Otherwise, they exist and are callable only to code included in that file. This is a simple matter of "attaching" them to the special exports object.

```
exports.POST = POST;
exports.GET = GET;
exports.PUT = PUT;
exports.DELETE = DELETE;
exports.GET_ALL = GET_ALL;
exports.CLEAR_DATA = CLEAR_DATA;
```

If you want, you can actually expose these functions with different names than they are designated internally in the source file. Though in this case, we want them to be what they are called in the file so that the function names become the names of the attributes added to exports. Once that's done, you can call these functions, which would be considered methods now of the object returned by the require() call that imports this module.

Summary

In this relatively short chapter, you saw the rather simple code that makes up the DAO that the server code in `main.js` uses to work with MongoDB. You saw how this code performs queries, entity creations, updates, and deletions. You also saw how this code presents an API to the main code of the server by exporting functions and creating a "proper" Node.js out of it.

In the next chapter, we'll look at the technology that will allow us to take this web app and make it a true mobile app, namely, PhoneGap.

Part 3

Putting It All Together

Opportunity is missed by most people, because it is dressed in overalls and looks like work.

—Thomas Edison

One rage every three months is permitted. Try not to hurt anyone who doesn't deserve it.

—Ron Swanson

Intellectual growth should commence at birth and cease only at death.

—Albert Einstein

The good news about computers is that they do what you tell them to do. The bad news is that they do what you tell them to do.

—Ted Nelson

People say nothing is impossible, but I do nothing every day.

—Winnie the Pooh

Chapter 9

Introducing PhoneGap

Now that My Mobile Organizer is complete—that is, both the client app and server-side API are in place—it's time to talk about mobilizing this application.

That's where a new piece of technology comes into play: *PhoneGap*. With this tool, we'll be able to transfer the app into a native application—more or less—that will run across multiple mobile platforms including Android and iOS.

While it's entirely possible simply to put the client app on a web server and have people access it with their web browser, that's not a true native app experience, like many people expect these days. You can't just go and download your app from the app store on your device—Google Play[1] for Android or the App Store for iOS. That's a piece of the puzzle that we need to supply, and PhoneGap is exactly what we need to pull off that trick!

The Problems with Mobile Development

Mobile development has historically been a bit tricky if you had it in your head to support multiple platforms. If you wanted an app to run on Android, iOS, Windows Phone, BlackBerry, and so on, you faced a Herculean task. The only real option for a long time was to write multiple applications using native toolkits specific to each platform. You'd write your app in Objective-C for iOS, in Java for Android, in .NET for Windows Phone, and in C++ for BlackBerry. Sure, you could design the code of the application in such a way that rewriting it for each platform was slightly easier, but it was still *rewriting it* for each platform, so a little easier or not, it was still a major chore.

This is a form of fragmentation: the market itself is fragmented with the multiple platforms available. This fragmentation makes life difficult for a developer, unless you choose not to support some platforms, and that's usually not a great idea if you want to reach the widest possible audience.

---

[1]Google Play is the main store for Android, but it's technically not the only one. Amazon has its own store for its Kindle devices (which can also be accessed from a non-Kindle device with the right app installed), and Barnes and Noble has its own store for its Nook devices (which are limited to those devices only). In addition, other relatively minor independent stores exist, but for the majority of Android users, the Google Play store is the main store.

Even today, this situation hasn't entirely disappeared. In some situations, this is still the development model used; that is, writing the same app over and over again using the different technologies that target specific platforms is at times the best choice. This is often the case with games, for example, where performance is at a premium. Writing a native version for a given platform will usually result in better performance, albeit at the cost of maintenance (and *actual* cost, in terms of hiring more developers!).

However, rewriting code for each platform is becoming less and less the approach that most developers take in favor of (overall in most ways) better choices such as cross-platform libraries that let you write a single code base that runs on multiple platforms (well, *mostly* a single code base anyway). Libraries such as Corona, for example, allow you to do this, and they do so rather well in many situations.

In this context, HTML+JavaScript+CSS can also be viewed as such a cross-platform tool. It's not always thought of like that, but that's what it is in effect. You target this "platform" made up of these three technologies, and as long as a mechanism is available on a given platform to execute your application, it will generally work across platforms. As it happens, a web browser is exactly that mechanism! Using these technologies, we can avoid a number of forms of fragmentation.

Before we talk about that, though, let's look at the forms of fragmentation we're trying to avoid in the first place, that is, the forms of fragmentation that come along with true native development that make it harder than we'd like it to be.

Fragmentation of User Experience

Another problem with mobile development across multiple platforms is that of providing a consistent user experience. Each platform has its own UI design and patterns to which native apps need to adhere. That means the application will look, feel, and function differently in terms of its UI from one platform to another.

> **Note**   Some argue that this is actually a good thing. If all iOS apps look and function the same basic way, then the experience for an iOS user is consistent across apps, for example. While this is undoubtedly true, it means that cross-platform development will always lead to an app working differently, or at a minimum looking differently, across platforms. Which approach is better is a matter of some debate, although a company like Apple that puts a lot of thought into its user experience, and by extension a lot of pressure on its developer community to adhere to its standards, probably doesn't have quite as much debate about it as do we developers who want to support multiple platforms.

Some developers try to enforce consistency across platforms, regardless of whether their app is consistent with other apps on any given platform, so they try to achieve something like the diagram shown in Figure 9-1.

Figure 9-1. A consistent UI across platforms

In this model, it's still a good idea to try to come up with a user interface that at least takes into account the basic design cues of each platform. In other words, while this model allows developers to create any UI they can dream up, it's probably better to keep in mind the design of other applications on the platforms you're going to support and try to come up with a design that isn't way out in left field.

Fragmentation of Features

It's also true that not all platforms are created equal, as Figure 9-2 shows. Android, for example, has the notion of widgets while iOS does not. If your application's basic functionality depends on widgets, the experience will be different, perhaps drastically so, on iOS.

	iOS	Android	BlackBerry	hp webOS	Windows	SYMBIAN
Accelerometer	✓	✓	✓	✓	✓	✓
Camera	✓	✓	✓	✗	✗	✓
Compass	✓	✓	✗	✗	✗	✗
Contacts	✓	⚠	✓	✗	✓	✓
File	✗	✓	✓	⚠	✗	✗
Geolocation	✓	✓	✓	✗	✓	✓
Media	⚠	⚠	✓	✓	⚠	✗
Notification	✓	✓	✓	✗	✓	✓

Figure 9-2. PhoneGap API availability: not all mobile OSs are created equal

This means your application may have considerably different capabilities running on one platform than it does on another platform by necessity. Especially for users who might jump between platforms, that's not going to endear them to your application, more so if they lose features they depended on previously.

Caution   Please be aware that Figure 9-2 is *not* meant to be all-inclusive, nor is it even meant to be 100 percent accurate! Constructing a proper chart like this that covers all of the platforms that PhoneGap supports and that accurately reflects the current state of affairs would require a *much* bigger chart than this with many footnotes below it. This chart is really just meant to give you, at a glance, an estimate of what's available. However, and more importantly, it is designed to illustrate that there are most definitely differences across platforms, and PhoneGap won't solve all of your problems in terms of cross-platform development!

Fragmentation of Development Tools

Another problem is that of the various development tools. Developing an iOS application, for example, requires you to have a Mac. If you're more of a Windows user, like I am, that's a bit of a problem. Even if you're a Mac user, you still need to have Xcode installed to do iOS development. You don't need to have Xcode installed for Android development; however, you do need the Android SDK (you may or may not have a true IDE on top of that). Table 9-1 shows just some of the myriad tools and technologies with which you'll need to be familiar.

Table 9-1. I hope you have a lot of time on your hands!

Mobile Platform	Development Machine Platform	Programming Language	Development Tool
iOS	MAC / OS X Only	Objective-C	Xcode
Android	Windows / Mac / Linux	Java	Eclipse, ADT
BlackBerry	Windows / Mac / Linux	Java	Eclipse, ADT
Symbian	Windows / Mac / Linux	C++	Carbide.c++
webOS	Windows / Mac / Linux	HTML, JavaScript, CSS or C++	Eclipse
Windows Phone	Windows Only	C#/VB, .NET, Silverlight or WPF	MS Visual Studio

Each platform has its own SDK if nothing else, and you'll need to install them all for the platforms you want to support. That aside, you'll still need to learn different languages, APIs, and platform-specific tools. While it's true that a capable developer can generally jump between technologies without too much difficulty, there's no question that it slows them down and sometimes leads to less optimal designs. Something that works great in Objective-C might not work as well in Java, architecturally speaking. Being able to optimize a design across technologies is a huge task no matter how capable you are!

The "Native Experience," Courtesy of PhoneGap

Now let's go back to what I proposed earlier; that is, building an app with HTML+JavaScript+CSS that runs in a browser on a mobile device should avoid all of that fragmentation—at least in theory. HTML, JavaScript, and CSS are all standards-based technologies, which means that aside from some relatively minor differences here and there, an app written using them will generally look, feel, and function consistently across platforms. That sure sounds like the Holy Grail of mobile development, doesn't it? Especially if we narrow the scope a bit to HTML5, which to most people actually means the combination of HTML5, CSS3, and the latest version of JavaScript (and that's what *I* will mean by HTML5 from here on out), you can make a strong case for it being exactly that.

There's still a significant problem to deal with, though: the "native experience." What I mean by that is the experience that a user has of downloading an app to their device from an online store that appears to run like any other native app written with Objective-C for iOS or Java for Android, for example. Yes, they can point their web browser at a URL and launch your app, and in some ways that's better, as it ensures that they always run the latest code. However, it's not the same thing, and people seem to prefer not having to do that. (I make this statement based on the popularity of apps.)

Is there a way to accomplish that goal with these technologies? Of course there is: PhoneGap.

What Is It?

PhoneGap is a framework that allows you to use standardized web technologies to build mobile applications. In short, you more or less build your application using HTML5 as you always would and then package it using PhoneGap to create a native application. This application can be built to target multiple platforms, and it can then be offered for download in each platform's online app store. The application, to the end user, looks and works just like any other application. It gets an icon in the launcher, for example, which launches the app without opening their web browser.

Not only does PhoneGap provide this native "wrapper" around your HTML5 application code, but it also provides a robust collection of JavaScript APIs that you can (optionally) use to gain access to the native device capabilities that your HTML5-based application running in a web browser otherwise wouldn't have access to use. Things such as gyroscopes, accelerometers, GPS, databases, and more, are made available to you via these APIs. While you certainly can write an application that doesn't use them, you often will want to incorporate them in order to provide all of the capabilities that users expect from a modern mobile app.

The underlying goal of PhoneGap is to offer, effectively, a runtime that provides parity across platforms. Develop a PhoneGap application using standard HTML5 technologies, one that targets the PhoneGap APIs where necessary, and the result is that your app will work the same across all supported platforms without you having to lift a finger to achieve that goal. In other words, it's Nirvana!

A Brief History

PhoneGap was birthed at an event in San Francisco named iPhoneDevCamp in 2008 as a means to deal with the issue that many developers run into when starting iOS development, which is that Objective-C can be challenging or, at the very least, unfamiliar even to experienced developers. Although somewhat less true today because of the popularity of iOS development, it was certainly true in 2008.

PhoneGap quickly gained popularity because it provided experienced web developers with an avenue into native iOS development using technologies with which they were already comfortable, rather than having to learn Objective-C and a completely new way of doing things. Then, in 2009, PhoneGap won the People's Choice Award at O'Reilly Media's Web 2.0 conference. That's when people really started to take notice, and it was the catalyst for PhoneGap usage to explode quickly.

Though originally created by a company named Nitobi, PhoneGap was purchased by Adobe in 2011. Shortly thereafter, Adobe contributed the PhoneGap code base to the Apache Software Foundation where it lives now under the name Cordova.

Don't let this confuse you! In simple terms, Cordova is the underlying library, while PhoneGap, still very much alive and kicking under the Adobe banner, is the most commonly used *distribution* of Cordova, so to speak. Perhaps a better way to put it is that it is analogous to how WebKit relates to Safari: WebKit powers Safari, and, in the same way, Cordova powers PhoneGap. Yes, that also means there could be other competing versions of Cordova, and it also means that PhoneGap could have different capabilities than the basic distribution of Cordova (in fact, it does: PhoneGap Build, an important element of which you'll see plenty shortly).

How Does This Black Magic Work?

I've been using the term *native app* a bit loosely here with regard to PhoneGap. In fact, PhoneGap apps are actually "hybrid" apps, not *true* native apps. The difference is that a hybrid app runs within a WebView, which handles rendering the UI, rather than the native toolkit of the underlying OS platform.

A *WebView* is something that nearly all modern mobile OSs have. Some platforms have different names for it, but probably the most common one is WebView. Whatever it's called, it's a specific UI component that can be embedded directly into the UI of a native application. Typically, this is used to show things such as online help content or registration pages—any web site really that the application needs.

This is done without launching a separate web browser, and I'm sure you can see how that's a handy capability for any app to have! A WebView differs from a web browser in that it doesn't have typical web browser controls such as the back, forward, and home buttons. Instead, it's just the viewport portion of a browser—the blank canvas onto which HTML is rendered. Beyond being simply handy for a native app, though, it's the key to PhoneGap!

At the most basic level, PhoneGap is not much more than a native app with a UI that is nothing but a full-screen WebView control within which your HTML5 web app is launched. From there on, your app works as if it were running in a web browser—which, of course, it *actually is*, as far as the HTML and JavaScript is concerned! Remember, though, it's a web browser that doesn't *look* like a web browser to the user, since it doesn't have the usual navigation controls or other "chrome" around the rendering surface of a typical browser. The canvas on which your app renders its UI is the entire screen of the mobile device effectively, just as is the case for a native app.

It's really one of the more clever ideas to come along, but it's also quite simple and obvious after the fact, which, of course, is a hallmark of any great idea.

There is, of course, slightly more to it than that. Every WebView control allows for one other key capability: the ability of JavaScript code to call native code, be it C/C++, Objective-C, or Java, depending on the OS.

Getting PhoneGap and Writing a Simple App

Getting started with PhoneGap depends on having Node.js installed, along with npm. Assuming you do already, all you need to do is to execute the following command from a command prompt. (Don't forget that you probably need to prefix these with sudo on a Mac or *nix machine.)

```
npm install -g phonegap
```

In addition, you may need to install Cordova separately.

```
npm install -g cordova
```

From the previous two chapters, you know exactly what those commands are doing: installing PhoneGap and Cordova as global Node.js libraries. PhoneGap itself doesn't depend on Node.js, but part of what is installed when you execute this command is a command-line tool that can do many useful things, chief among them being to create a skeleton PhoneGap app for you.

```
cordova create myApp
```

This command will create a basic PhoneGap app in the directory myApp under the directory in which you run the command. This will create a number of files, but perhaps the most important are index.html and js/index.js. Both of these files are found in the www directory created by the cordova command, and that's where all of your application files should go. You'll also find a css directory for your stylesheets, img for your images, res for icons, and spec for some necessary support code about which you don't typically need to be concerned.

> **Note**   In most cases you can use the command phonegap instead of cordova. However, it appears that cordova is meant to be the One True Command going forward, so it's best to use that.

The entry point into the app, index.html, looks like this:

```
<!DOCTYPE html>
<!--
    Licensed to the Apache Software Foundation (ASF) under one
    or more contributor license agreements. See the NOTICE file
    distributed with this work for additional information
    regarding copyright ownership. The ASF licenses this file
    to you under the Apache License, Version 2.0 (the
    "License"); you may not use this file except in compliance
    with the License. You may obtain a copy of the License at

    http://www.apache.org/licenses/LICENSE-2.0

    Unless required by applicable law or agreed to in writing,
    software distributed under the License is distributed on an
    "AS IS" BASIS, WITHOUT WARRANTIES OR CONDITIONS OF ANY
     KIND, either express or implied. See the License for the
    specific language governing permissions and limitations
    under the License.
-->
<html>
    <head>
        <meta charset="utf-8" />
        <meta name="format-detection" content="telephone=no" />
        <meta name="viewport" content="user-scalable=no, initial-scale=1, maximum-scale=1,
minimum-scale=1, width=device-width, height=device-height, target-densitydpi=device-dpi" />
        <link rel="stylesheet" type="text/css" href="css/index.css" />
        <title>Hello World</title>
    </head>
    <body>
        <div class="app">
            <h1>PhoneGap</h1>
            <div id="deviceready" class="blink">
                <p class="event listening">Connecting to Device</p>
                <p class="event received">Device is Ready</p>
            </div>
        </div>
        <script type="text/javascript" src="phonegap.js"></script>
        <script type="text/javascript" src="js/index.js"></script>
        <script type="text/javascript">
            app.initialize();
        </script>
    </body>
</html>
```

This is all of the boilerplate code that is just enough to produce a working PhoneGap app. Don't get too hung up on the details, because we'll be changing this in the next chapter when My Mobile Organizer is PhoneGap-ified, so to speak. The one thing to note is the call to `app.initialize()`. This is effectively where your application code begins to execute. The app object is defined in `index.js`, as shown here:

```
/*
 * Licensed to the Apache Software Foundation (ASF) under one
 * or more contributor license agreements. See the NOTICE file
 * distributed with this work for additional information
 * regarding copyright ownership. The ASF licenses this file
 * to you under the Apache License, Version 2.0 (the
 * "License"); you may not use this file except in compliance
 * with the License. You may obtain a copy of the License at
 *
 * http://www.apache.org/licenses/LICENSE-2.0
 *
 * Unless required by applicable law or agreed to in writing,
 * software distributed under the License is distributed on an
 * "AS IS" BASIS, WITHOUT WARRANTIES OR CONDITIONS OF ANY
 * KIND, either express or implied. See the License for the
 * specific language governing permissions and limitations
 * under the License.
 */
var app = {
    // Application Constructor
    initialize: function() {
        this.bindEvents();
    },
    // Bind Event Listeners
    //
    // Bind any events that are required on startup. Common events are:
    // 'load', 'deviceready', 'offline', and 'online'.
    bindEvents: function() {
        document.addEventListener('deviceready', this.onDeviceReady, false);
    },
    // deviceready Event Handler
    //
    // The scope of 'this' is the event. In order to call the 'receivedEvent'
    // function, we must explicity call 'app.receivedEvent(...);'
    onDeviceReady: function() {
        app.receivedEvent('deviceready');
    },
    // Update DOM on a Received Event
    receivedEvent: function(id) {
        var parentElement = document.getElementById(id);
        var listeningElement = parentElement.querySelector('.listening');
        var receivedElement = parentElement.querySelector('.received');
```

```
        listeningElement.setAttribute('style', 'display:none;');
        receivedElement.setAttribute('style', 'display:block;');

        console.log('Received Event: ' + id);
    }
};
```

The initialize() method is the one called, which then calls bindEvents(), which in turn adds an event listener for the deviceready event. Events are discussed under "Events" in the "Here Comes the APIs" section in this chapter, but in short, this event is fired when the app is loaded and ready for your application code to begin executing. Because this is a basic app, the event listener, onDeviceReady(), doesn't do a whole lot; it calls on the receivedEvent() method to update some DOM elements to indicate that the app has been loaded.

You would change or remove much of this entirely in your own application, and in fact, you could do *none* of this and have a fully functional app wrapped in PhoneGap. Defining an app object, hooking the deviceready event, and calling initialize()—all of this is entirely optional. In fact, you don't even technically need to import the phonegap.js file as done in index.html here. All of this is simply what the command-line tool generates to give you a solid foundation on which to build.

It's worth noting that earlier versions of PhoneGap did not have any of this. Earlier versions were simply an archive that you downloaded and extracted, and then you were done. There was no installation with Node.js or with npm or a command-line tool. You had to add the files to the appropriate skeleton app, and there were different versions for each platform. PhoneGap is growing up fast to be sure!

Once you have the skeleton application, the next step is to augment it with some platform-specific data. To do so, navigate to the directory created by the cordova create command, test in this case, and execute the following command:

cordova platform add android

Assuming you have the prerequisite tools installed, namely, Java and Apache Ant, as well as the Android SDK, then after that command, you'll find that a new platforms/android directory is created in your project, which contains a batch of Android-specific files. These are the files that the Android SDK tools need to build your app into a true Android app. You need to add platform support for each platform you want to support, be it iOS, BlackBerry, webOS, and so on.

Adding platform support just adds some boilerplate files to your project for each platform. The next step is to create a true platform-specific source project. Continuing this Android example, to build an Android version of your application, you then execute this command:

cordova build android

The result is that in platforms/android, you'll find the source code for a 100 percent native Android application. In fact, you can launch this app in an emulator, assuming you have one set up. To do so, simply execute the following command:

cordova emulate android

The emulator you had previously configured as part of your Android development environment setup should launch with your app running in it. The same basic steps work for all platforms that PhoneGap supports, although each has its own quirks.

A Simpler Build Approach: PhoneGap Build

As you saw in the previous section, creating a PhoneGap app is a simple matter of putting some web app content into a template or skeleton app that PhoneGap creates for you and then adding some PhoneGap-specific hooks into the page initially loaded (this latter part being optional). Some command-line tools that PhoneGap (and Cordova beneath it) provides make it all straightforward.

However, you also may have noticed that it can take a significant amount of effort to set up a development environment specific to each platform that you want to support. I used Android as an example in the previous section, and in that case, you need to install a Java SDK, Apache Ant, and the Android SDK first. Each platform you intend to support requires you to download, install, and get familiar with one or more native SDKs and tools (and OSs in some cases).

Over on the iOS side, for example, first you'll need to own a Mac, since the tooling required runs only on OS X. If you already have a Mac, then great—you're ahead of things. However, if you don't own a Mac, that's the first significant hurdle to jump. After that, you'll need to install Xcode, Apple's IDE. Then comes the iOS SDK, as well as registering for developer certificates and such with Apple. While developing for iOS isn't especially difficult compared to any other mobile platform, there are definitely a few more steps involved than with many other platforms if you aren't already set up to do it.

For BlackBerry, Windows Phone, Bada, webOS, or any other platform you intend to support, the story is similar. In all cases, unless you're already familiar with the tools and technologies, there will be a learning curve, whether steep or not, and that's only *after* you acquire and set up the tools.

In short, if you want to support multiple platforms, then you're going to have to install multiple sets of tools and learn to use them. In some cases, you will even have to deal with different operating systems because some tool chains don't work on all operating systems that you might want to use. It can be a huge, time-consuming, complex pain in the tuchus, as my mom used to say!

Thankfully, there is a *much* simpler solution that takes virtually all of this pain away: PhoneGap Build. While the next chapter deals with that extensively as part of the process of building the My Mobile Organizer app and deploying it, a simple description is provided here. *PhoneGap Build* is a cloud-based solution offered by Adobe that allows you to upload your application's source code, plus a small XML configuration file that provides some details needed by the servers that then builds your application for a number of platforms and ultimately makes download links available to you. You simply upload an archive of your app, and after a few minutes, you'll be able to download versions for iOS, Android, Windows Phone, BlackBerry, webOS, and Symbian (the supported platforms at the time of this writing). You don't need *any* tooling or SDKs installed on your local machine, nor do you need to use a specific OS.

It really is a fantastic service, and you'll see it in full action in the next chapter.

Here Comes the APIs

In addition to providing the native "wrapper" that your HTM5-based application needs to run on a mobile device as a native (well, hybrid anyway!) application, PhoneGap also provides a set of JavaScript APIs that you can optionally use to interact with various device capabilities. These APIs also provide additional functionality in a cross-platform fashion that you can use to enhance the functionality of your application beyond what HTML5 allows.

> **Note**   Some of what's in these PhoneGap APIs is provided by HTML5 natively. However, the PhoneGap APIs smooth out some of the differences that you might otherwise encounter from one platform to another. The beauty of writing to the PhoneGap APIs is that your app will work today, but over time as HTML5 support is enhanced, the PhoneGap team can simply delegate to the HTML5-native functions more and more.

Let's take a quick tour of the APIs that are available. This is in no way, shape, or form meant to be an exhaustive API reference. Quite the contrary. This is meant only to give you a high-level overview of the capabilities that the APIs provide. The PhoneGap documentation (http://doc.phonegap.com) is where you should go for all of the nitty-gritty details you'd need to truly make use of these APIs.

Most of the APIs are exposed to your JavaScript code as objects added to the navigator object that most browsers provide. These objects usually provide methods for you to use and attributes that convey information you may find useful. Exposing the APIs this way means you should be able to use virtually any JavaScript library you'd like without fear of any name clashes with PhoneGap itself, with a few exceptions.

It's important to realize that, on many devices, permission must be given for many of these APIs to be used. Permissions for a PhoneGap app are configured in various configurations and manifest files. For example, let's say you want your app to be able to take pictures on an Android device. In that case, you would modify the config.xml file under app/res/xml and add this:

```
<plugin name="Camera" value="org.apache.cordova.CameraLauncher" />
```

You would also need to modify app/AndroidManifest to include the following:

```
<uses-permission android:name="android.permission.WRITE_EXTERNAL_STORAGE" />
```

On iOS, a config.xml file in the root directory of the app would need to include this:

```
<plugin name="Camera" value="CDVCamera" />
```

Once again, the PhoneGap documentation for each API spells this out in detail for you, and you'll need to look this up any time you want to use these functions.

Lastly, it's important to note that although these APIs are meant to provide a cross-platform coding experience, in reality it's not that simple. Many of these APIs have quirks on specific platforms about which you'll need to be aware. In fact, some APIs may not even be supported on specific devices, or methods supported on one platform may not be supported on another. There may well be instances where you simply can't use a given API or specified method because it won't work on one platform or another, and the function is core to your application. In that case, you'll need to get extra-creative! A bit of app redesign might be in order to work around the limitations.

Once again, the API documentation states all these quirks and even offers suggestions in some cases for working around them. If I had to put a number on it, I'd say that something like 70 percent of what's available in the APIs will work consistently across platforms for you. (That's just a guess, though; please don't hunt me down with Sentinels[2] if I'm wrong!) PhoneGap can take you a long way, but it's not a panacea for perfect cross-platform HTML5 development.

In short, it's important always to consult the API documentation when using a new PhoneGap API to ensure that you understand both the permission requirements and the quirks of the API about which you're interested.

Accelerometer

Most modern mobile devices have an *accelerometer*, a sensor that tracks changes in motion relative to the device's current location, or previously recorded location, relative to three axes of movement. This allows you to detect things such as the device being bumped, rotated, or flipped over, to name a few.

Access to this API is provided through the `navigator.accelerometer` object. Through this object, you have a number of methods available to you. For example, the `getCurrentAcceleration()` method allows you to get the current values along the three axes.

```
navigator.accelerometer.getCurrentAcceleration(
  function(acceleration) {
    alert("X=" + acceleration.x + ", Y=" + acceleration.y +
      ", Z=" + acceleration.z);
  }
);
```

This gets a single moment-in-time value, calls a callback function, and passes it the information. What if instead you want to track movement over time? The `watchAcceleration()` method is perfect for that.

```
var wid = navigator.accelerometer.watchAcceleration(
  function(acceleration) {
    alert("X=" + acceleration.x + ", Y=" + acceleration.y +
      ", Z=" + acceleration.z);
  },
  function() { alert("error"); },
  { frequency : 3000 }
);
```

---

[2]Word is that the Sentinels, those mutant-murdering giant robots from the X-Men universe, are set to make a big appearance in the upcoming (as of this writing) movie *Days of Future Past*. That's exciting news for any comic book geek!

This will update the acceleration every three seconds (3 * 1,000 milliseconds). The value returned by watchAcceleration() is a value you can pass to clearWatch() to stop accelerometer monitoring. (This is very much like the usage of setInterval(), and although I haven't checked, it's a good bet that's how this API works under the covers.)

Camera

The PhoneGap APIs make it easy to take a picture with a mobile device that has a camera. This is exposed by being able to launch the camera app on the device like so:

```
navigator.camera.getPicture(
  function(imageData) {
    var image = document.getElementById("myImage");
    image.src = "data:image/jpeg;base64," + imageData;
  },
  function() { alert("Failure"); },
  { quality: 50, destinationType : Camera.DestinationType.DATA_URL }
);
```

This will fetch an image from the camera and insert it onto the page via the myImage <img> element (which is assumed to already be on the page). Alternatively, if you use the destinationType: Camera.DestinationType.FILE_URI option, then you can get a URI to the image instead of the base64-encoded image data (the URI is passed to the callback instead).

Many options are available in that third-argument options object, including quality and sourceType, as you can see in the example. Just some of the others are encodingType, which allows you to specify whether you want a JPG or PNG file back; targetWidth and targetHeight, which allow you to scale the returned image; and cameraDirection, which lets you choose whether to use the front-facing or rear-facing camera, assuming the device has both.

Capture

The Capture API provides access to the audio, image, and video capturing capabilities of the device. This is a bit different from just launching the camera app and grabbing a picture from it.

Let's start with audio first, though. This API allows you to launch the devices' native audio capture app easily.

```
var captureSuccess = function(mediaFiles) {
  var i, path, len;
  for (i = 0, len = mediaFiles.length; i < len; i += 1) {
    path = mediaFiles[i].fullPath;
  }
};

var captureError = function(error) {
  alert("Error code: " + error.code, null, "Capture Error");
};
```

```
navigator.device.capture.captureAudio(
  captureSuccess, captureError, { limit : 2 }
);
```

The limit parameter in the options argument passed to captureAudio() specifies the maximum number of recordings to be taken. Once the asynchronous call returns, the captureSuccess() function is called, and you can do something interesting with the files recorded at that point, whatever that may be.

Capturing images is just as easy using the captureImage() method, but this works similarly to the Camera API, so it's a little less interesting perhaps. The captureVideo() method, on the other hand, is also available if you're interested in capturing video, and using either method looks exactly like using captureAudio(). The previous example will work for either changing captureAudio() to captureImage() or captureVideo(). The API is nicely consistent that way.

In addition to the limit option, which is available for all three methods, you can also do things like setting the duration of recording for both audio and video, and you can set the capture mode for audio and video to determine the format. Actually, mode is a good example of one of the places where device-specific quirks comes into play because mode isn't supported on all platforms, and the actual modes supported differ from platform to device platform.

Compass

Many devices nowadays have a compass built into them that provides your app with the ability to determine the direction in which the device is pointing, and working with this sensor is a simple matter of using the PhoneGap Compass API. This API looks a lot like the Accelerometer API. For example, getting a one-time directional heading can be accomplished easily.

```
navigator.compass.getCurrentHeading(
  function(heading) {
    alert(heading.magneticHeading);
  }
);
```

The magneticHeading attribute provides a value from 0 to 359.99, the degrees in a circle obviously, with magnetic north being at the top of the circle. You can also get the trueHeading value, which gives you a similar value but one that is relative to the geographic North Pole this time. You can also get the headingAccuracy so that you can tell the deviation in degrees between the reported heading and the true heading.

In addition to getCurrentHeading(), you can get a continuous heading reading with the watchHeading() method, and it works the same way as watchAcceleration() from the Accelerometer API does. Of course, there's a clearWatch() method available too, which allows you to stop monitoring the compass.

Connection

The Connection API is one of the simpler PhoneGap APIs, yet it is also one of the more important. Unlike the other APIs, the Connection API provides no methods for you to call. Instead, the connection object added to the navigator object contains just a few attributes.

The first one is the most important: type. The value of this attribute tells you the current type of connectivity the device has. A simple example of using type might look like this:

```
var cs = navigator.connection.type;
var states = {};
states[navigator.connection.UNKNOWN] = "Unknown";
states[navigator.connection.ETHERNET] = "Ethernet";
states[navigator.connection.WIFI] = "Wi-Fi";
states[navigator.connection.CELL_2G] = "Cell 2G";
states[navigator.connection.CELL_3G] = "Cell 3G";
states[navigator.connection.CELL_4G] = "Cell 4G";
states[navigator.connection.CELL] = "Cell Generic";
states[navigator.connection.NONE] = "No connection";
alert(states[cs]);
```

The Connection API also provides the constants that you see used as keys in the states object, and these constants let you determine the current device's connection state. This API does not provide a "connection watch" mechanism like the Accelerometer and Compass APIs, but you can, of course, do that yourself with setInterval(). (That's probably not advisable, however, as checking connectivity status can be a somewhat expensive operation on some devices.)

As I said, this is one of the simpler APIs that PhoneGap offers, but it's a vitally important capability for nearly any modern mobile application, as many, or maybe even most of them, need connectivity of some sort.

Contacts

Working with the contacts available on the device is something that many applications need, for example, to dial a number associated with the contact. PhoneGap provides the Contacts API for these needs, and it's another simple API, although not quite as simple as Connection. It provides just two methods, create() and find(), allowing you both to create new contacts and to find existing ones and retrieve data about them. Here's an example of both:

```
var c = navigator.contacts.create(
  {"displayName" : "Kiera Cameron"}
);

c.note = "I am a note";
c.save();

var opts = new navigator.contacts.ContactFindOptions();
opts.filter = "Kiera";
opts.multiple = true;
navigator.contacts.find(
  ["displayName", "note"]
  function(contacts) {
    alert(
      "Name = " + contacts[0].displayName + ", Note = " + contacts[0].note
    );
  };
```

```
  function() { alert("error"); },
  opts
);
```

The `create()` method returns a Contact object that contains fields such as `displayName`, `phoneNumbers`, `emails`, `addresses`, `birthday`, `note`, and lots more. Although you can pass as much of this data to `create()` as you like, you can always edit a Contact object after the fact and then call `save()` on it, as shown for saving a note.

The `find()` method allows you essentially to query the contacts database on the device, although the simplest use case would be as follows:

```
navigator.contacts.fund( ["*"], function(contacts) { }, function(error) { }, { });
```

This would return all of the fields available for all of the contacts. However, in the example, only contacts with the name Kiera in the `displayName` field (or note field) will be returned. In addition, by setting the `multiple` option attribute to `true`, we get back an array of zero or more Contact objects. Alternatively, setting that attribute to `false` results in just a single Contact object, or `null`, being returned.

Device

The Device API is another simplistic API but a useful one. This is another API that has no methods in it. It's just a collection of attributes. Unlike most of the other APIs, the object `device` is found in global scope since it's a member of the `window` object, not an attribute of the `navigator` object. So, you can simply write this:

```
alert(device.model);
```

The attributes available are as follows:

- `model`: Specifies the name of the device model. The device manufacturer determines this value, and it could even be different for various versions of the same product.

- `cordova`: Gets the version of Cordova (PhoneGap) in use.

- `platform`: Returns the operating system the device is running. Some values you could see here are Android, BlackBerry, iOS, webOS, WinCE, and Tizen. You could see other values as well, and again, you could even see different values for different OS versions.

- `uuid`: Provides access to the device's Universally Unique Identifier (UUID) to your code. The format and algorithm used to generate this UUID is entirely manufacturer-dependent, and some devices and/or OS versions won't even allow you to retrieve this information; also, it is not necessarily unique for the device but instead unique per application (and per install of the application). In other words, you probably don't want to count on this as a true unique device identifier!

- `version`: Gets the operating system version. The format of this may not be consistent across devices and OSs.

The key thing to remember here is that you should use the values available through this API with extreme caution. If nothing else, you'll probably need to write a lot of extra logic to account for all the various versions of a given value you might get, along the lines of the following:

```
if (device.model == "galaxy" || device.model == "GalaxyS3" || device.model == "SGS4") {
  // Do something for Samsung Galaxy devices
}
```

That's not especially pretty code to be sure, and more importantly, it will likely be brittle when new versions come out or even after an over-the-air update changes the value for existing devices. As I said, *use with caution!*

Events

The Events API is arguably not an API at all, but since it is listed as such in the PhoneGap documentation, who am I to argue? The Cordova library underlying PhoneGap provides a number of life-cycle events that your code can hook into to perform tasks at appropriate times. The events you can watch for are simply strings that you use with the native document.addEventListener() method, and the available strings, event names in other words, are listed in this API.

An example, and arguably the most important, is deviceready, which you can use like so:

```
document.addEventListener("deviceready"),
  function(eventInfo) {
    // Do work
  }, false
);
```

This event is particularly important because every PhoneGap application will use it. (There may be an exception to that rule, but I've never seen it.) This event fires only after Cordova has fully loaded, which is different from the plain old onLoad event handler with which you're familiar because onLoad actually fires before Cordova has loaded, which means that if your application code tries to call Cordova functions before the deviceready event fires, then errors will occur. Typically, you hook up the deviceready event listener in an onLoad event handler.

The other events available include the following:

■ pause: This event fires when the application is put in the background.

■ resume: This event fires when the application is brought back into the foreground.

■ online: When the connectivity status of the device changes to a network-connected state, this event fires.

■ offline: When the connectivity status of the device changes to an offline state, this event fires.

■ backbutton: This event fires when the user taps the back button on their device, assuming the device has a back button, of course!

- ▓ `batterycritical`: When the battery charge level reaches the device-specific critical level, this event fires. This is a good trigger for your application to save data to avoid any loss if the battery drains completely.

- ▓ `batterylow`: This event fires when the battery reaches the device-specific low level, which is always before the `batterycritical` event fires (although how much before is entirely dependent on the thresholds the device uses).

- ▓ `batterystatus`: This event fires when the status of the battery's charge changes by at least 1 percent. This allows you to get continual updates on the charge remaining if you need it.

- ▓ `menubutton`: This event fires when the user taps the menu button on their device, assuming the device has a menu button.

- ▓ `searchbutton`: If the device has a search button, this event will fire when it is tapped.

- ▓ `startcallbutton`: This event fires when the start call button is tapped, if any.

- ▓ `endcallbutton`: This event fires when the end call button is tapped, if one exists on the device.

- ▓ `volumedownbutton`: This event fires when the volume up button is activated. Most devices have a physical volume control rocker switch, so this allows you to be informed of it being pressed in the up direction.

- ▓ `volumeupbutton`: This is the opposite of `volumedownbutton`, of course!

Notice in the previous example that the `deviceready` handler callback function is passed an `eventInfo` object. This object contains attributes specific to the event that provides information about the event. As an example, the object for a `batterylow` event contains a `level` attribute with a value of 0 to 100, describing the current charge remaining. Not all events provide objects, so be sure to consult the documentation if you need information about a particular event to see what is provided.

Geolocation

The Geolocation API provides your app with the ability to use the physical location–sensing capabilities of the device. With it, you can determine the location of the user in the real world based on latitude and longitude. Note that this doesn't necessarily mean GPS capability, as in using a GPS receiver to interpret signals from satellites in space, although that is definitely part of it. The broader definition of geolocation, in terms of global positioning, can also be achieved by other means including IP address, RFID, Wi-Fi, and Bluetooth data, at a cost of accuracy (over a true GPS location fix).

At the end of the day, this is secondary to the fact that this API allows you to determine the position of the user on Earth, regardless of method. The API looks and works very much like the Accelerometer and Compass APIs in that there are three primary methods, `getCurrentPosition()`, `watchPosition()`, and `clearWatch()`, all on the `navigator.geolocation` object.

```
navigator.geolocation.watchPosition(
  function(position) {
    alert(position.coords + " / " + position.timestamp");
  },
  function(error) { alert(error); },
  { enableHighAccuracy : true, timeout : 5000, maximumAge : 60000 }
);
```

Here the inlined callback function will be called any time a change in position is detected. The position object passed to this callback allows you to retrieve the coordinates (coords) of the new position, which is an object that contains attributes such as latitude, longitude, altitude, accuracy, altitudeAccuracy, heading, and speed. The position object also includes a timestamp to tell you when the location fix was last updated.

By default, the accuracy of the position will be determined using network capabilities, but if you want a higher, true GPS-based location, the option enableHighAccuracy must be set to true. This applies for watchPosition() and getCurrentPosition() equally. The timeout option specifies how long, in milliseconds, to wait for a location fix (5,000 milliseconds, or 5 seconds, in this case), and maximumAge tells the OS how old a cached location can be for your code to accept it (60 seconds here).

Globalization

The PhoneGap Globalization API, as found in navigator.globalization, is a (mostly) informational API that gives you access to details about the user's locale and time zone, and it provides some functionality based on it. It delivers a series of fairly obvious methods to get at various pieces of that information. All of these methods are asynchronous, as are most of the PhoneGap APIs, so you'll supply a success and, optionally, failure callback. Some of the methods accept a third options object argument as well.

Here are some quick examples of using this API:

```
navigator.globalization.getPreferredLanguage(
  function (language) { alert(language.value); },
  function () { alert("Error"); }
);
```

This will display the preferred language of the current user. If you're interested in their locale instead, you can do the following:

```
navigator.globalization.getLocaleName(
  function (locale) { alert(locale.value); },
  function () { alert("Error"); }
);
```

Finally, if you'd like to get the pattern string for formatting and parsing dates according to the client's user preferences, you can use the following:

```
navigator.globalization.getDatePattern(
  function (date) { alert(date.pattern); },
  function () { alert("Error"); }
  { formatLength : "long", selector : "date and time" }
);
```

The getDatePattern() example shows the usage of some options. You can choose whether you want the format string for long or short dates, as well as medium and full dates. You can choose whether you want the format string for just a date, just a time, or a date and time combined.

The following are the other methods available:

- dateToString(): Returns a date formatted as a string according to the client's locale and time zone. Note that "returns" is a bit of a misnomer here, as it's really "returning" the formatted date to the callback function. This is still an asynchronous call, as is the case for the other methods here that actually do something other than just provide you with information. Also note that the term *client* here refers to the combination of the device and the user and the preferences that are currently in effect for them.

- stringToDate(): Parses a string version of a date formatted based on the client's locale preferences and the time zone of the device, and it returns a proper Date object from it.

- getDateNames(): Returns an array of either the names of the months or the days of the week according to the client's preferences.

- isDayLightSavingsTime(): Returns whether daylight saving time is in effect for a given date using the client's time zone and calendar.

- getFirstDayOfWeek(): Returns the first day of the week according to the client's user preferences and calendar.

- numberToString(): Returns a number formatted as a string according to the client's user preferences.

- stringToNumber(): Parses a number formatted as a string according to the client's user preferences and returns the corresponding number.

- getNumberPattern(): Returns a pattern string for formatting and parsing numbers according to the client's user preferences.

- getCurrencyPattern(): Returns a pattern string for formatting and parsing currency values according to the client's user preferences and ISO 4217 currency code.

InAppBrowser

The InAppBrowser API allows your app to open a web browser, the special InAppBrowser component specifically, and show a given web page without leaving your application. The API itself is made available through the window.open() function, with which you're probably already familiar since it's part of the DOM API. The InAppBrowser API simply enhances that existing function.

An example of using this API might look like this:

```
lec = function(event) {
  alert("Error: " + event.message);
  iab.removeEventListener("loaderror", lec);
};
```

```
iab = window.open("http://www.apple.com", "_blank", "location=yes");
ref.addEventListener("loadstart", function(event) { alert(event.url); });
ref.addEventListener("loadstop", function(event) { iab.close(); });
ref.addEventListener("loaderror", lec);
ref.addEventListener("exit", function(event) { alert(event.type); });
```

There are a couple of interesting things here to note. First, the key thing is that when you call `window.open()`, the second argument is the target in which to load the page. The value `_blank` is needed to open the page using the InAppBrowser. If you use `_self`, your app is essentially replaced, as the page you specify will open in the Cordova WebView component hosting your application. You can also specify `_system`, which will open the page in a separate system browser instance.

The third argument specifies features for the InAppBrowser control. The `location` attribute specifies whether to show the location bar. In fact, `location` is the only cross-browser option available; all others are dependent on the underlying OS. For example, on an iPhone, you can specify `allowInlineMediaPlayback` to turn HTML5 media playback on or off, or you can specify `transitionstyle` to specify the transition to use between pages.

Once you call `window.open()`, you'll have a reference to the InAppBrowser instance. With that, you optionally can attach event handlers. In this example, the `loadstart`, `loadstop`, and `loaderror` events are hooked. In the case of `loaderror`, an external function is specified. This is important because, in that function, the event is detached with `removeEventListener()`. This wouldn't be possible for the inlined functions for `loadstart` and `loadstop`, for example, because you need a reference to the callback function when using `removeEventListener()`, and no such references exist when using anonymous inline functions.

Notification

In all of the little examples in this chapter so far, I've used the basic JavaScript `alert()` function. As you might imagine, that's not ideal on a mobile device. Fortunately, PhoneGap provides a better approach in the Notification API.

This API provides five methods on the `navigator.notification` object.

- `alert()`: Shows a custom alert or dialog message. Most implementations of Cordova use a native dialog box for this, but some may use the basic JavaScript `alert()` anyway, reducing your customization options (discussed after this list).

- `confirm()`: Shows a customizable confirmation dialog.

- `prompt()`: Shows a customizable prompt dialog. The difference between a confirm dialog and a prompt dialog is that `confirm()` has only buttons while `prompt()` has a text input field.

- `beep()`: Causes the device to play its default beep sound.

- `vibrate()`: Causes the device to vibrate if it supports haptic feedback.

All of these functions are asynchronous in nature, except for beep() and vibrate(), which doesn't need a callback function as the others do, as you can see here:

```
navigator.notification.alert("Hello there",
  function() { },
  "Hello From The App", "Thanks"
);

function showConfirm() {
  navigator.notification.confirm(
    "Are you sure you want to exit?",
    function(buttonIndex) {
      alert("You tapped button #" + buttonIndex);
    },
    "Exit Confirmation", "Yes,No"
  );
}

function showPrompt() {
  navigator.notification.prompt(
    "Please enter your name",
    function(results) {
      alert("You tapped button #" + results.buttonIndex +
        " and entered " + results.input1
      );
    },
    "Name Entry", [ "Ok", "Exit" ]
  );
}

navigator.notification.beep(3);
navigator.notification.vibrate(3000);
```

First, the alert() function is used to show a basic alert where the title of the dialog is "Hello from The App," the text in the dialog is "Hello there," and there is a single button labeled "Thanks." The inlined callback function is called when the dialog is dismissed.

The showConfirm() function is demonstrated next. This time, the dialog has a title of "Exit Confirmation" and text of "Are you sure you want to exit?" There will be two buttons labeled "Yes" and "No." When either is tapped, the inlined callback function is called, and it displays which button was tapped by its index.

The showPrompt() function is very much like showConfirm(), except that this time, the value the user enters in the text field is displayed in the callback.

The beep() and vibrate() functions are shown last. For beep(), the argument 3 simply means to beep three times. The 3000 passed to vibrate() means to vibrate the decide for 3 seconds (1,000 milliseconds * 3).

The "Standard" APIs

The APIs discussed so far are PhoneGap APIs specifically, that is, things that Cordova provides. Three other APIs are part of the PhoneGap API, but they're a little different in that they're really facades over the W3C-standard APIs. They are File, Media, and Storage. As such, they aren't defined by Cordova but by a standards committee. I'll touch on them briefly so that you have some exposure to them and what they can do, but they are in a sense outside of the scope of this chapter, so this won't be a full exploration of them.

Files

The File API that PhoneGap provides is directly based on the W3C's File API, which allows you to read, write, and navigate the local file system of the device, with some security restrictions in place, of course, depending on the device and OS.

From a high-level perspective, working with the File API boils down to a few specific tasks. The first of these is to request a file system with which to work. This file system is the basis from which all other operations proceed.

```
window.requestFileSystem(LocalFileSystem.PERSISTENT, 1000,
  function(fileSystemObject) { },
  function(fileErrorObject) { }
);
```

The first argument is the type of file system being requested. This can be PERSISTENT, as shown, or TEMPORARY. Anything stored on a PERSISTENT file system can be cleared only if authorized by the user, whereas the browser can clear TEMPORARY storage. The second argument is the amount of storage, in bytes, that the app requires for storage. The third argument is the callback function to call when the file system is retrieved. This is passed an instance of FileSystem. The fourth argument is if the file system can't be obtained, and it is passed an instance of FileError.

The FileSystem object is how you will work with files and directories after that. For example, to read a file, you write this:

```
window.requestFileSystem(LocalFileSystem.PERSISTENT, 1000,
  function(fileSystem) {
    fileSystem.root.getFile("info.txt", null,
      function(fileEntry) {
        fileEntry.file(
          function(file) {
            var reader = new FileReader();
            reader.onloadend = function(event) {
              alert(event.target.result);
            };
            reader.readAsText(file);
          },
          function(e) {
            alert("error: " + e);
          }
        );
      },
```

```
      function(e) {
        alert("error: " + e);
      }
    );
  },
  function(e) {
    alert("error: " + e);
  }
);
```

Once the FileSystem object is obtained, the getFile() method of its root member is called. This means that the file will be read from the root of the file system, not a subdirectory. The getFile() method returns to its success callback (the first function passed to it, which is the same pattern for all of these methods) only a FileEntry object, which is an object that *represents* a file on a file system. It's not the file itself *per se*; it doesn't contain the file's content, for example, just some metadata about it such as whether the entry is a file or directory (isFile and isDirectory attributes), its name (the name attribute), and its full path (fullPath attribute). This object, though, is how you can then read the actual file contents, but before that you need to get a File object based on it, which is where the file() method of the FileEntry object comes into play. That returns to its success callback a File object. A File object contains "concrete" information about the file (or directory) including its type and size and the last time the file or directory was modified via its lastModifiedDate attribute.

Once you have a File object based on the FileEntry in which you're interested, you then use a FileReader to read the file. As with all of the File API, this is an asynchronous operation, so once you create an instance of it, you set an event handler on it for the onloadend event. Then kick off the reading with a call to readAsText(), and when the file is completely read into memory, the specific callback will be called, passing to it an event object. Most importantly, that object contains the contents of the file in its target.result attribute.

Writing a file follows the same basic pattern, with some small differences.

```
window.requestFileSystem(LocalFileSystem.PERSISTENT, 1000,
  function(fileSystem) {
    fileSystem.root.getFile("info.txt", { create : true },
      function(fileEntry) {
        fileEntry.createWriter(
          function(writer) {
            writer.write("Hello!");
          },
          function(e) {
            alert("error: " + e);
          }
        );
      },
      function(e) {
        alert("error: " + e);
      }
    );
  },
```

```
function(e) {
  alert("error: " + e);
}
);
```

This time, rather than creating a `FileWriter` manually, the `createWriter()` method of the `FileEntry` object is used to get an instance, which is passed into the callback and is then used to write some content to the file. Also note that the second argument to `getFile()` is an `options` object, in this case with a single option, `create`, to indicate that we want the file created if it doesn't already exist.

A number of other objects make up the File API, including the following:

- ▓ `DirectoryEntry`: This object represents a directory on the file system. It serves the same purpose as `FileEntry` and has many of the same capabilities.

- ▓ `DirectoryReader`: This is much like `FileReader`, but in this case, it allows you to iterate over its children, whether other directories or files.

- ▓ `FileTransfer`: This object contains methods for uploading and downloading files from servers using HTTP or HTTPS multipart requests.

Media

The Media API provides the ability to record and play back audio files on a device. As of this writing, you need to be a bit careful with this particular API because the PhoneGap API docs state that it doesn't match the W3C standard and therefore is in flux. (It might even be entirely deprecated in the future.) Because of this, I won't go into too much detail, but I'll give you a quick overview.

This API is built around the notion of a Media object. You create this object like so:

```
var m = new Media("http://server.com/music.mp3",
  function() { alert("success"); },
  function(error) { alert("error"); },
  function(status) {
    if (status == Media.MEDIA_NONE) { alert("No media"); };
    if (status == Media.MEDIA_STARTING) { alert("Playback starting"); };
    if (status == Media.MEDIA_RUNNING) { alert("Playing now"); };
    if (status == Media.MEDIA_PAUSED) { alert("Playback paused"); };
    if (status == Media.MEDIA_STOPPED) { alert("Not playing"); };
  }
);
```

As part of the creation, you specify callback functions for successful loading and error handling, as well as status changes (optionally). The first argument is a path to the audio file you want to play, whether on the Web, as shown here, or just a plain old file name available to your application locally.

Once you have a Media instance, you can call methods on it to control playback.

- ▓ `getCurrentPosition()`: Returns the current position within an audio file. This is an asynchronous method, so it requires callbacks for success and failure.

- ▓ `getDuration()`: Returns the duration of an audio file. This synchronous method returns the duration, so no callbacks are required.

- ▤ `play()`: Starts or resumes playing an audio file. This is a synchronous method, so no callbacks are required.

- ▤ `pause()`: Pauses playing an audio file. This is a synchronous method, so no callbacks are required.

- ▤ `release()`: Releases the underlying OS's audio resources. This is a synchronous method, so no callbacks are required.

- ▤ `seekTo()`: Moves the position within the audio file. Pass to this synchronous method a milliseconds value to which to seek.

- ▤ `startRecord()`: Starts recording an audio file. This is a synchronous method, so no callbacks are required. When using this method, the source you pass to the Media constructor as the first argument will not be a full path; it will just be a file name. That is, of course, the file that will be created from the recording.

- ▤ `stopRecord()`: Stops recording an audio file. This is a synchronous method, so no callbacks are required.

- ▤ `stop()`: Stops playing an audio file. This is a synchronous method, so no callbacks are required.

Storage

The PhoneGap Storage API is one you've already seen in action to some degree in the form of localStorage. Therefore, I won't talk about that again. However, I will talk about the SQL database capabilities this API provides.

The W3C Web SQL Database specification is what this API implements, and that specification is an implementation of a relational database using SQL to work with it. On many devices, it is implemented using the lightweight, embeddable SQLite database engine, but this is not something about which you typically need to be concerned, and indeed the specification doesn't say anything about what engine should be used—it's entirely up to the platform developers.

Working with these SQL databases is actually quite easy. The first step is to open a database.

```
var db = window.openDatabase("myDB", "1.0", "myDB", 100000);
```

The first argument is the name of the database. The second is a version number, which is purely for your own information. (For example, if you update your app and increment the version number, you can later query the existing database to see whether it's a previous version and upgrade it if that's the case.) The third argument is a display name used by some tooling (although it can, and probably in many cases is, the same as the first argument). The final argument is the requested size of the database.

This method returns a `Database` object that you then use to execute transactions. For example, to create a table, you can do the following:

```
db.transaction(
  function(transaction) {
    tx.executeSql("DROP TABLE IF EXISTS myTable");
    tx.executeSql("CREATE TABLE IF NOT EXISTS myTable (id UNIQUE, username)");
  },
```

```
    function(error) { alert(error); },
    function() { alert("Success"); }
);
```

As you can see, as is true of all operations against a database, this is done within a transaction context obtained by calling the `transaction()` method of the `Database` object. The first argument to this method is a function that is responsible for executing one or more SQL update queries (meaning not literally SQL update queries but any SQL that updates the database). The second argument is a callback function in case of an error, and the third argument is a function to be called if the operation is successful.

That's how you can modify the database structure, insert records into tables, or update records, but what about queries that return data? It works much the same.

```
db.transaction(
  function(transaction) {
    tx.executeSql("SELECT * FROM myTable", [],
      function(transaction, resultSet) {
        var len = resultSet.rows.length;
        for (var i = 0; i < len; i++){
          alert("id = " + resultSet.rows.item(i).id +
            ", username =  " + resultSet.rows.item(i).username
          );
        }
      },
      function(error) { alert(error); },
    );
  },
  function(error) { alert(error); },
  function() { alert("Success"); }
);
```

You'll notice that the `executeSql()` method also accepts a success and failure callback reference. They are optional, however, which is why you don't see them in the update example. When reading, though, it only makes sense that you'll want to do something with the data returned in the `ResultSet` object passed to the callback. This object, most importantly, contains a `rows` array, which contains the actual results of the query. As a result, you can iterate over that collection and, perhaps as in the example, display the fields from each row returned.

The error object returned to any of the error handler callbacks is an instance of `SQLError`, and it conveys to you information about why the operation failed through its code property. For example, if the data you're trying to save is too large for the database, you might see a value of `SQLError.TOO_LARGE_ERR` in that field.

Summary

In this chapter, you got your first look at PhoneGap, a toolkit for creating cross-platform HTML5-based applications. You saw how it provides a mechanism to run these applications as (more or less!) true native applications that can be sold in the various app stores for different platforms. You saw how PhoneGap provides a robust collection of APIs for working with native device capabilities, which abstracts the platform differences away and allows you to maintain a single code base.

In the next chapter, we'll look at PhoneGap Build, a cloud-based facility for building applications that removes the need to install native SDKs on your desktop to build your mobile apps. This is the true final step to creating a native mobile version of My Mobile Organizer!

The Final Build: Going Mobile with PhoneGap

You know how in *Star Wars, Episode VI: Return of the Jedi* it all leads up to Luke's final battle against Darth Vader in front of the Emperor? All of the training, all of the hardship, all of the kissing of sisters leads inexorably to that singular point? Well, here we are, light saber in hand, standing before the Emperor over Endor!

In the previous chapters, we built My Mobile Organizer, from its jQuery Mobile client side to the Node.js+MongoDB back end, with associated libraries helping along the way. We brought PhoneGap into the conversation to start going down the path of mobilizing the app in a cross-platform manner.

Now it's time for the final step: throwing the code at PhoneGap Build to create a native app that can run on iOS, Android—what have you. However, we're going to go a bit further here and talk also about adding some PhoneGap API goodness to the app. We'll also discuss the steps involved in publishing your app to one of the app stores for the two most popular platforms, iOS and Android, as well as some related stores for Android-based devices from specific vendors.

The first step is the PhoneGap Build. You've heard me say many times throughout this book that "this isn't all that tough," or something similar, and PhoneGap Build is no different! It amounts to little more than zipping up your code, uploading it to the PhoneGap Build servers, and then having some patience! A short while later, usually measured in a few minutes, you'll have native-packaged applications for a number of platforms ready to transfer to your device for testing.

There are, however, two steps that you'll need to do first, signing up for a PhoneGap Build account and configuring your application for building, so let's talk about them first.

Get Ready: Signing Up

The first thing you'll need to do is to sign up for a PhoneGap Build account. To do so, visit
`https://build.phonegap.com` and click the big Get Started! button next to the floating robot over the
scrolling sky. (I know, it sounds crazy, but that's what's there and it actually looks cool!) When you
click the button, the page will automatically scroll to a section that outlines your plan choices, as
shown in Figure 10-1.

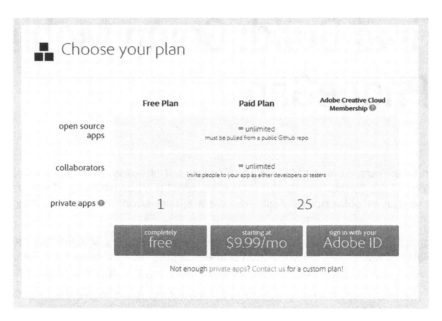

Figure 10-1. PhoneGap Build plan options

If you happen already to have an Adobe Creative Cloud account, then you are all set! Simply
sign in with your credentials for that service, and you're good to go. You will have the ability to
create 25 separate private apps within PhoneGap Build, and you can then manage and build them
independently. You'll also have the ability to have unlimited open source apps.

PUBLIC VS. PRIVATE APPS

The difference between public and private apps for the purposes of PhoneGap Build is simply where the source code of
the project is hosted.

Although it's not strictly necessary, PhoneGap Build focuses a bit on using Git and GitHub for your development. If you're
unaware, Git is a source control system created by Mr. Linux himself, Linus Torvalds. GitHub, at `www.github.com`, is an
online service that makes use of Git, provides a more user-friendly web-based interface to it, and adds extra collaboration
features. GitHub offers free use of its services, with premium services optionally available. You can host your code there
and allow others to help work on it if you want.

Whether you use GitHub to create a repository of your code or create your own Git repository, that repository either is publicly accessible to all or is private and accessible only by a select group—even just you. Simply put, if your code is in a publicly accessible repository, then it is considered a public app in the eyes of PhoneGap Build. Conversely, if your code lives in a repository that is not publicly accessible, then the app is private as far as PhoneGap Build goes.

While you can make PhoneGap Build obtain your source code from a private repository directly, if you have one, more frequently when creating a private app you'll simply upload a ZIP archive to PhoneGap Build. That way, if you prefer Subversion for your source control, for example, as I do, you can still use PhoneGap Build just fine. The service is in no way dependent on Git or GitHub, although it's certainly designed to work with the popular GitHub service rather well.

The difference in the number of private apps allowed is the big differentiating factor in the PhoneGap Build plans available to you.

If you don't have an Adobe Creative Cloud account and you don't want to sign up for one and if you think you're going to be using PhoneGap Build a lot, then you also have the option of signing up for PhoneGap Build services alone for $9.99 per month. This allows you up to 25 private apps, just like having an Adobe Creative Cloud account does.

Both of these options also provide for an unlimited number of public apps as well as an unlimited number of collaborators. A *collaborator* in PhoneGap Build means someone who can test or even build your app. A collaborator is either a *designated tester*, which means they have read-only access to your account and can download completed builds, or a *developer*, which means they can initiate builds as well. You add collaborators for each app by e-mail address, and by doing so; PhoneGap Build sends an automated e-mail to that person, which provides information about registering for a PhoneGap Build account as well as a link for the app's site on PhoneGap Build where the app downloads and build process control can be found.

In addition to those two paid plans, and most relevant for the purposes of this book, is the free option Adobe makes available to you. Using this option, you still get an unlimited number of public apps and an unlimited number of collaborators, but you are now limited to a single private app. Of course, you can remove an existing app to make room for another at any time, and so as long as you're working on only one app at a time, this would be sufficient. The free service also, from my experience, is subject to longer lines in terms of queuing for a build to occur. In other words, you might wait five minutes for your build to complete instead of 30 seconds if you have a paid plan. That's a small price to pay in my mind. Either way, for what we need to do here and now, it's perfectly fine.

Once you select your plan, you'll be asked to create an account. You can do this either by creating an Adobe ID or, if you already have a GitHub account, logging in. If you create an Adobe ID, you'll be greeted with the screen in Figure 10-2.

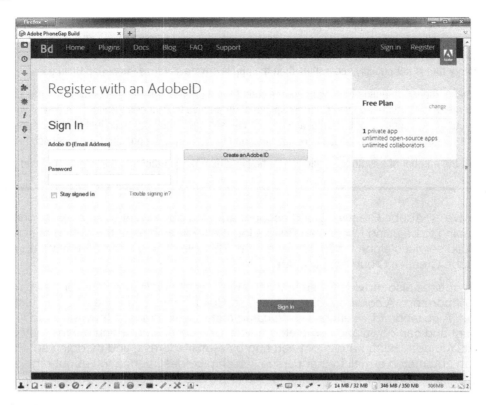

Figure 10-2. Creating an Adobe ID account

Incidentally, if you choose to go this route and later decide to sign up for Adobe Creative Cloud services, then you can use this same account to have some consistency across all of your Adobe offerings.

Once you create the account and accept the end-user license agreement (because it wouldn't be cool with all of the lawyers if you didn't have to accept a EULA somewhere!), then you'll find yourself staring at a screen very much like the one shown in Figure 10-3. At this point, you have a choice. You can either create a new private app by supplying the URL to a Git repository (or connect to your GitHub account if you have one) or upload a ZIP archive of your application. For the purposes of this book, that's all we'll be doing; the usage of Git and GitHub will be an exercise left to you, dear reader, if that's something about which you're interested.

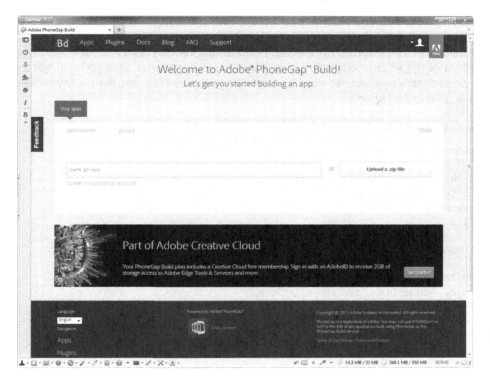

Figure 10-3. *Creating your first app in PhoneGap Build*

You also have the choice of creating a new app from an open source Git repo, which really means a public app. To do so, as with a private app, you either supply the URL to a private Git repo or connect to your existing GitHub account.

However, I'm jumping the gun a bit here! Before you upload an app, there's another step that you generally will have to take, and that's to create a configuration file to include in your uploaded archive.

Get Set: The Configuration File

Creating a configuration file is, in fact, optional. Instead, you can configure the app using the web interface provided by PhoneGap Build. However, I suggest you use a configuration file, since that way your app will be a bit more self-contained and you can make all of your changes locally before shipping them off to PhoneGap Build. The alternative is a bit of a split in that your source code will be local but the configuration of your build will be in the cloud. I prefer keeping it all together. In any case, the flexibility exists to take either approach, and it's entirely up to you for which you prefer, but I'm going to discuss the configuration file approach here.

The configuration file is based on the W3C's widget specification, which you can read about in all its gory details at www.w3.org/TR/widgets. If you're not the type to peruse big, complex specification documents, read on!

The configuration file, which you'll name `config.xml` and place in the root directory of the app alongside the `index.html` file that serves as the app's starting point, is where you specify metadata about your application that informs PhoneGap Build about various parameters it needs to build your application. Most of the information you can put in this file is optional, and you can get away with a small subset of all that is available to you. Listing 10-1 is the `config.xml` file for My Mobile Organizer. As you can see, it is rather spartan.

Listing 10-1. The config.xml File for My Mobile Organizer

```
<?xml version="1.0" encoding="UTF-8" ?>

<widget xmlns="http://www.w3.org/ns/widgets"
  xmlns:gap="http://phonegap.com/ns/1.0"
  id="com.etherient.MyMobileOrganizer"
  version = "1.0.0">

  <preference name="phonegap-version" value="2.9.0" />

  <name>My Mobile Organizer</name>
  <description>My Mobile Organizer</description>
  <author href="http://www.etherient.com" email="fzammetti@etherient.com">
    Frank W. Zammetti
  </author>

</widget>
```

The first required element is the `<widget>` element. This must be the root element that lets PhoneGap Build know you're following the widget specification. This element has a number of attributes, but only `id` and `version` are required.

The `id` attribute is the unique identifier of your application, which must be unique across all apps built using PhoneGap Build. The way you ensure this without meeting up with every other developer in the world and coming to some sort of arrangement is to use reverse-domain name naming. This is typically seen in Java package names, and it is simply your domain name backward, plus an app name. For example, I own the domain name `etherient.com`, so `com.etherient.MyMobileOrganizer` fits the bill. Now I only have to ensure the final portion of that, `MyMobileOrganizer`, is unique within the domain I control. I'm not averse to arguing with myself at times, but I'm sure even I can manage this level of cooperation with myself!

The `version` attribute is a free-form field, but typically the value is in the common `major.minor.patch` form, as you can see. Optionally, you can supply a `versionCode` attribute, which applies only to Android builds. This integer value represents the version of your app relative to other versions. This allows your code to do a comparison of values to see whether it needs to perform any sort of upgrade/downgrade conversions. Again, though, this is optional, even for an Android build.

The `<name>` and `<description>` elements, children of the root `<widget>` element, are not actually required by the widget spec, but the PhoneGap Build documentation calls them out as required, so it may be true that they are required for the build servers to process the file. I suggest treating them as required in any case, as they are elements you'll likely *want* to supply because they are used on the Your Apps page of your PhoneGap Build console, as shown in Figure 10-4.

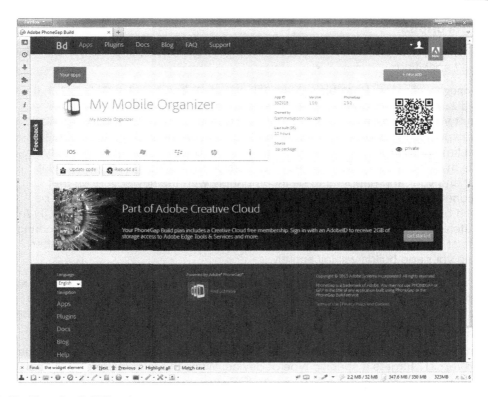

Figure 10-4. The PhoneGap Build Your Apps page

The larger "My Mobile Organizer" is the value of the `<name>` element, and the smaller "My Mobile Organizer" below it is the value of the `<description>` element. Whether the `<description>` element is required or not, if you have more than one app, you'll want to see that sort of information on the page to help keep things straight I'm sure.

The other element present in the `config.xml` file for My Mobile Organizer is `272103_1_En`. This is entirely optional, but it is a good idea to provide, especially if you're working with multiple developers.

Preferences

Beyond the basic elements and attributes are zero or more `<preference>` elements, children of the `<widget>` element. These are how you provide additional information to PhoneGap Build to use to build your application. Each `<preference>` element has a `name` attribute and a `value` attribute, the values of which are dependent on the preference you're setting.

Some preferences are global and apply to all platforms, while others set platform-specific configuration.

Global Preferences

Here is a list of the global preferences allowed, their possible values, and the default value if the preference isn't specified:

- phonegap-version: Possible values: 2.0.0, 2.1.0, 2.2.0, 2.3.0, 2.5.0, 2.7.0, and 2.9.0. Default value: 2.9.0. Defines which version of PhoneGap you want your app to be built with. In the config.xml file for My Mobile Organizer, I've specified version 2.9.0, for example, which happens to be the default at the time of this writing. While this preference is optional, I prefer to specify this myself because that ensures what version my builds use. If you leave it out and your app happens to be incompatible with the newer version that PhoneGap Build uses by default, then you'll have a build that appears to be valid but doesn't quite function properly when used. Note that if you specify this preference, all build types will be set to that version. You can, of course, change this at any time. Note too that if you specify an unsupported version number, then your app builds will fail entirely.

- orientation: Possible values: default, landscape, and portrait. Default value: default. Determines the initial screen orientation that your app will have. The default value effectively means to use whatever orientation the device is in when the app is launched (or is rotated to by the user).

- target-device: Possible values: handset, tablet, and universal. Default value: universal. Targets a specific type of device. While this is considered a global preference, currently it is effectively an iOS-only preference because only iOS differentiates device types like this. For iOS builds, the default means a universal app will be built that can run on all form factors supported by iOS.

- fullscreen: Possible values: true or false. Default value: false. Specifies whether the app should launch full-screen. When true, the status bar at the top of the screen is hidden.

iOS-Specific Preferences

There are a number of iOS-specific preferences.

- webviewbounce: Possible values: true or false. Default value: true. This determines whether the screen will "bounce" when it is scrolled beyond the top or bottom of the screen.

- prerendered-icon: Possible values: true or false. Default value: false. This determines whether iOS will apply its default gloss effect to the app's icon on the user's home screen.

- ios-statusbarstyle: Possible values: default, black-opaque, and black-translucent. Default value, default. This determines the style of the status bar when your app is run. The default is a gray status bar. Note that although black-translucent is supported, the PhoneGap WebView in which your app runs does not extend beneath the status bar, so it will appear identical to black-opaque once your app is running.

- detect-data-types: Possible values: `true` or `false`. Default value: `true`. This controls whether the OS automatically turns certain data types, such as phone numbers and dates, into links.

- exit-on-suspend: Possible values: `true` or `false`. Default value: `false`. This determines what will happen when your app is suspended. If `true`, it will be terminated entirely, for example, when the user presses the home button.

- show-splash-screen-spinner: Possible values: `true` or `false`. Default value: `true`. This determines whether the spinner seen when your app launches is displayed on the splash screen.

- auto-hide-splash-screen: Possible values: `true` or `false`. Default value: `true`. If set to false, the splash screen must be hidden using a JavaScript API; PhoneGap will not do it by default like it will when set to `true`.

BlackBerry-Specific Preferences

For BlackBerry, only a single specific preference is supported.

- disable-cursor: Possible values: `true` or `false`. Default value: `false`. This allows you to prevent a mouse icon/cursor from being displayed when your app is running.

Android-Specific Preferences

Finally, Android has a few specific preferences available.

- android-minSdkVersion: Possible values: any integer value. Default value: 7. Allows you to specify the minimum version of Android that your app requires to run. This corresponds to the `usesSdk` attribute in the `AndroidManifest.xml` file. The default value 7 corresponds to Android 2.1 (Eclair).

- android-maxSdkVersion: Possible values: any integer value. Default value: none. This goes hand-in-hand with the `android-minSdkVersion`, and it allows you to set the maximum version of Android that your app supports. It is somewhat unusual to see this value set, but if you know, for instance, that your app is incompatible with a newer version of Android, then you can use this to ensure that users with a newer version can't attempt to run your app and have a bad experience as a result.

- android-installLocation: Possible values: `internalOnly`, `auto`, and `preferExternal`. Default value: `internalOnly`. The values `auto` or `preferExternal` allow the app to be installed on an SD card. Note that this can lead to unexpected behavior, and it is usually not a good idea. You'll need to do some research on that if you think your app needs to be installable to external storage so that you fully understand the potential pitfalls of doing so.

- splash-screen-duration: Possible values: any numeric value (milliseconds). Default value: 5000 (5 seconds). This lets you specify for how long to display your app's splash screen.

- load-url-timeout: Possible values: any numeric value (milliseconds). Default value: 20000 (20 seconds). This lets you specify how long things such as Ajax calls are allowed to go for before they time out.

Other Supported Elements

Beyond the `<preference>` elements, a number of other elements are available to you as children of the `<widget>` element, which can be useful for various things.

Icon Support

Your app can include a number of icons to support *various* platforms, devices, and configurations. The `<icon>` element, of which you can have as many as you need, allows you to accomplish that.

The `<icon>` element is optional, and if no `<icon>` elements are present in your config file, then an icon of the PhoneGap logo will be used as your application's icon. This element supports three attributes. The first is `src`, which is required and specifies the location of the image file relative to your `www` directory. The `width` attribute, which is optional, is the width of the icon in pixels. While not required, this (and `height`) are recommended for the same reason that you usually want to supply them on an `<img>` tag on a web page: it boosts performance somewhat. The `height` attribute serves the same purpose for the vertical size of the icon.

Unless otherwise specified in your config file, each platform will try to use the default `icon.png` found in the root of your application. In addition, you can specify platform-specific icons that must be in specified formats. Aside from `icon.png`, for iOS you can supply a number of other files.

```
<icon src="icons/ios/icon.png" gap:platform="ios" width="57" height="57" />
<icon src="icons/ios/icon-72.png" gap:platform="ios" width="72" height="72" />
<icon src="icons/ios/icon_at_2x.png" gap:platform="ios" width="114" height="114" />
<icon src="icons/ios/icon-72_at_2x.png" gap:platform="ios" width="144" height="144" />
```

Each of these corresponds to various configurations including iPhone, the original iPad, and iPads with Retina displays. Please refer to the PhoneGap Build documentation for more specifics on these. (This is a common comment about all of these elements actually, but I'm only providing a general overview here, not every particular.)

For Android, you can supply icons for the various display types.

```
<icon src="icons/android/ldpi.png" gap:platform="android" gap:density="ldpi" />
<icon src="icons/android/mdpi.png" gap:platform="android" gap:density="mdpi" />
<icon src="icons/android/hdpi.png" gap:platform="android" gap:density="hdpi" />
<icon src="icons/android/xhdpi.png" gap:platform="android" gap:density="xhdpi" />
```

For BlackBerry, icons must be smaller than 16KB; in addition, they provide for a hover state for the icons.

```
<icon src="icons/bb/icon.png" gap:platform="blackberry" />
<icon src="icons/bb/icon_hover.png" gap:platform="blackberry" gap:state="hover"/>
```

For Windows Phone, a regular icon and a tile icon are supported.

```
<icon src="icons/winphone/icon.png" gap:platform="winphone" />
<icon src="icons/winphone/tileicon.png" gap:platform="winphone" gap:role="background" />
```

webOS provides the ability to specify a default icon as well as a mini icon seen in notifications.

```
<icon src="icons/webos/icon.png" gap:platform="webos" />
<icon src="icons/webos/miniicon.png" gap:platform="webos" gap:role="mini" />
```

As you can see, a number of icon options are available to suit all of your needs across all of the device types and configurations.

Splash Screens

A *splash screen* is what the user sees while your app is loading and initializing. PhoneGap Build allows you to define these through the use of `<gap:splash>` elements, of which you can have as many as needed to support various platforms (or you can have none, of course, since this is entirely optional).

One of these elements can have `src`, `gap:platform`, `width`, and `height` attributes, just like the `<icon>` element previously discussed. Like most icon files, your splash screens should be saved as PNG files. Here's an example:

```
<gap:splash src="splash/ios/Default-568h@2x~iphone.png" gap:platform="ios" width="320" height="480" />
```

Since the `<gap:splash>` element is optional, if not supplied, the default `splash.png` supplied by PhoneGap will be used. As with icons, though, you can specify different splash screens for various platforms, devices, and configurations.

Caution   If you do not supply the `gap:platform` attribute, the referenced image will be copied to *all* platforms, increasing the size of their application packages.

In the case of iOS, support similar to the icons is present.

```
<gap:splash src="splash/ios/Default.png" gap:platform="ios" width="320" height="480" />
<gap:splash src="splash/ios/Default_at_2x.png" gap:platform="ios" width="640" height="960" />
<gap:splash src="splash/ios/Default_iphone5.png" gap:platform="ios" width="640" height="1136" />
<gap:splash src="splash/ios/Default-Landscape.png" gap:platform="ios" width="1024" height="748" />
<gap:splash src="splash/ios/Default-Portrait.png" gap:platform="ios" width="768" height="1004" />
<gap:splash src="splash/ios/Default-Landscape_at_2x.png" gap:platform="ios" width="2048"
height="1496" />
<gap:splash src="splash/ios/Default-Portrait_at_2x.png" gap:platform="ios" width="1536"
height="2008" />
```

For Android, once again, the different display densities are supported.

```
<gap:splash src="splash/android/ldpi.png" gap:platform="android" gap:density="ldpi" />
<gap:splash src="splash/android/mdpi.png" gap:platform="android" gap:density="mdpi" />
<gap:splash src="splash/android/hdpi.png" gap:platform="android" gap:density="hdpi" />
<gap:splash src="splash/android/xhdpi.png" gap:platform="android" gap:density="xhdpi" />
```

BlackBerry is simpler, and it supports only a single splash image.

```
<gap:splash src="splash/bb/splash.png" gap:platform="blackberry" />
```

Windows Phone, similar to BlackBerry, has a single splash screen; but unlike BlackBerry, iOS, and Android, it must be in JPG format.

```
<gap:splash src="splash/winphone/splash.jpg" gap:platform="winphone" />
```

Custom URL Schemes

A custom URL scheme is an iOS-only feature that allows your app to register custom URL schemes for app handling purposes. Here's an example:

```
<gap:url-scheme name="com.acme.myscheme" role="None">
  <scheme>pgbr</scheme>
  <scheme>pgbw</scheme>
</gap:url-scheme>
```

You can have as many `<gap:url-scheme>` elements as you want or none at all. The `name` attribute, which is optional, defaults to the application bundle ID, which must be unique. (If any are duplicated, then the build will fail.) The role must be one of `Editor`, `Viewer`, `Shell`, or `None`. This attribute is optional and defaults to `None` if not specified. As a child of a `<gap:url-scheme>`, at least one `<scheme>` element must be present.

Features

The `<feature>` elements can be used to specify which features your application is using. If you specify features of the PhoneGap API, those will be expanded to the appropriate permissions for your application.

For example, if you're going to use the Geolocation API, you should add a `<feature>` element like so:

```
<feature name="http://api.phonegap.com/1.0/geolocation"/>
```

The necessary permissions for Android, iOS, BlackBerry, and so on, will be added to your final application build automatically—no messing with native config files required!

Here's a list of the currently supported features and the native permissions to which they map:

- `http://api.phonegap.com/1.0/battery`: Android—BROADCAST_STICKY
- `http://api.phonegap.com/1.0/camera`: Android—CAMERA; Windows Phone—ID_CAP_ISV_CAMERA and ID_HW_FRONTCAMERA
- `http://api.phonegap.com/1.0/contacts`: Android—READ_CONTACTS, WRITE_CONTACTS, and GET_ACCOUNTS; Windows Phone—ID_CAP_CONTACTS
- `http://api.phonegap.com/1.0/file`: Android—WRITE_EXTERNAL_STORAGE

- http://api.phonegap.com/1.0/geolocation:
  Android—ACCESS_COARSE_LOCATION, ACCESS_FINE_LOCATION, and
  ACCESS_LOCATION_EXTRA_COMMANDS;
  Windows Phone—ID_CAP_LOCATION

- http://api.phonegap.com/1.0/media: Android—RECORD_AUDIO,
  RECORD_VIDEO, and MODIFY_AUDIO_SETTINGS;
  Windows Phone—ID_CAP_MICROPHONE

- http://api.phonegap.com/1.0/network: Android—ACCESS_NETWORK_STATE;
  Windows Phone—ID_CAP_NETWORKING

- http://api.phonegap.com/1.0/notification: Android—VIBRATE

- http://api.phonegap.com/1.0/device:
  Windows Phone—ID_CAP_IDENTITY_DEVICE

Access Elements

The `<access>` element provides your app with access to resources on other domains. This allows your app to load pages from external domains that can take over your entire WebView element, essentially taking the place of your application from the user's perspective.

Two special cases for this element are supported. First, a blank access tag in the form of `<access />` denies access to any external resources. A wildcard version in the form of `<access origin="*" />` allows access to any external resource.

The more common usage scenario is to declare specific domains accessible like so:

```
<access origin="http://www.etherient.com" />
```

You can also use the `subdomains` attribute to allow access to any subdomain of the specified domain.

```
<access origin="http://www.etherient.com" subdomains="true" />
```

So now, `products.etherient.com` will be accessible as well.

> **Caution**   The behavior of the `<access>` element is heavily dependent on the platform to which you're deploying. The PhoneGap Build documentation contains information and links to additional reading about this behavior.

Plug-ins: Extending What's Already Good to Make It Great

Another element that is available in `config.xml` is the `<gap:plugin>` element. This allows you to use PhoneGap plug-ins with a minimum of effort.

Before I describe that element, let's talk about what a PhoneGap plug-in is in general. In short, a *PhoneGap plug-in* is an extension to PhoneGap. Such an extension adds capabilities to your applications. In a sense, it lets you add on to the PhoneGap API and then use the additions in your application code as you would any of the PhoneGap APIs described in the previous chapter.

A plug-in consists of two parts: a JavaScript API for your app to interact with and a bit of native code that implements the underlying functionality of that API. Plug-ins, by design, allow for the implementation to be specific to a given platform, while the API with which you interact remains consistent across all supported platforms. If you've been paying attention, you'll realize that this describes all of the PhoneGap APIs very well!

You can develop your own plug-ins, of course. Doing so will require you to get into native code, meaning Objective-C for iOS, Java for Android, C# for Windows Phone, and so on. It also means you'll need to have a Mac for iOS development. However, there are many plug-ins available for you to use without going through that effort and avoiding that bit of native development entirely, which is the point of this book after all! In addition, PhoneGap Build makes it even a little easier by providing an element in the configuration file that allows you to skip even the step of obtaining the plug-in code on your own and including it with your application!

> **Tip**   Plug-ins by their nature may not be supported on all of the platforms that you intend your app to run on. Because of this, it's important to design your app such that it degrades gracefully when the features that the plug-in uses aren't available on a given device. This is actually a true statement of some parts of the basic PhoneGap API because some of those functions may not be available on certain platforms as well. With those APIs, though, they are designed to reach as broad of an audience as possible, while that may not always be true of plug-ins. The basic point is that, as you design, simply consider and code your app as to what happens when a given feature isn't available on a given device.

A `<gap:plugin>` element specifies a PhoneGap plug-in that you want to include in your application. This is a two-step process. First, make sure the plug-in is supported by PhoneGap Build. While you can use plug-ins that aren't supported natively by PhoneGap Build, in such cases it will be your responsibility to include the appropriate code with your archive. For the "supported" plug-ins, that code will be added to your app on the fly, making it easy to use those plug-ins. Second, include any necessary `<script>` tag in your app to import the plug-in's JavaScript code.

> **Note**   Technically speaking, the native code is included by virtue of the `<gap:plugin>` element, but PhoneGap Build also injects the appropriate JavaScript file that results from that element. It's still your job to include that JavaScript file in your `index.html` file; it won't do that for you.

For example, to use the Barcode scanner plug-in that adds the ability to scan and recognize bar codes to your app, add this element:

```
<gap:plugin name="com.phonegap.plugins.barcodescanner" />
```

The `name` value is a unique plug-in ID that uses the same reverse-domain scheme as the ID for your app. You can optionally include a `version` attribute that will allow you to specify the precise version of the plug-in to use; otherwise, PhoneGap Build will choose the latest version known to it. You can also do some fancy tricks like `version=">=2.2.1"` to specify a minimum version to use or version="<=2.2.1" to specify that you want to use a version no newer than 2.2.1. You can also use the tilde (~) operator to specify fuzzy versions, meaning that PhoneGap Build will ensure that the latest version of a plug-in with the same major version is used. For example, you can do version="~2". This would cause the latest 2.x version to be used, but not a version with a different major version number (meaning that no 1.x versions and no 3.x versions).

In addition, the <gap:plugin> element can have child <param> elements, each with a name and value attribute. This allows you to pass configuration information to the plug-in. The documentation for each plug-in will spell out what configuration parameters are available.

To complete this example, the final step would be to add the following in your index.html file:

```
<script src="barcodescanner.js"></script>
```

Now you'll be able to do things like this in your application code:

```
var scanner = cordova.require("cordova/plugin/BarcodeScanner");

scanner.scan(
  function (result) {
    alert("We got a barcode\n" +
      "Result: " + result.text + "\n" +
      "Format: " + result.format + "\n" +
      "Cancelled: " + result.cancelled
    );
  },
  function (error) {
    alert("Scanning failed: " + error);
  }
);
```

The PhoneGap Build documentation includes a current list of all of the plug-ins supported and the requisite usage information you'll need to use them. Some are supplied by Adobe, while others are supplied by third parties, and the list is expanding all of the time.

At the time of this writing, here's the list of available plug-ins, the ID for each, and the latest version available. (This is a point-in-time list, remember, and you'll want to look at the current list if and when you decide to use the plug-in capabilities.)

- *American Bible Society Biblesearch*: org.americanbible.biblesearch, 1.0.6. The American Bible Society has produced this JavaScript library to ease the use of the Bible Search API (http://bibles.org/pages/api) in Cordova/PhoneGap applications. This plug-in allows you easily to search the Bible, locate specific passages, and get information about specific books, chapters, and verses.

- *AppAvailability*: com.ohh2ahh.plugins.appavailability, 0.1.0. This plug-in allows you to check whether another app is installed on the device. It requires a package name on Android, com.facebook.katana for example, and an URI scheme for iOS, fb:// for example.

- *BarcodeScanner*: com.phonegap.plugins.barcodescanner, 0.6.0. Simply put, this plug-in allows your app to scan bar codes. 'Nuff said.

- *Bluetooth Serial*: com.megster.cordova.bluetoothserial, 0.2.0. This plug-in allows you to add Bluetooth serial communication capabilities to your application.

- *Child Browser*: com.phonegap.plugins.childbrowser, 4.2.1. It provides a lightweight browser window for viewing pages external to the host application along with the ability to return easily to the application. This is handy for showing online documentation, for example.

- *Facebook Connect*: com.phonegap.plugins.facebookconnect, 0.3.2. This is the official plug-in from Facebook for Cordova/PhoneGap apps to use. It allows you to use the same JavaScript code in your PhoneGap application as you would use in your web application to integrate with the popular Facebook platform. This plug-in even handles logon and authentication for you!

- *FastCanvas*: com.adobe.plugins.fastcanvas, 1.0.1. FastCanvas is a PhoneGap plug-in that implements a very fast, 2D, HTML5 Canvas-compatible (mostly anyway) rendering surface for Android. On other platforms, it silently falls back on the native Canvas implementation so that your app will still work there, even if at a degraded performance level. While FastCanvas attempts to look and behave like the HTML5 Canvas, it supports only a subset of the HTML5 Canvas API, focusing on what benefits most from hardware acceleration. If you're thinking "Ah ha! Games!" with this, you're right, although it's not exclusively for game development, of course.

- *GAPlugin*: com.adobe.plugins.gaplugin, 2.1.1. This plug-in allows you to post usage information to your Google Analytics account.

- *NFC*: com.chariotsolutions.nfc.plugin, 0.4.5. This plug-in provides the ability for your app to use Near Field Communication (NFC). With it, you can read and write NDEF messages to NFC tags or share with peers that also support the protocol.

- *PowberManagement*: com.simplec.plugins.powermanagement, 0.1.2. This plug-in controls power management features so that an application can better manage its power usage on iOS and other supported platforms.

- *PushbPlugin*: com.adobe.plugins.pushplugin, 1.3.3. This plug-in allows your application to receive push notifications on both Android and iOS platforms. The Android implementation uses the Google Cloud Messaging service to accomplish this and Apple APNS Notifications on iOS.

- *Pushwoosh*: com.pushwoosh.plugins.pushwoosh, 3.0.0. Like PushPlugin, Pushwoosh allows your app to receive push notifications. They differ in the underlying communication technology used to receive those messages.

Go: Starting the Build

With a config.xml file written and added to the root of your application, it's time to kick off a build. The first step to doing this is a simple one: create a ZIP archive from your application's directory. For example, in the source code bundle for this book, you'll find a client directory (as well as a `client_augmented` directory, but we'll get to that shortly). If you look at the contents, you'll see that it's nothing but HTML, JavaScript, CSS, image files, and, of course, that `config.xml` file. Zip up that directory, and you'll have an archive ready to be shipped off to PhoneGap Build.

> **Note**   When I say, "zip up that directory," I mean you should zip up the contents of the directory, not the directory itself. Put another way, after you zip it up, copy the archive file to an empty directory somewhere else and try to extract it. When you do so, you should not see a client directory created in the empty directory. Instead, you should see the contents of the client directory "spill out," so to speak, directly into the previously empty directory into which you're extracting the archive. If you create the archive from a GUI, you should be selecting all of the contents of the client directory and zipping that up, not selecting the client directory itself.

After initially signing up for PhoneGap Build and logging in, you'll see a screen like the one shown in Figure 10-5.

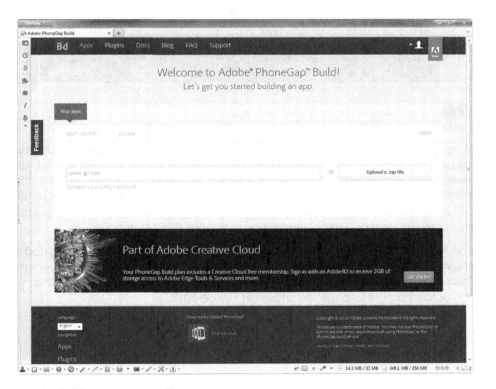

Figure 10-5. PhoneGap Build, at your command!

If you've already uploaded an app, which is what we'll be doing next, then you will instead see a list of your apps, as shown in Figure 10-6, with one or more applications listed. You can get to this screen later too by clicking the Apps link at the top of the page.

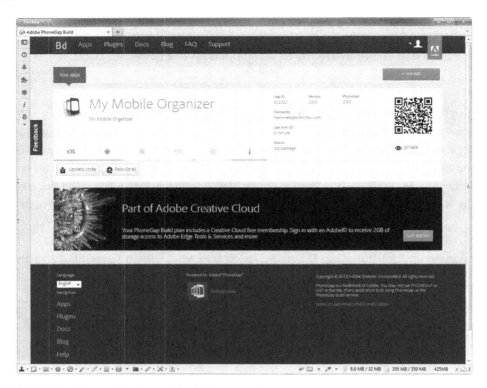

Figure 10-6. All of this has happened before, and it will happen again

However, let's assume that this is indeed your first app. In that case, you'll need to decide whether you're working on a public or private app. If it's a public app, click the open source tab and enter or paste in the address of your public Git repo or connect with your GitHub account as directed. However, assuming that you're following along for the purpose of this book, make sure the private tab is selected, which it is likely by default; you can see that you have the choice of supplying the address for a private Git repo or, again, connecting with your GitHub account.

The third option available, which is what's most relevant here, is the big honkin' "Upload a .zip file" button. Make sure you've properly zipped up the client directory, as previously described, and click the button. Then browse to where the ZIP file is located and select it. Once you do this, you'll be greeted with an upload progress page, as shown in Figure 10-7.

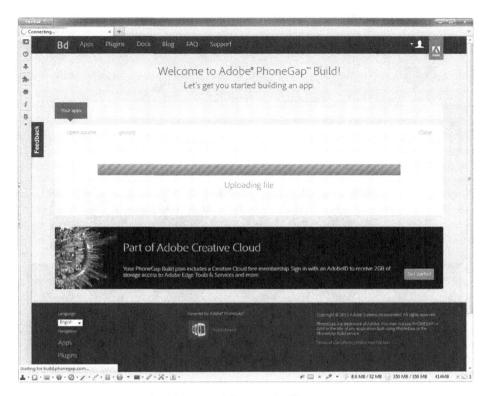

Figure 10-7. We're making progress now! (Get it? Progress? Progress bar?!)

For My Mobile Organizer, since it's not a very big app, it won't take more than a few seconds to upload. This isn't the end of the process, though! All that you've done is ship the code to the PhoneGap Build servers—you haven't actually begun a build. To do that, you need to take some action on the next screen, Figure 10-8, that you'll see once the upload completes.

Figure 10-8. App uploaded and ready to build

The simplest sequence of events now is to click the "Ready to build" button. Doing that, and nothing else, will start the builds for all supported platforms.

However, you also have the choice of enabling debugging and enabling hydration. I'm going to skip the Enabled Debugging option for now entirely. We'll come back to it later, but let's discuss hydration briefly.

Hydration is an option that provides two main benefits to developers and potential testers or your app alike. The first benefit is that compilation times are improved significantly. Second, updates are effectively pushed directly to a device running the application. The way that this is accomplished is that a special native binary is compiled that acts as a container for your mobile application. This is much like what PhoneGap does anyway, of course, but this version of the binary has some additional capabilities baked in. The result is that, whenever a developer uploads a new build, testers of the app, which may in fact be just the developer and not someone else, will be notified when they restart the application that a new version is available. If that person decides to run the new version, that new version will automatically be retrieved from the PhoneGap Build servers, and it will replace the existing version on their device.

For a single developer project, hydrating an app probably doesn't buy you a whole lot (although it is arguably a bit more convenient to update your on-device app). For a team of developers or when you have actual app testers involved, as is common in the later stages of development, this is a handy mechanism indeed.

Note   You can hydrate an app after the fact as well very easily just by clicking the button on the app details page on the PhoneGap Build console, which is essentially what I've been describing in this section. See the PhoneGap Build documentation for further details.

Whether you hydrate or not or enable debugging or not (something, again, that I'll get to a little later in this chapter), when you're ready to go, click that "Ready to build" button. Doing so yields the screen in Figure 10-9.

Figure 10-9. A build running

You can't see it in a static screenshot, of course, but the little bars under each of the target platforms are an animated progress indicator. This isn't terribly useful, especially if you have old eyes like me! Instead, click the app title, the big "My Mobile Organizer" here, and you'll be greeted with an expanded version, as shown in Figure 10-10.

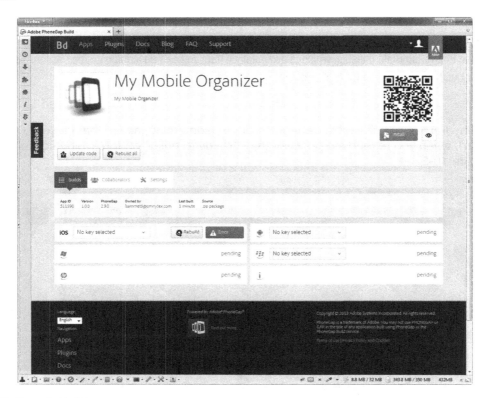

Figure 10-10. Expanded build process

Here you can see that most of the builds are still in progress and so are pending.

Crossing the Finish Line: The Output Files

Each of the supported platforms uses its own native bundle formats, but all of them are archives containing platform-specific code. On iOS, the format is IPA. For Windows Phone, it's a XAP file. For webOS, we're talking about an IPK. For Android, the answer is an APK. BlackBerry uses a JAD file, and Symbian uses a WGZ file.

Notice that the iOS build has failed, and it seems to have to do with not having a key selected, based on the text in the drop-down. In fact, if you click the Error button, which is red (you'll have to take my word for that since you can't tell here!), it will explicitly tell you this and provide a link for information on dealing with this situation. This is an additional step required for iOS only, and I'll discuss that later in this chapter; it's actually not a big problem to deal with.

> **Note**   Android and BlackBerry also support the notion of keys, but for those, the build won't fail if you don't supply one because default keys are available from PhoneGap Build. For testing, these keys are sufficient, but for a final, "production" build, you'll need to supply your own keys, just as you do for iOS (which requires them even for development purposes. (Again, I'll touch on this a bit later.)

After some time, your screen should look like Figure 10-11, with all builds (except iOS, as just mentioned) available for download.

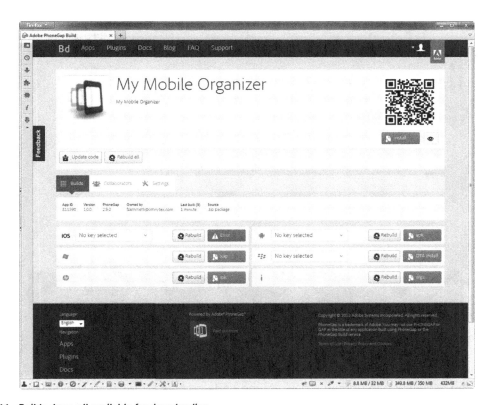

Figure 10-11. Builds done, all available for downloading

That is, in a nutshell, all it takes to build an app with PhoneGap Build!

At this point, you can download the bundle for each platform using the buttons next to each and install those bundles onto a real device, or an emulator, and begin testing your app (except for iOS, as there's a problem with keys to deal with there, but that will be dealt with in the "Deploying to iOS Devices" section).

The Install button in the top right is another nice way to get at those bundles. The page you get when you click it can be provided to your testers so that they have one, consolidated place to go to get any of the builds, without having to parse any of the "technical" details you see on the app info page. In addition, you can rebuild an individual platform if you need to (for example, after adding a key for iOS) by clicking the Rebuild button next to the build for each platform. Finally, you can click the "Rebuild all" button to kick off a build of all platforms at once.

Also, at this point, you can add collaborators on the aptly named Collaborators tab, as you can see in Figure 10-12.

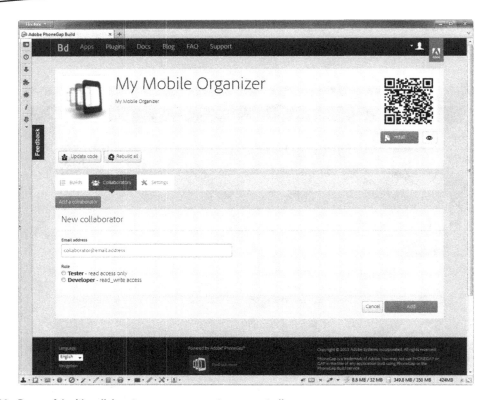

Figure 10-12. *Be careful with collaborators; some may get you arrested!*

In addition, there are settings that you can manipulate about your app, as shown in Figure 10-13. The Settings tab allows you to upload a new source code archive for building (which you can also do by clicking the "Update code" button above the Builds, Collaborators, and Settings tabs), as well as add hydration and debugging capabilities to your app. You can also decide whether only approved collaborators can download your app (in addition to you, of course), which is the case by default.

Figure 10-13. *Basic settings*

If your source code archive *did not* include a config.xml file, then you can alter some of the available settings here as well. In the case of My Mobile Organizer, a note is displayed saying that you should instead update the file and then push a new archive including it to the servers to make changes to those config values. Figure 10-14 shows these available config options and that warning message.

Figure 10-14. *Configuration options*

Finally, if you scroll the Settings tab to the bottom, you'll see a Danger Zone section. While this implies that you should run screaming from the room, you should probably fight that urge. I'll be honest here: I wasn't able to find any concrete information on what this section is. Based on the title, I was thinking that you'd see any sort of problems that might cause your build to fail—that sort of thing. However, I tried a number of different, on-purpose mistakes, and I could never get such messages to show up there, so that assumption may be wrong. In any case, what *is* there for sure is a button that allows you to delete the app, and certainly that's important. Come to think of it, I suppose "Danger Zone" could simply mean "Here are functions that are dangerous if you misuse them." That makes sense too, doesn't it? Whatever the case, that button allows you to get rid of the app entirely, which is helpful on the free account where you can have only one private app. Deleting an existing one to make room for another is common.

Getting Files Onto Your Device

As described in the previous section, the native bundles for each platform for which your app was successfully built are easily downloadable from the app info page or the Install page. However, that tells you nothing about how to get that bundle onto a real device or an emulator. Let's talk about that now, shall we?

> **Note**   I'm only going to describe Android and iOS here. I feel justified in doing that since those two platforms account for 90+ percent of all smartphones in the world as of the first quarter of 2013. You'll be on your own for any other platform, although I can tell you, generally, that they all look more or less similar to either Android or iOS, so after reading this section you'll at least have a clue should you want to deal with those platforms as well.

Deploying to iOS Devices

To deploy to an iOS device, you'll first need a Mac, as the development tools you'll need to use to do so are available only on a Mac. The key thing beyond that is that you need to set up a provisioning profile. This is what ties your development devices to your team or what allows you to publish to the App Store. Before you can even deal with profiles, though, you'll need to do a few things.

First, you'll need to register as an Apple developer at https://developer.apple.com/programs/register. Once there, you'll find a link to install Xcode, Apple's integrated development environment for iOS and Mac development. Go ahead and install that, if you don't already have it installed.

Once you do that, you need to authenticate your computer and create a certificate request. A signing certificate is a component that identifies you, and it becomes part of a provisioning profile, along with other information about the app and the devices on which it can be installed. To get started, you'll launch the Keychain Access tool found in the utilities folder of your Mac. Next you'll select the Certificate Assistant ➤ Request A Certificate From A Certificate Authority menu. You'll be asked to provide some information, such as e-mail address, name, banking information (so you can get paid!), and so on. Walk through the process as directed until you come to the end where you'll save the generated key.

Note   Before you can deploy to an actual device and publish to the App Store, you'll also need to cough up the $99 annual fee Apple requires to join its iOS developer program. You can sign up for a developer account without paying this fee up front to gain access to iOS development documentation and tools, but until you pay your dues, you will be able to use the iOS simulator only for development, not physical devices. More relevant for this book, you won't be able to do what follows in terms of deploying your app to a real device.

Next, log on to the iOS Dev Center web site at `https://developer.apple.com/devcenter/ios/index.action`. Once there, click the Members link up top. This will bring you to a screen with a link for Certificates, Identifiers, and Profiles. Go ahead and click that link. Once there, click Devices in the left column, and then click the Add Devices button. Add any devices on which you intend to develop, including their unique device ID, which you can find in iTunes when your device is connected. (You may need to click the serial number you see on the Summary tab to get this, depending on the version of iTunes you are running.)

After your devices are added, while still in the provisioning portal, click Certificates on the left and then click the plus sign. You will then select the device generated in the previous step. In a few seconds, your certificate will be generated, and you'll be able to download it. Do so, and then double-click the file in Finder to add the certificate to your computer.

After that, you need to create a new app ID. On the left, in the provisioning portal, click App IDs, and then click the plus sign. Fill in the required information (description, bundle identifier, and so on) and click Submit. Your app ID will be created.

At this point, you are now ready to create a provisioning profile. This is done from the Provisioning link on the left side of the provisioning portal. Assuming you are doing development, select the Development tab. (When you're ready to publish your app, the process is the same except that you'll create a distribution profile via the Distribution tab.) Once there, enter the required information, including the app ID you created as well as selecting the devices with which the profile will work, and then click Submit.

Now launch the Xcode Organizer tool on your Mac, as shown in Figure 10-15, which you can find on the Windows menu after you launch Xcode. Once there, click the Devices tab up top. Then, under the Library heading on the left, select Provisioning Profiles. Next click the Refresh button. The profile you just created should appear there.

Figure 10-15. The Xcode Organizer

As you can see, the process for getting an iOS build ready for deployment to a device is fairly involved. However, once all of the prerequisites are done, the process really boils down to a few simple steps.

> **Note**   The provisioning profile you create here is what you enter on the PhoneGap Build page to allow that build to be successful.

Creating an iOS App Store Package

One other step that you'll need to be familiar with at this point is how to create an iOS App Store Package, better known as an *IPA file*. You'll need to do this when you're ready to distribute your app to the App Store or when you're going to use TestFlightApp.com, as described in the "TestFlightApp.com" section, which is coming up shortly!

To create an IPA file, follow these steps:

1. Create a folder named `Payload`, making sure to use that specific capitalization, somewhere on your Mac.

2. Put the `.app` file that PhoneGap Build generated for you into it.

3. Zip up the folder in Finder.

4. Rename the resultant archive to `xxx.ipa`, where xxx is anything you like.

Yep, that's it! The IPA file will now be ready to ship off to the App Store (assuming you used a valid distribution provisioning profile when you built it) or to `TestFlightApp.com`.

Now that you can build an iOS app that is deployable to one of your registered development devices, how do you actually go about getting it onto said devices? Here, as with Android, you have a couple of choices.

First, you can use the Xcode Organizer tool. To do this, first connect the device to your Mac. Then launch Xcode Organizer, and look for the device name under the Devices header on the left. You should find the device with a green indicator next to it. Next, expand the device menu and select Applications. Click the Add button, and then navigate to the folder where the `.app` file that the PhoneGap Build generated for you is stored and select it. The app should then be installed on the device.

Alternatively, you can use iTunes to install your app. To do this, open iTunes and connect your device. Then drag the `.app` file into the Library in the upper left. You should then see the app available for installation in the Apps tab, and you can install it like any other app.

TestFlightApp.com

A third option, which I like quite a bit, is a site called `TestFlightApp.com`. (In case you haven't had your morning coffee just yet, that's the URL too!) This site allows you to distribute your app to beta testers without them needing to do anything special in terms of setting up SDKs or any of that.

The process is simple: you sign up for a `TestFlightApp.com` account first. Next you invite users to be part of your testing via tools available on the site. This process will also collect the device IDs of those users. You then add those IDs back onto the iOS Provisioning Portal page. You finally build your app as always and upload it to `TestFlightApp.com`—and that's it! Test users will receive an e-mail notification that the app is available. The e-mail will provide a link for them to use to install the app so that they can begin testing it.

This process requires an API file, which was described in the "Creating an iOS App Store Package" section. Other than that, though, the process is very straightforward (oh, and did I mention free?)!

> **Caution** `TestFlightApp.com` also offers an SDK that allows you to hook in some good telemetry and statistics capturing. In addition, the site is currently working on an Android version of its services that, when ready, will help streamline beta testing on that platform as well (and there's a nice symmetry to using a cloud-based service for testing deployments when you're also using such a service to do the builds in the first place, isn't there?).

Deploying to Android Devices

So now that you have a packaged version of your application in APK form for Android in hand, courtesy of PhoneGap Build, how exactly do you get it on a device to play with? You can install it to the emulator that comes with the Android SDK as well, if you prefer, and the procedure for that versus a physical device isn't much different. There's actually a number of ways you can accomplish this task, the first of which is to use the Android Debug Bridge (ADB).

ADB is a tool that comes with the Android SDK, so if you don't have the SDK installed, you'll either need to visit http://developer.android.com and install it or use one of the other methods described next to get the app onto an Android device.

Once you have it installed, then all you need to do is to execute this from a command prompt:

```
adb install -r app.apk
```

> **Note**   You'll need to ensure that the `tools` and `platform-tools` directories under the Android SDK directory are in your path for this to work.

As long as `app.apk` is in the current directory, executing that command will push the APK onto the first device ADB finds attached to your PC. If you have an emulator running, it will be that device. If you have an actual Android phone attached via USB, it will be installed to that device.

Note that you'll also need to ensure that the USB debugging option is enabled on the device. The USB debugging option is found under Developer Options in your devices' Settings menu, although you may have to perform a little "trick" to enable this option. (This "trick" depends on your version of Android, but it typically involves tapping the Android version field on the About device screen a number of times.) Figure 10-16 shows this screen for reference.

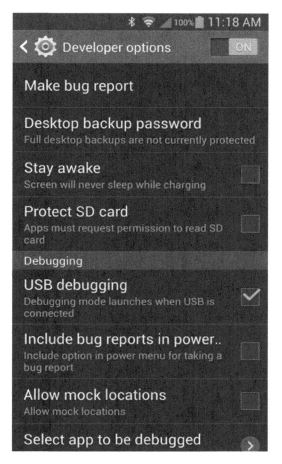

Figure 10-16. *USB debugging option enabled*

In addition, you'll also need to enable the "Unknown sources" option, which allows for installation of apps from sources other than the Play store. This is under Security in Settings, as shown in Figure 10-17.

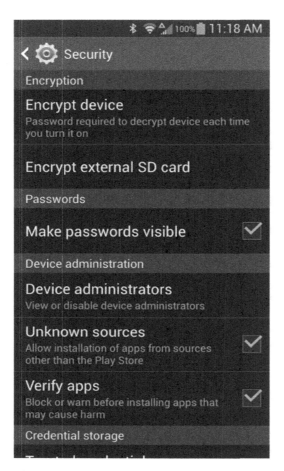

Figure 10-17. "Unknown sources" option enabled

Another way to get the app onto your device is simply to copy the APK file to your device when it's attached in USB mass storage or MTP mode (depending on OS version). You'll then have to browse to the file on the device with the file system browser of your choice and open it. You should again get the usual installation pop-up at that point.

Another approach, and the technique I personally use most because it is arguably the simplest and most convenient, at least in my mind, is to create a share to a directory on my PC. Next I make sure that the APK is present in that directory, and then I use a file system browser on my device, such as FX File Explorer, ES File Explorer, or Astro File Explorer (all of which most fittingly have SMB capabilities), to browse to that share and directly launch the file. This approach is nice because I don't have to bother with USB cables, making sure that drivers are installed, that the adb sees my device properly, and all that stuff that can sometimes get tricky with Android development. I also don't have to worry about uploading to a web server (of course, the web server could be running locally, which would make that approach not much different from this one frankly). It's still a two-step process, as all of these are, but now it's very straightforward. In addition, when I'm testing on multiple devices, it's easy since the same APK is always at the same location and I can browse to it any time I like to install it.

Augmentation: Adding Some PhoneGap API Goodness

Now that you're familiar with how to build My Mobile Organizer using PhoneGap Build and you've seen how to deploy that app onto mobile devices or emulators to test, let's take things to the next level and use some of those PhoneGap APIs to augment the functionality of the app as it stands. In reality, some of the APIs have been used already. Do you remember the code that checks for network connectivity? Well, that's part of the API. So too was the code for dealing with localStorage. Now, let's add some functionality with some other APIs, a few of which aren't even defined as part of HTML5.

In the code package for this book, you'll find the `client` directory, of course, which has been discussed in previous chapters. You'll also find a `client_augmented` directory. That directory is the focus of this section. It contains the client portion of My Mobile Organizer, just as in the original `client` directory, but this version includes the PhoneGap additions that we're going to discuss next.

Would You Like a Side of Geolocation with That?

First, let's add the ability to record the location where the user was at the time they created an item. For the sake of brevity, I'll add this only to notes; I'll leave it for you to add to the other entity types as an exercise. Recall that the code of the app is written to be generic across the board, so how it's done for notes would be how it's done for the other entity types with little change. In fact, a big part of what we'll do here will cover those other entities automatically.

The first step is preparatory in nature: we'll need a way to confirm that the save actually works. To do that, let's add a read-only field to the `notePage.html` file. It will be another text field on the note entry form, but it will be marked as read-only. Simply add the following after the `noteText` field:

```
<label for="noteGeolocation">Geolocation At Time Of Creation</label>
<input type="text" name="geoLatLong" id="noteGeoLatLong"
  readonly="true">
```

Good, that gives us a place to see the saved data now, and the user won't be able to enter it themselves, as that's the job of the API. We'll save a simple latitude and longitude value as a comma-separated string constructed from the data returned by the Geolocation API. That way, if we want to parse that string later for some reason, it's a simple call to the string's `split()` method.

Because of the commonality of the code throughout the app, we need only to modify the doSave() function in `main.js` to make this work (from a client perspective, that is). Since this is shared by all entity types, this change will allow geolocation information to be saved for all types, in fact, but only notes will show it upon retrieval. Instead of showing individual changes, in its place I'll show you the new version of the function and then explain what's different. Here it is:

```
function doSave(inType, inGeoLatLong) {

  if (!validations["check_" + inType](inType)) {
    $("#infoDialogHeader").html("Error");
    $("#infoDialogContent").html(
      "Please provide values for all required fields"
    );
    $.mobile.changePage($("#infoDialog"), { role : "dialog" });
    return;
  }
```

```
$.mobile.loading("show");

$("#" + inType + "Entry").hide();
$("#" + inType + "List").show();
$("#" + inType + "Menu" ).popup("close");

var httpMethod = "post";
var uid = "";
if (updateID) {
  httpMethod = "put";
  uid = "/" + updateID;
}

var finalSave = function(inType) {

  var frmData = getFormAsJSON(inType);

  updateID = null;
  document.getElementById(inType + "EntryForm").reset();

  $.ajax({
    url : ajaxURLPrefix + "/" + inType + uid, type : httpMethod,
    contentType: "application/json", data : frmData
  })
  .done(function(inResponse) {
    frmData = frmData.slice(0, frmData.length - 1);
    frmData = frmData + ",\"__v\":\"0\",\"_id\":\"" + inResponse + "\"}";
    window.localStorage.setItem(inType + "_" + inResponse, frmData);
    populateList(inType);
    $.mobile.loading("hide");
    $("#infoDialogHeader").html("Success");
    $("#infoDialogContent").html("Save to server complete");
    $.mobile.changePage($("#infoDialog"), { role : "dialog" });
  })
  .fail(function(inXHR, inStatus) {
    $.mobile.loading("hide");
    $("#infoDialogHeader").html("Error");
    $("#infoDialogContent").html(inStatus);
    $.mobile.changePage($("#infoDialog"), { role : "dialog" });
  });

};

if (inType == "note") {
  navigator.geolocation.getCurrentPosition(
    function(position) {
      $("#" + inType + "EntryForm [name=geoLatLong]").val(
        position.coords.latitude + "," + position.coords.longitude
      );
      finalSave("note");
    },
```

```
      function(error) {
        $("#" + inType + "EntryForm [name=geoLatLong]").val(
          "Not Available"
        );
        finalSave("note");
      }
    );
  } else {
    finalSave(inType);
  }

} // End doSave().
```

If you compare this to the original version, you'll see that it's the same up until the line where the finalSave() function is created, which is new. What I've done is to take the remainder of the code from the original doSave() function and wrap it in the finalSave() function. The code within finalSave() is, again, the same as what was in doSave(); it's just wrapped in a function now. However, we need to have a function like this because, after finalSave() is fully defined, you'll notice a block of code that is a call to the Geolocation API. The issue here is that the call to navigator(). geolocation.getCurrentPosition() is asynchronous, so we can't have the call to the server occur before that API call returns. With finalSave() defined, we can call that from within the callback to the Geolocation API (in both success and error cases). Of course, this is done only for notes. For any other entity type, finalSave() is immediately called, and things proceed as they always have.

Inside the function passed as the first argument to navigator().geolocation.getCurrentPosition(), the success callback, the form field we just added has its value set to one constructed from the returned location. Then finalSave() is called, passing the entity type that was originally passed in to doSave(). This causes the server to be called and the entity created or updated as usual. If an error occurs, the second function passed to navigator().geolocation.getCurrentPosition() does the same thing, but the value of the field is "Not Available" in this case.

> **Note**   While this will work on a modern desktop browser as well, at least in Firefox, if you choose to not share your location, the app will hang because neither callback to getCurrentPosition() executes. Frankly, I'm not sure if this is by design or if it is a bug in the API. (I expected the error handler to be executed, but it's not.) It's not a big deal; it's just something to be aware of as you test. As a rule, you shouldn't expect all of the PhoneGap APIs to work on the desktop, because they're obviously designed for mobile devices. The ones that *do* work are likely going to be the only ones supported by HTML5 natively. (There has been talk of a "desktop shim" for PhoneGap, essentially the native code implemented to allow all the APIs to work on desktop machines, but as of this writing it's not yet available, at least not in a usable form.)

One small change is needed in the server code, in DAO.js to be specific. In the definition of the note schema, we just need to add to the list of fields.

```
geoLatLong : "string"
```

The rest of the server code is identical. I told you that writing the code like this would make it easy to extend later.

Smile, It's Camera Time!

Up until this point, I've cheated a little bit: the PhoneGap APIs used, even including the Geolocation API, are provided by HTML5 itself, not PhoneGap. That's why they work on your desktop machine as well, assuming that you have a current browser at least. This means you don't even need PhoneGap to make them work. You may even have noticed that, thus far, My Mobile Organizer doesn't seem to import any PhoneGap JavaScript. Well, it more than *seems* that way; it very much *is* the case!

This time around, let's pick an API that isn't part of HTML5 (at least, not yet): the Camera API. To make this work, we have to get some PhoneGap JavaScript into our application. So, we head on over to phonegap.com, download something, and add a .js file to the project, right? Wrong!

We're in the world of PhoneGap Build now, and to paraphrase Doc Brown, "Manually add files? Where we're going, we don't manually add files." Hmmm, I may have that quote slightly wrong,[1] but you get the point.

No, we have to make just one small addition to the index.html file to get the code we need. Simply add the following <script> tag:

```
<script src="phonegap.js" type="text/javascript" charset="utf-8"></script>
```

You can, in theory, add it just about anywhere in the <head> of the document, but I put it right after the viewport <meta> tag so that I know it's loaded as soon as possible. Now if you run the app on your desktop, that link will result in a 404 Not Found error, although it won't cause the app to fail to load. This doesn't really matter since the Camera API won't work on a desktop anyway.

However, something magical happens when you send the archive to PhoneGap Build: it will automatically inject the phonegap.js file, using the version of specified configured in the config.xml file (or the latest version if no such specification is present). From that point on, you have access to all of the PhoneGap APIs, not just the ones that are really part of HTML5 anyway, the Camera API being one of them.

The next thing to do is to add some UI elements to use the API. Let's do this in the contactPage.html file. We'll add a button that lets you take a picture of someone as part of his or her contact record.

> **Note** I'm going to cheat just a little more here and not actually *do* anything with the picture. It won't be saved or anything; this will just demonstrate getting the picture from the camera app on the mobile device. However, it would be a fantastic exercise for you to save the picture to the database and then show it when the item is retrieved.

---

[1]This is a joking reference to the famous quote by Dr. Emmett Brown at the end of *Back to the Future*: "Roads? Where we're going, we don't need roads."

Add the following markup right after the markup for the contact e-mail field:

```
<img src="" id="contactPicture" border="4"
  style="width:320px;height:320px;">
<button type="button" data-theme="e" data-icon="plus"
  onClick="getContactPicture();"
  id="contactGetPictureButton">Take Picture</button>
```

The `<img>` tag is where the picture taken will be injected once it's captured, and the button triggers a call to the getContactPicture() function, which we'll add at the end of `main.js`. That function looks like this:

```
function getContactPicture() {

  navigator.camera.getPicture(
    function(inImageData) {
      document.getElementById("contactPicture").src =
        "data:image/jpeg;base64," + inImageData;
    },
    function(inMessage) {
      alert(inMessage);
    },
    { quality : 20,
      destinationType : navigator.camera.DestinationType.DATA_URL }
  );

}
```

The `navigator.camera.getPicture()` method is the one we'll use, and it launches the camera app on the device and then returns the image to My Mobile Organizer. There the success callback, the first function passed to that method, sets the source of the `<img>` tag we just added a moment ago to display the picture that was taken. If an error occurs, a plain old `alert()` is used to let the user know what happened.

The third argument to `navigator.camera.getPicture()` is an object that contains options for the call. The `quality` of the picture, vis à vis how much compression will be applied, is set to 20, which is fairly low, but as it happens, anything higher will cause Android to not work. If you were doing this for real, you'd probably want to check the platform on which the app is running and change the quality accordingly so that iOS and other platforms don't have their quality unnecessarily degraded because of Android.

We also tell the method what we want to get back from the call, and that can be either a URL to the image or, as is the case here, a base64-encoded string representing the image. This is useful because we can use the Data URL scheme to set the source of the `<img>` tag, which is, in a sense, "embedded" in the page from that point on. In fact, the Data URL scheme was created exactly for that purpose: being able to embed binary data, usually images, in an HTML document and avoid having the browser make a second request for the image after parsing the document. Here it simply avoids the intermediary step of having to save the image. (The camera app may do that anyway, but that's not our concern from the perspective of My Mobile Organizer.)

Now if you do only the steps outlined so far, you'll find that clicking the button doesn't do anything. That's because we're missing one last piece of the puzzle, and that's telling PhoneGap Build what features the app needs so that it can add the appropriate platform-specific permissions to the native builds. Accessing the camera is a "privileged" operation on most mobile platforms, so permission must be given in whatever way each platform does that. On Android, for example, the user will see the permissions listed at the time the app is installed, as shown in Figure 10-18.

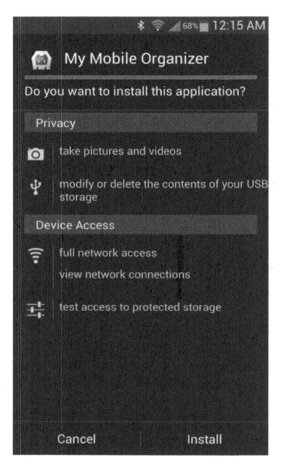

Figure 10-18. Android permissions dialog

To ensure that the proper platform-specific permissions are included, simply add the following to config.xml:

```
<feature name="http://api.phonegap.com/1.0/camera" />
<feature name="http://api.phonegap.com/1.0/file" />
```

That's all PhoneGap Build needs to include those permissions, and that's the last thing needed to make this work! Rebuild the app, click Take Picture on the contacts entry page, and you'll find that the camera app now launches and that the picture you take will be displayed where the <img> tag is afterward.

There's a lot more you could do here such as saving the picture, as previously mentioned, but also rotating it and sizing it appropriately for that `<img>` tag (which you probably would want to size dynamically, not statically, as I did). However, as an example of getting PhoneGap API code working, this does the trick nicely.

Whole Lotta Shakin' Goin' On: Haptic Feedback

Let's do another example of PhoneGap API usage, this time with some haptic feedback or, in other words, vibration. Let's make it so that any time the user clicks any of the navbar items on the bottom, the device vibrates briefly.

The first step is to add the appropriate `<feature>` tags to the `config.xml` file. This time, there's only a single one to be added.

```
<feature name="http://api.phonegap.com/1.0/notification" />
```

Once that's in place, we need to add an `onClick` handler for each of the navbar items in the home page (`index.html`) and each of the entity pages (`appointmentPage.html`, `contactPage.html`, `notePage.html`, and `taskPage.html`). For example, here's the navbar markup in the footer from `index.html`, with the `onClick` handlers added:

```
<div data-role="footer" data-position="fixed">
  <div class="ui-loader-background"></div>
  <div data-role="navbar" class="cssNavBar">
    <ul>
      <li><a href="appointmentPage.html" class="cssNavAppointmentPage"
        onClick="navigator.notification.vibrate(500);"
        data-icon="custom" data-prefetch="true"
        data-iconpos="notext"></a></li>
      <li><a href="contactPage.html" class="cssNavContactPage"
        onClick="navigator.notification.vibrate(500);"
        data-icon="custom" data-prefetch="true"
        data-iconpos="notext"></a></li>
      <li><a href="notePage.html" class="cssNavNotePage"
        onClick="navigator.notification.vibrate(500);"
        data-icon="custom" data-prefetch="true"
        data-iconpos="notext"></a></li>
      <li><a href="taskPage.html" class="cssNavTaskPage"
        onClick="navigator.notification.vibrate(500);"
        data-icon="custom" data-prefetch="true"
        data-iconpos="notext"></a></li>
    </ul>
  </div>
</div>
```

The argument passed to `navigator.notification.vibrate()`, 500, is the number of milliseconds to vibrate. Half a second seems reasonable to me, so 500 milliseconds it is!

Another Kind of Shaking: Accelerometer Access

Let's do one final augmentation of My Mobile Organizer and use another PhoneGap API in the progress: the Accelerometer API. We'll add a feature so that when the user shakes their device, they will have the ability to clear their data, rather than having to click the button on the About screen. Of course, the confirmation dialog will be reused, since accidentally losing your data simply because you jostled your phone probably wouldn't be such a good thing!

For this to work, there are no <feature> elements to add. Accelerometer access isn't privileged on any supported platform, so there are no permissions to be granted. (More precisely, they are granted by default on most platforms that even have such a permission, but either way, as a developer, we're good to go without doing anything, and that's the point.)

Accomplishing this goal requires us to do two things. First, we need to add an event listener for the special PhoneGap-provided deviceready event, like so:

```
$(document).on("deviceready",
  function() {
    shake.startWatch(function() {
      $.mobile.changePage("#confirmClear");
    });
  }
);
```

Add that code to main.js in the EVENT HANDLERS section. This calls the startWatch() method of the shake object, which takes a callback function as an argument. That callback does nothing but shows the existing confirmation page, which effectively takes care of clearing the data if the user elects to do so.

"Hold up!" I hear you say. "What's this shake object thingamajig?" Well, as it happens, the meaning of the term *shake* isn't something that PhoneGap knows. In fact, the underlying platform probably doesn't either—it knows only about raw accelerometer data. We can certainly access the accelerometer data from our app using the PhoneGap API, as briefly described in the previous chapter when we looked at the Accelerometer API a little bit. From that, we can reason out what a shake might be in terms of what the raw data looks like during that event. If we track the accelerometer data over time and look for a certain delta between two moments in time, a delta that crosses some threshold, then that may be a good description of what accelerometer data looks like for a physical shake event.

If that sounds a little complicated, don't worry! While it's not rocket science, I'd just as soon not have to get into that level of detail myself. I'd much rather have some high-level abstractions to work with instead.

Fortunately, a developer by the name of Lee Crossley, who works for a company called Click Innovate out of Manchester, UK, has created shake.js, a small bit of code that encapsulates all of these details and provides a simple API for us to use by way of a shake object that it creates. The code is posted on GitHub at https://gist.github.com/leecrossley/4078996. I've simply taken that code and added it to the end of main.js. (Arguably, it's better to have a separate shake.js file, since this is third-party code, but the difference in this case isn't big enough to worry about, I say.)

The shake object provides two methods: `startWatch()` and `stopWatch()`. You call `shake.startWatch()`, passing it a callback function, and when the code in the `shake` object detects a shake event, the callback is called. If you decide to stop watching for shake events, simply call the `shake.stopWatch()` method. The code added for this augmentation never uses this method, so life is even easier in this use case.

Yep, that's all there is to it. Thanks, Lee!

When Things Go Wrong: Debugging

Things are about to get *seriously* wild around here!

PhoneGap Build provides a way to debug your application, which is, frankly, amazing. This facility is based around an open source tool named weinre (pronounced "winery"). The name *weinre* is short for WEb INspector REmote. What it allows you to do is debug an application remotely, and what it gives you to do this is a tool that is similar to Firebug or Web Inspector for WebKit-based browsers or similar to the Chrome Developer Tools. Things such as inspecting the DOM or viewing console logs are all possible with weinre. In addition, multiple weinre clients can be debugging the same application simultaneously, which gives a whole new meaning to the phrase *pair programming*!

You can install weinre locally if you like, which is normally done using the `npm` command-line tool. You can also download a binary package manually at the weinre home page at `http://people.apache.org/~pmuellr/weinre/docs/latest`.

As with all things PhoneGap Build, you can even do it in the cloud if you prefer! Let's walk through the steps. First, do you remember that "Enable debugging" button on the Settings tab of the app info page on the PhoneGap Build console? Well, you need to click that bad boy! This will trigger a new build, and the appropriate debugging code will be injected automatically. There are no code changes for you to make, no settings to set, and no `config.xml` entries, just a button click and a few moments for the builds to complete.

Once the builds complete, you need to reinstall the app on your mobile device or emulator. Once you do, launch the app. You shouldn't really notice any differences immediately, except that the app takes an extra second to start. Otherwise, it should appear to run normally.

Now, though, with the app running, head back to the console page on the PhoneGap Build site and click the new Debug button that you should see next to the "Update code" and "Rebuild all" buttons. You'll first be greeted with the pop-up in Figure 10-19.

Figure 10-19. A little warning, to make life interesting

This message indicates that no debug server was specified in `config.xml`. Most of the time, you'll probably want to use your own weinre instance, but that isn't actually required. Instead, click the Attempt Debug button, and you should, after a few seconds, wind up on a page that looks like Figure 10-20.

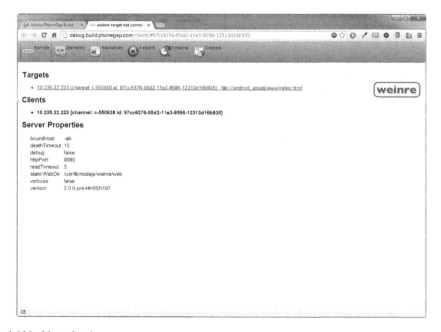

Figure 10-20. Look kids, it's weinre!

The list of targets is the list of apps currently running that are connected to this weinre instance, which is hosted by Adobe. There will likely be the only one, as you see here, so go ahead and click that link to select it for debugging. Next, click the Elements icon up top. What you should see as a result, assuming that you're still on the home page of the app, is what is shown in Figure 10-21.

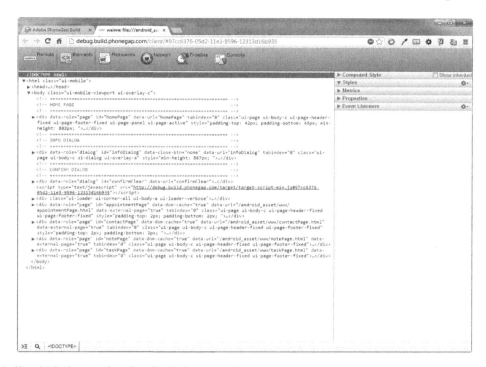

Figure 10-21.   Yes, that's the actual markup for the home page!

> **Note**   You can return to the list of targets at any time by clicking the Remote icon in the upper left.

Think about what you're actually looking at for a moment: that's the actual markup that is displayed in the WebView control inside the PhoneGap container running on your mobile device, and you're seeing this *from across the Internet*! Better still, you had to do virtually nothing other than to click a couple of buttons!

That's more than a little amazing if you ask me. However, as they say, wait, there's more!

Go ahead and, on this page, click the triangle next to the `<div>` with the ID `homePage`. That will expand the markup. Now hover over various sections of that markup, and watch your mobile device as you do. As if by magic, the sections of the app corresponding to the markup over which you're hovering will highlight!

If you're amazed by that, check this out: click the icon in the lower left that looks like a greater-than sign with three lines next to it. That's the console. Once you do, enter this and hit Enter:

```
$(".ui-title").text("hello!")
```

Your screen should look like the one shown in Figure 10-22 at this point. (What's on the right might be a little different, since I was exploring the markup a little more during this process.) Look back at your mobile device, and what do you see? Yes, the header text "Welcome!" has been changed to "Hello!"

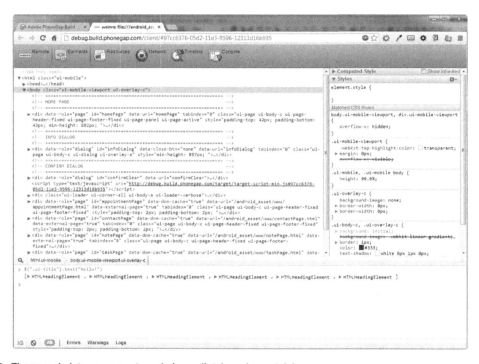

Figure 10-22. The console lets you execute code immediately and remotely!

> **Note**   In fact, the headers on all of the pages have changed, but that's just a result of the selector used as is, which is just fine to demonstrate this concept.

Isn't that pretty darned cool?

> **Note**   The weinre tool works only in WebKit-based browsers at the moment, which is why these screenshots are in Chrome and not my usual browser, Firefox. Ask me how I found that out.

You can execute any arbitrary JavaScript code you like here. You can also expand the styles on the right, whether declared in stylesheets or computed, and alter things there to change what you see on the screen immediately as well. You can, of course, inspect all of the elements on the page, including all of their properties.

You can even explore things like LocalStorage, as shown in Figure 10-23, where you can see a task that I've saved. In addition, note the text in the console that says "doSave() called." That's the result of a `console.log()` call that I added to the `doSave()` function. Yep, you can do all the logging you like and be able to access that remotely too!

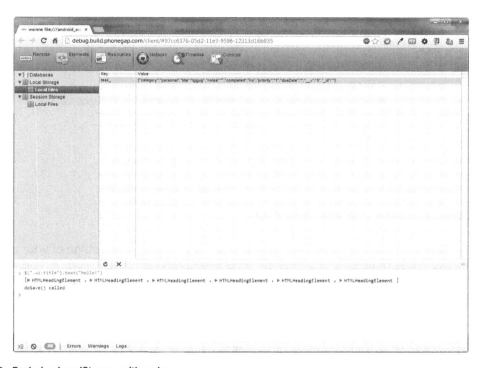

Figure 10-23. *Exploring LocalStorage with weinre*

Would you like to see the request that was done to save that task? That's easy enough; just head over to the Network task, and you'll see a list of all recorded network traffic made via Ajax (see Figure 10-24). You can click each to drill down into the details to see exactly what data was sent, what the response was, the headers that were involved, and so on.

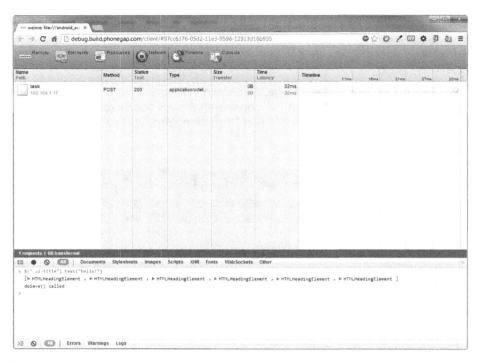

Figure 10-24. A network request recorded while saving a task

Finally, the Timeline icon allows you to view events that occur during the lifetime of your application. Currently, only two types of events can be seen: timers/intervals (which are recorded only if you click the record button at the bottom) and user-specified events. You can create a mark on the timeline by calling `console.markTimeline("xxx")`, where xxx is any label you'd like to see.

> **Note**   The Console icon up top just expands the console at the bottom to take up the whole window.

How Do I Run a Local weinre Server?

Using the Adobe-hosted weinre instance is fine for playing around, but you'll likely want to set up your own instance to do any real work for performance reasons if nothing else. Doing so is quite easy, and it begins with installing weinre. As I mentioned earlier, npm is the way to do this.

```
npm -g install weinre
```

Go ahead and run that command, and you're ready to go! You can then run weinre from a command prompt by executing this:

```
weinre
```

This will start a web server at `http://localhost:8080` that will look just like the hosted weinre instance and function just the same but running on your local machine.

Now, to use this instance, you'll need to add some information into `config.xml` to let PhoneGap Build know you are using a private instance (and, incidentally, to get rid of that pop-up message from earlier when you click the Debug button). The XML to add is as follows:

```xml
<feature name="debug-server" required="true">
  <param name="domain" value="http://aaa.bbb.ccc.ddd"/>
  <param name="key" value="xxx"/>
</feature>
```

The domain value `aaa.bbb.ccc.ddd` is the IP address of the machine on which weinre is running. The key value `xxx` is the unique ID of your app.

That's all there is to it! From there on out, you can use your own local instance, which will almost certainly be faster than the public instance, not to mention more secure.

The Final Step: Distributing Your Application

Now that the application is fully coded, augmented, built, and even debugged, let's talk about distribution. Sit here at my knee, children, and let me spin you a tale. Time was, I reckon, far back in history around the year 2000. I remember as if it were…just 13 years ago!

Microsoft had come out with what I thought was a pretty cool mobile operating system: PocketPC (later renamed to Windows Mobile and now of course Windows Phone, but I'll stick with PocketPC since that's the time frame to which I'm referring). Back then, when you made an app to sell for PocketPC, you had to do it all yourself. This means you created a web site, did some custom programming to handle purchases and registrations, and coded all that good other stuff. You put your app up there, and then you went about advertising in whatever way you could.

The upside to that approach was complete control and a 100 percent profit. Everything you made went right into your pocket, and you could create any sales model that made sense. You could go out and purchase banner ad space that linked back to your site for purchases. You could even possibly form a partnership with another developer to include an advertisement for your game when they started up theirs, and vice versa. Whatever you could dream up and make work, it was all up to you. Now, it didn't take long for people to think to themselves: "Self, there's got to be an easier way!"

Before you knew it, there were storefront sites popping up all over the Web. These sites would do all of the hard work for you: advertising, credit card processing, handling of returns, and so on. They would do this all in exchange for a percentage of your sales. All you had to do was give up a little bit of coin from each sale, and, in return, your hassle level went way down.

This worked fairly well, but people who wanted apps still had to know about these sites. They had to go visit them in the relatively primitive web browser on their device, or, as was more common at the time, they would do so on their PC, download the installation file, manually copy it to their device, and then execute it there to be installed. It wasn't a particularly pleasant experience, truth be told, but it worked for the most part.

Today, of course, we have what are really the descendants of those storefront sites. The Apple App Store, Google Play store, the Amazon Appstore for Android, and all of them serve the same basic purpose. They also work in much the same way: for a percentage of each sale, and in some cases small up-front fees, they will take care of most of the details of selling your apps for you.

In today's world, they go a step further (and some, a lot further). These are, to varying degrees (as will be discussed in the remainder of this chapter), "curated" experiences. This means that, in contrast to the old days, where the storefront sites would generally sell any app (and of course you could still always sell them yourself for sure), the companies that run these new app stores do some degree of quality control on the apps they sell. There are requirements you have to meet and guidelines you have to follow.

The benefits, however, are great: we very much live in an app-centric world right now. People with their fancy, uber-powerful smartphones consider apps when they think of things to do with their devices. As part of that mind-set, they are very much trained to go to the app stores provided to them, and, in some cases, that's the only way to get apps onto their device (without resorting to nonstandard techniques at least).

These modern-day app stores also absolutely dwarf those old storefront sites both in terms of the volume of apps available and in terms of profit potential for you. Simply put, even if there are other ways that you might sell your apps, if you aren't in these modern stores, you are almost certainly giving away money. (And if money isn't your primary motivating factor, then you're giving up exposure as well.)

So, what are the major app stores today, and what does it take to get into them? Well, as I said, that's not a simple "one-size-fits-all" answer. It's actually a spectrum. Let's start by discussing the one that is generally acknowledged as being the trickiest to deal with in most regards in the eyes of most developers.

The Only Game in Town for iOS: The Apple App Store

As mentioned earlier, you'll need to pay the $99 fee to get into the iOS developer program before you can publish to the App Store. Once you do that, the process isn't very much different from publishing to Google Play. Everything you need is at the Apple Developer Center web site: `https://developer.apple.com/membercenter`.

Being published in the Apple App Store is a more difficult experience than with other stores, because Apple takes a much more proactive role in ensuring quality. It does a far more in-depth review of your applications and has a much more stringent set of guidelines that you'll need to follow. The process also takes much longer, sometimes weeks. The result, though, is that apps that make it through the process are all but guaranteed to be of a certain quality level and to have a certain degree of consistency across the board.

You can find the app review guidelines at `https://developer.apple.com/appstore/guidelines.html`, and I highly suggest studying them before you submit your app for review. It's far from atypical to fail the App Store's review the first (or even the second or third) time! Thus, the more familiar you are with the guidelines and the more you strive to adhere to them, the better your chances are of passing on the first try. It should be noted that, if you do fail, subsequent review rounds tend to happen quite a bit faster.

Publishing to the Apple App Store

Figure 10-25 shows what you'll see when you visit the Apple Developer Center site and log in after becoming a member.

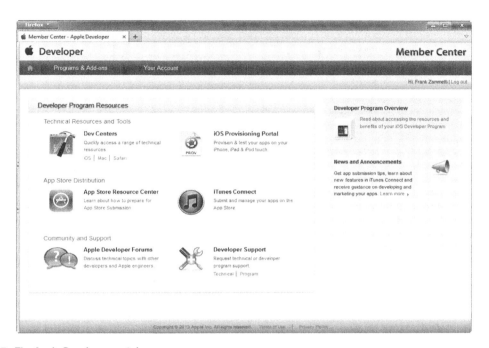

Figure 10-25. The Apple Developer portal page

Once there, you'll use iTunes Connect to begin the process. When you click that link, you'll be greeted with the window shown in Figure 10-26.

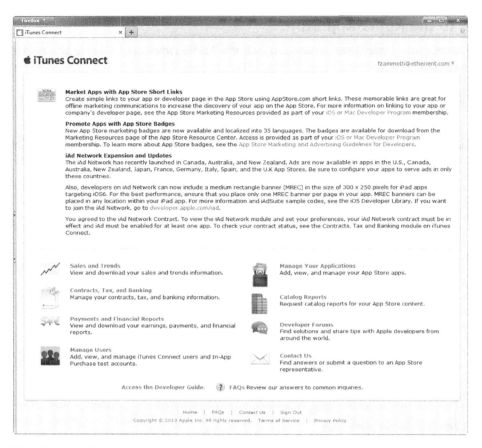

Figure 10-26. iTunes Connect site

Click the Manage Your Applications link, and you'll be brought to a page that lists all of your existing apps, if any, but most important will be the Add New App button. Once you click that, you'll be guided through the process of creating an iTunes Connect app record, which you can think of as a "stub" for your new application. You'll enter some basic application information as in other stores, and eventually, at the end, the record will be created.

You'll be returned to iTunes Connect, and you will need to select the option to manage your new application. You will then have to fill out an export compliance questionnaire and then finally click the Ready to Upload Binary button. The status of the record will then change to Waiting for Upload.

Click the Upload to App Store button, and the Application Loader (see Figure 10-27) will be launched. This app will walk you through the process of uploading your IPA file in a few simple steps.

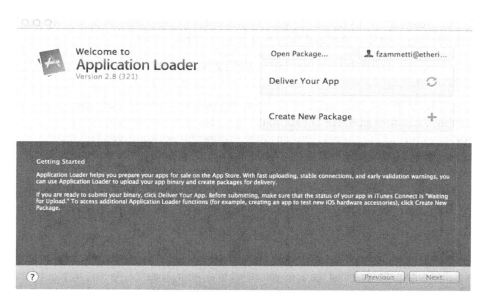

Figure 10-27. *Application Loader*

You simply click the Deliver Your App button and follow the directions. Note that you will be able to do this only if the record on the iTunes Connect site is in Waiting for Upload status, so be sure it is before launching Application Loader.

Once the binary is uploaded, your app will be pending review, and then it's just the waiting game of crossing your fingers and hoping it gets through review unscathed! If you do need to make changes based on the review, you'll follow the same basic steps outlined here and again click the Ready to Upload Binary button in the iTunes Connect site to upload the new version through Application Loader.

Eventually, though, your app will be published, and, with a little luck, you'll be putting your kids through college with money to spare in no time!

Google Play

Google Play (http://play.google.com) is the latest iteration of the store Google has built for its Android platform. While there are a number of other stores for Android, Google Play is what you might call the canonical store, and it is certainly the most popular overall. It also happens to be the one with possibly the least barrier to entry.

You can get going with Google Play in just a few minutes! All it takes is a few simple steps.

1. Register for a Google Play publisher account at (https://accounts.google.com/ServiceLogin?service=androiddeveloper&passive=1209600&continue=https://play.google.com/apps/publish/v2/&followup=https://play.google.com/apps/publish/v2/).

2. Pay the $25 registration fee when you sign up.

3. Wait approximately 48 hours for your registration to be processed. (It may be considerably less, but it could take this long in some cases.)

4. If you intend to publish only free apps, then you're done when your registration is processed.

5. If you intend to sell your apps, then you also need to set up a Google Merchant account at `https://accounts.google.com/ServiceLogin?service=sierra&ltmpl=seller&continue=https://checkout.google.com/merchantSignInRedirect`. You can go ahead and do this while you're waiting for your registration to process.

Once you're alerted via e-mail that your registration is complete, you can log on to the developer console (`https://play.google.com/apps/publish`) and publish an app at your convenience.

> **Tip**   A unique feature of Google Play, and one that is incredibly handy, is the ability to browse for apps on your PC and then automatically install the apps you select to an Android device. As long as your device is known to Google Play, you'll be able to select it from a list when you click the Install button for a given app, and the app will magically be installed in just a few seconds!

Google takes 30 percent of each sale; 70 percent goes to you. Google handles all the details of sales and refunds for you, and it may even do some small degree of advertising on your behalf (although it's nothing to count on for your only advertising). You are paid each month via your Google Merchant account, which results in a direct deposit to the checking account you put on file. There are no recurring fees either, just the initial $25. That's quite a low barrier to entry!

Publishing to Google Play

Adding a new application is a simple systematic process that the developer console guides you through. Along the way, you'll need to enter a host of information including the application title, description, recent changes (if updating an already published app), categories for your app to appear under in Google Play, URLs for your website, pricing information, and other basic information about the app. You'll also have the opportunity to upload screenshots and even link to demonstration videos of your app in action.

Naturally, you'll have to upload the APK you generated as well, signed with a cryptographic key created using the Java SDK tools. Once you do all of this, it should take less than an hour in most cases for your app to appear in Google Play.

Unlike the Apple App Store, Google Play is extremely lenient when it comes to the apps it publishes. There are some automated test tools that run against your APK to ensure validity and to weed out some obvious malware, but generally you can publish anything you like without a problem.

Note Some people think Google Play is too lenient, but it's entirely a matter of opinion. Some people prefer the more stringent Apple curation approach, while others think the Google approach is more open. Certainly, it can't be argued that it is easier and faster to get an app published in Google Play, and virtually anyone can do it, but whether that's a good or bad thing is for the customer to decide. As an app developer, you certainly want to be in as many stores on as many platforms as possible to maximize your earning potential.

Updating your app later is similarly easy: just go back into the developer console, edit your app, upload the new APK (and screenshots if needed), update the meta-information, and click a button. Usually in only a few minutes, your new version will be available to the world.

If you are charging for your app, the Google Merchant account you created can be accessed (http://checkout.google.com/sell) to see all of the sales you've had and all of the refunds given. You can also get financial reports there for tax purposes.

Overall, there really isn't much to working with Google Play! Once you know how to create an APK using the steps discussed earlier in this chapter and you have the necessary account(s) set up with Google, it's really just entering some information and clicking a few buttons.

Other App Stores: Amazon Appstore for Android and Barnes & Noble Nook Store

As I mentioned, the Google Play store is the One App Store To Rule Them All™ for Android or, at least, that's probably what Google would want you to think. It isn't, strictly speaking, the only game in town, though.

With the release of the Kindle device, which is Android-based, Amazon has created its own store, pedantically named the Amazon Appstore for Android. However, Amazon's store isn't just for Kindle devices; you can install its store app (www.amazon.com/mobile-apps/b?ie=UTF8&node=2350149011) on any Android device (as long as you set your device to allow installation of third-party apps from unknown sources; see your device's security settings for these options).

Once you do so, you'll be able to browse Amazon's collection of apps, which includes much of what you find on Google Play. There might be a few other gems unique to the Amazon store as well. In addition, Amazon has, from the first day that its store went live, given away one app free daily. As with Android apps in general, if you get an app free that normally isn't, then you'll still "own" the app and can install it later.

Tip In case it didn't occur to you, even if you don't intend to use Amazon's store, generally I still suggest visiting it daily to get the free app. That way, if down the road you decide you want a given app, you may find that you in fact already "own" it thanks to Amazon!

Nominally, Amazon charges a $99 annual fee to publish to its store. However, it is "currently" waiving that fee. I put currently in quotes because it has actually been waiving that fee from the beginning! Amazon may well stop waiving it at some point, but it seems like a bit of marketing on its part to continue waiving it. Like Google, Amazon takes a 30 percent cut of each sale. However, there's no extra merchant-type account to deal with. The single account you create (`https://developer.amazon.com/welcome.html`) takes care of all of this in one place. Payment is monthly with Amazon as well, and again it is a direct deposit.

Submitting an app is very much like the Google process, and it requires substantially the same information. The difference, though, is that Amazon does some deeper verification of your app, and it even does a little bit of quality control (albeit very little, it seems). There is also a longer waiting period for an app to be published initially—sometimes up to two weeks. Updates tend to be processed much quicker, however.

Barnes & Noble also has a store specific to its Nook devices. Unlike Amazon, however, this store truly is specific to those devices; that is, you cannot access the Nook store from a non–Barnes & Noble device.

Overall, the process is similar to both Google Play and the Amazon Appstore, and the fees involved are similar in terms of setting up an account and selling your apps. However, Barnes & Noble is the most stringent of the three when it comes to reviewing your app. In fact, it has been known to reject apps that aren't of "sufficient quality." At other times, you may have to go through the review process a few times to get all the kinks worked out to Barnes & Noble's liking before your app is published.

> **Note** My own experience with Barnes & Noble was like this. My game, *Engineer*, had to go through review three times before it was accepted, whereas it had no trouble getting into the Google Play store on the first try and only had one round of tweaks to get through even Apple's stringent review process. Each time, there was something I had missed that didn't meet Barnes & Noble's app guidelines, which are available to you once you create a developer account, so it was certainly all on me. I strongly suggest becoming familiar with these guidelines before you begin writing your apps, though; that's the real point here. I can tell you from experience that it will make your life a lot easier down the road!

As I mentioned earlier, it's a good idea to be in as many stores as possible in order to reach as large an audience as possible. Of course, the technologies used to build My Mobile Organizer give you the ability to be on as many devices as possible, which is an underlying goal throughout this process! No Android stores are difficult to get into, nor are they difficult to deal with once you're in them, so I definitely encourage you to get into as many as possible.

Summary

We covered quite a bit of ground in this, the final chapter of our adventure together! You saw how to write a configuration file to control PhoneGap Build, and you then learned how to ship off an archive of your application, including the configuration file, to the servers for building it. You learned that you have some choices in getting your source code into the cloud beyond the archive approach, specifically Git and GitHub.

You got a glimpse of what PhoneGap plug-ins are all about, and you learned that PhoneGap Build provides support for them through a simple configuration-based mechanism. You saw how they allow you to extend the functionality of your apps without mucking about with native code. You also studied how to kick off a build and the native bundles that result from that process.

You learned about augmenting the application with PhoneGap-specific APIs to enhance its functionality, without writing any native code.

Finally, you learned about app distribution models for Android and iOS, and you saw what's involved in taking the bundles produced by PhoneGap Build, getting them onto devices for testing, and ultimately getting them into app stores for wider distribution.

Now, as we reach the end, I hope you've enjoyed the journey we've taken together. I hope that you've learned quite a bit from the process and that you are now ready to take your web development skills into the world of mobile. I hope that you had a few chuckles along the way too! Now go, have fun, and be productive (and name a child after me as a thank-you)!

Index

▇ M

R

S

T

U

V

W, X, Y, Z

Get the eBook for only $10!

Now you can take the weightless companion with you anywhere, anytime. Your purchase of this book entitles you to 3 electronic versions for only $10.

This Apress title will prove so indispensible that you'll want to carry it with you everywhere, which is why we are offering the eBook in **3 formats** for only $10 if you have already purchased the print book.

Convenient and fully searchable, the PDF version enables you to easily find and copy code—or perform examples by quickly toggling between instructions and applications. The MOBI format is ideal for your Kindle, while the ePUB can be utilized on a variety of mobile devices.

Go to www.apress.com/promo/tendollars to purchase your companion eBook.